500 Social Media Marketing Tips: Essential Advice, Hints and Strategy for Business: Facebook, Twitter, Pinterest, YouTube, Instagram, Snapchat, LinkedIn, and More!

Fall 2018 Edition

Copyright © 2012 - 2018 by Andrew Macarthy

Cover and internal design © Andrew Macarthy

Website: http://www.andrewmacarthy.com
Facebook: http://www.facebook.com/500socialmediatips
Twitter: http://www.twitter.com/andrewmacarthy
Instagram: http://www.instagram.com/500socialmedia

*** My *Premium Content Bundle* is a selection of incredibly useful social media marketing resources - instantly downloadable - to help you reach and surpass your social media marketing goals. Learn more at www.andrewmacarthy.com/premium ***

D0051424

1

Table of Contents

Why Your Business Needs Social Media Marketing!

Over the last decade, social media marketing has become an indispensable tool in the arsenal of brands and businesses of all kinds, with opportunities to build relationships, engage with customers, and increase sales like never before – and the stats back it up. Market research analysts at Technavio estimate that annual global social commerce revenues will exceed $165 billion by 2021 - up 34% from 2017., and in a Social Media Examiner poll conducted in 2017, 92% of respondents said that social media marketing is now important to their business. If you're not using social media at all or your current strategy isn't working for you as well as you'd hoped, now is the time to make a change. You are about to learn hundreds of expert hints and tips to effectively market your business across all of the most popular social media platforms including Facebook, Twitter, YouTube, Instagram and Pinterest. Each chapter is grouped broadly into several sections including profile optimization, content strategy, and advice on paid advertising.

Since the first edition of this book was published in 2012, social media marketing has evolved massively. One of the most significant changes is the shift from brands simply broadcasting marketing messages on social platforms to an environment where engaging with fans and fostering communities around a product or an idea has become imperative to success. Instead of a simple drive to rack up the highest number of followers on a social media profile as a marker of authority or success, businesses are opting to take a customer-first approach in their content, as well as building niche communities, encouraged by changes on major social media platforms such as Facebook, where meaningful interactions are given priority over public, overtly-promotional content.

As things stand, success in social media marketing results from building strong and long-lasting relationships with customers and professional contacts, and sharing the type of content and expertise that they will want to share with their friends, family, and colleagues. This approach will help to attract and keep loyal customers and connections, and encourage them to become online ambassadors for your brand. While this approach is a world away from traditional marketing, this open, two-way conversation is now what billions of consumers around the world expect from the businesses and brands in which they invest time and money. Direct selling *does* have a place within the social media marketing ecosystem, but as you'll learn, it is no longer the direction that the vast majority of brands will want focus on.

I hope you find all of the following advice helpful, whether you're a complete social media novice or an already-savvy marketer looking for some extra expert tips to drive your business onto bigger and better things. Do let me know how you get on by getting in touch via my social channels!

Andrew.

Before You Begin: Key Considerations For All Social Media Marketing

Peer pressure, success stories in the media and general hype tell today's business owners that having a presence on social media is essential. That's not to say a business couldn't do well without utilizing social networking, but they'd certainly be missing out on a myriad of opportunities to build and grow. However, one of the biggest mistakes that a brand can make is to leap into social media marketing with no real clue of what they are going to do with it - only the vague hope that if they just simply start posting on a few social sites, it will somehow – through the magic of the Internet – turn them into a billion-dollar company overnight. While there is a possibility that you will get lucky (probably not "billion-dollar lucky, mind you) in most cases this kind of "try it and see" approach will lead to unrealistic goal-setting, poor results, a huge waste of time, and ultimately a defeatist attitude that discourages you from the idea of social media marketing completely. To ensure that this *doesn't* happen to you – and to give you the best chance of success - I urge you to digest the key considerations for social media marketing detailed below. By the end of this chapter you will have a firm understanding of what kind of approach *works* for business on social media and how to pursue your efforts in a well-planned, logical manner.

Decide which social networks will work best for you

Unless you're a big company with the resources to plow full speed ahead into every potentially viable social platform, chances are you're better to focus on one or two "core" social networks first. It's better to excel on a couple of social networks than be mediocre on five or six. And while social media marketing tools are free to use, your time is a limited and valuable commodity. Indeed, depending on the type of business you run, not every social media site is going to suit your marketing, your audience, or what you are trying to achieve. To help you decide where to begin, identify the social networks where your target audience already hangs out, or use customer personas and research of social network demographics to judge where you will best be received. Joining Facebook is often the go-to choice for brands simply due to its sheer size and influence, but more "niche" communities with their own unique attributes - still with hundreds of millions of users, mind you - like Pinterest, Instagram, or LinkedIn, might be where you find you can make a bigger impact. You'll learn all about what each particular social network brings to the table as they are introduced in the chapters to come, but to start off, experiment with a couple of social networks where you can invest some significant time, track your progress, and then either build on your achievements with them, or steadily begin to experiment with other platforms on which you might have additional (or better) success.

Define and assess your goals

Before you start posting content to social media, it is useful to define the guiding themes and overall goals of your strategy, as these will help you shape the way you approach what may well become the linchpin in your marketing machine. I'm a fan of the SMART technique for creating actionable social media goals. Here's a breakdown; hopefully it'll help you too:

Specific: Be specific in what you want to achieve. Do you want to raise awareness of your brand? Increase sales? Improve customer service? Strengthen loyalty? Put a modest number or percentage on it.
Measurable: How will you know that your goal has been achieved? What analytics tools will you use to track your progress?
Achievable: Is your goal realistic? When you are just starting off, don't aim too high, at the risk of being deflated if you don't hit your projected goal; getting adept at all this stuff (particularly if you are approaching social media marketing seriously for the first time) takes a while.
Relevant: Is your goal aligned with your company's mission, vision and values?
Time: How soon do you want to have achieved the goal? To add a focus to your marketing, stick to one overarching goal at a time, e.g., *"I want to increase traffic to our website by 15% in the next 3 months"*.

For example, if you're a shoe store owner and you normally sell 20 pairs of shoes a day, why not aim to use social media to help you sell 25 per day? After a fair amount of time (at least a few months), evaluate where you are by using analytics tools, social insights (likes, followers, comments), and other metrics to help you track and measure your activity - you'll find lots more information on this shortly.

Perform an audit to help shape your content strategy

Carrying out an audit is one of the best ways to get an idea of a strategy for developing social media content that will resonate with your audience, and a great way to decide upon what content you should share with them. Take time to identify your audience's needs, desires, and interests on social media - ask yourself what problems you can help them overcome, what questions you can answer, what types of discussions they like to engage in, the type of content they prefer (e.g. text, photo, graphics, video), and when they are most likely to be around to see it. Tools like SEM Rush and TrueSocial Metrics are two popular paid options if you want to dig right down into the details, but you needn't spend a penny to get a good, general idea... especially if you use your competition to help you out! First, identify your competitors. You'll probably know them already, but a simple web search will tell you if you don't. Then visit their websites and social media profiles for a nose around. Make notes on how often your rivals publish blogs and status updates on social media (is it daily, every other day, weekly?), and which content seems to perform best for them based on the number of likes, comments, and shares. You can gain further insight by identifying how much of this content appears to be original versus that shared from other sources, and what the topics and tone of voice used are like. Use the information you gather to mirror successful types of content in your own social media strategy, but *also* to identify gaps and opportunities where you can improve on it.

Note: See the *Premium Content Bundle* chapter of this book to download a ready-made 24-question template to help your business plan and execute your social media strategy, and how to perform a simple competitor analysis.

Plan ahead with a social media content calendar
One of the stiffest tests facing brands on social media is to consistently publish high quality content for their fans. A company's social media presence that appears abandoned is the digital equivalent of turning the lights off. Because you're not updating online, people will assume that you're going out of business, even if the opposite is true. Consistency can really help to boost levels of engagement by enabling fans to anticipate your next post, and it will also foster a stronger relationship with your audience (who will keep coming back for more). One of the best ways to help get this right is by compiling a social media content calendar. An editorial calendar will allow you to plan your activity for weeks - or even months - in advance. This foresight will allow you to plan everyday posts as well as building seasonal themes into your updates, and prevent you from posting sub-par content just because you feel the urge to publish *something*. In addition to planning for the big holidays like Thanksgiving and Christmas, you will also be able to map out a strategy for "mini holidays" like July 4th or Valentine's Day, occasions where fans are actively searching on social media for deals, discounts, advice, etc. The ability to scan a social content

calendar regularly will also provide you with a way to step back from day-to-day posting and re-affirm your wider strategy. Of course, spontaneous posting to social media still has a place, but for the foundations of your marketing, a content calendar is highly recommended. One simple way to organize a content strategy (that can be used to populate your calendar and prevent yourself from becoming overwhelmed) is to create a daily theme across your social networks. For example: sharing a new blog post on Monday, asking a question on Tuesday, an infographic on Wednesday, a quote on Thursday, etc.

Note: Download my ready-to-use social media content calendar templates in the *Premium Content Bundle* chapter of this book.

Re-purpose content across social media

It is worth emphasizing that something that might be distributed as one piece of content in the real world (a press release, say), can be marketed as four or five content pieces for social media: blog about it, tweet, make a video, a story, share on Facebook, turn it into an infographic for Pinterest, etc. This is a fantastic strategy for making the most of your content creation, particularly if you are strapped for time or low on resources.

Drop old-style communication methods and get social – find and define your social voice

Successful social media strategy requires just that - a *social* strategy. Traditional marketing techniques like TV and newspaper advertising worked because the direction of communication could only go in one way (from brand to consumer) with little chance for reply, but social media means that this is no longer the case. Now that a two-way dialogue is firmly established and your brand is under the spotlight 24/7, you must resist the urge to talk *at* people, and adapt your tone of voice and communication methods to connect with them on a human level - speaking to them in a personable manner and listening with intent, rather than just hearing and doing nothing about it. This lesson applies the same whether you are a small business employing a handful of people, a multi-national company with thousands of staff, the owner of a "fun" business like a karaoke bar, or something more "serious" like a finance company. With that said, a good place to start is to define and use a tone of voice that matches your brand's core beliefs. By maintaining your fundamental beliefs across all web content, advertising and social media posts, you create parallel experiences, and these recognizable actions create expectations for customers and help drive them through your marketing funnel. Brands that define their social voice (and strive to maintain it in all of their social interactions) can cut through the noise and deliver a clear message that, ultimately, will deliver improved results.

Humanize your brand and be emotive; tell stories
People use social media to connect with other *people*, so lower your barriers and show fans the real you and the people behind your business' logo; be transparent, open, and authentic in all of your communication – authenticity often means being a little bit more open about what your business might traditionally share with customers. But there's a fine line – if you're consistently sharing posts about internal conflicts or your love life, that line has probably been crossed! Establish your *unique* voice, show a sense of humor, use everyday language, etc. And if being genuine endears customers to you, then they will be more likely to want to engage with your content, share it with others, *and* support you financially when the time comes to buy, by choosing you over another brand with whom they have no connection.

A genuinely human approach, especially with a focus on storytelling - the human brain's most primitive and powerful form of communication – has consistently proven to be a successful tactic on social media. It allows you to cut through the noise of the web as a whole, and through a combination of clever, emotive, surprising text and imagery, can snap people out of their autopilot-browsing; something we're all guilty of doing. As a brand, that's the moment you need to connect with customers, keep their attention as time moves on (if you aren't attempting to build momentum on social media, you're moving backwards), and ultimately win their trust, loyalty, and business. Here are a few "versus" examples to show how a little bit of thought into your language can make a big difference in the impact of your communication. Hint: the *preferred* language comes second in each example:

Putting emphasis on the customer: "We've just launched our new sunglasses range for summer, check it out!" vs "Earn your stripes by breaking boundaries in new Double Bridge shades // #ItTakesCourage to push yourself."

Providing clear value: "Read Our Best 26 Running Tips" vs "26 Running Tips That Will Help You Run Faster And Longer This Summer."

Building curiosity: "Study shows volunteering is key to improving your wellbeing." vs "71% see volunteering as key to improving wellbeing. Learn how your company can give back."

Keeping language simple: "Our research and calculations indicate that purchasing our air conditioning unit reduces the temperature of the home by an average of 10 degrees – how fantastic is that?" vs "We've done the math! Our sums show that our air conditioners make your home 10 degrees cooler, even on the hottest days!"

There's tons of advice for general content ideas in later chapters, to which the above language best practices apply, but for starters ask yourself: who are your customers? What are their stories? How does your product or service make their lives better? And how can you speak to them in a way that resonates?

Note: On the subject of image use for social media, studies show that images of humans (as compared to inanimate objects) - especially those smiling and making eye contact with the viewer - can help to drive conversion rates. Even if the product you are selling isn't tangible, e.g. data or financial services, you should still try to incorporate people and human faces into at least some of your images, whether they be of you, your customers, or simply people in stock images.

On a related note – and a powerful pairing to text alone – are emoticons or Emoji - fully-drawn, expressive emoticons and ideograms that have fast become a universal language all of their own, can add a whole new layer of fun and expression to your status updates. A study by Amex Open found that using emoticons in status updates increased comments by an average of 33%, while a separate investigation by Buddy Media discovered that posts with emoticons received on average 57% more likes, 33% more comments and 33% more shares. Perhaps more significant is that many social sites – Twitter, Instagram, and Facebook included - all support the use of Emoji –Instagram found that nearly 50 percent of all captions and comments include at least one emoji. So, it may well be worth experimenting with emoji to see how they can fit into your brand's posts.

So now you know that to succeed on social media, you need to maintain a cliché-free zone, with genuine communication, imagery, and stories that capture people's attention. As alluded to earlier, real people (especially on social media and especially the younger generation) don't respond to marketing speak, and will be quick to ignore you if they suspect it. Rather than trying to manipulate fans into buying products or service, showcasing you and your brand's true values and personality will go a long way to setting you apart from your competitors.

Don't over-promote: build relationships and provide value

The vast majority of social media users do not visit Facebook, Twitter, Pinterest, et al. to be given the hard sell by companies; they use them to interact with family and friends and to be entertained. If they do "like" or "follow" brands on social media, they often do so on a whim (think about the number of brands you "like" or "follow"). And all but the most passionate fans won't care to see every single post you publish (in fact, it is unreasonable to think that such a thing might be possible unless you spend a lot of money on paid promotion). Therefore, it is your job to convince people to enjoy having your business as something that is a big part of their everyday lives, and continue to earn your place in their feeds - don't see it as a right, see it as a privilege. You do this by building trusting and loyal relationships, by being friendly, sharing great content, helping people with customer service issues, etc. - with the odd promotional post in between, of course... which if the rest of your strategy is on target, your audience really shouldn't mind).

Ultimately, with social media content in mind, change your mindset from "what can we sell you?" to "what can we do to help you?", because in terms of choosing to follow a brand on social media, your fans will certainly be asking the question "what's in it for me?" With competition up and organic (non-paid) reach at an all-time low, it is crucial that the content you post touches people on a personal and emotional level. Some of the most powerful emotional triggers are humor, awe, anger, and even narcissism (stuff that, by sharing, makes the individual look good in front of their peers on social media).

Once you hit your stride, one useful exercise to help you keep on track is as follows: from time to time, stop and take a look at your last 10 social media posts and ask yourself this question: *"What value am I providing and what purpose am I serving?"* If you cannot clearly define the answer to this question, you should think carefully about amending your strategy to better reach audiences who are now smarter and savvier than ever before - people who easily see past weak content or an over-sale-sy message. Just as in the real world, social media followers will resonate with a brand that they can love and trust, much more than one whose sole purpose seems to be to encourage them to open their wallets at every opportunity. To reiterate the point I made above, you should strive to become a *seamless part* of their expected social media experience, not a jarring element that they want to skip past. All of this good work will build a positive image around your brand and slowly convert into sales.

Post consistently, with high quality content and stuff that resonates
As I touched on earlier, one of the toughest tests that brands face is to deliver consistent, high quality content for social media. Regardless of what or how often you post, never launch a presence on a social media channel, post for a few weeks, and then let its activity dry up! For most social networks, one, two or three updates per day is a good target. At a minimum, you should post at least a couple of times a week so that your content continues to appear in the news feeds of your most engaged fans. If you're really not in the position right now to pay much attention to social media, it is more important to be present than completely absent, even if that means putting aside just one day a month to update your social profiles with a link to your new blog post, uploading a video to YouTube, or giving insight into your work on your LinkedIn Company page. At least then, when the time comes that you're ready to expand your efforts, you have a foundation to build upon.

Once you're at that stage, consistency (do you notice I'm hammering this *consistency* point home?) is key. One of the main reasons that brands fail on social media is because they do not post enough. To single out Facebook as an example of a social network that a large majority of brands use, here's some wider perspective to explain why consistency is so important: When someone visits their Facebook News Feed, there are an average of 1,500 possible posts generated by site's complicated algorithm, and ordered by how likely the user is to interact with each piece of content - from friends, Pages, groups, events, etc. In addition, around half of users don't check Facebook every day. And of those that do, they only browse for around 30-60 minutes in total. For all of these reasons, the chance of all of your posts being seen *and* engaged with among all of that competition, is diminished considerably. In fact, without paid promotion (which we will look at later), Facebook makes it almost impossible for *all* of your fans to see *all* of your posts (the average being just 11%), and brands must now work hard to eek as much free, organic reach out of their Facebook activity as possible. In addition to the above, in order to make sure that as many people as possible encounter the content you post (either on the social network where it was originally posted or if shared elsewhere), the content used to promote your business (either directly or indirectly) must be worthy of fans' attention, i.e., the kind of entertaining, helpful, inspirational, *valuable* stuff that people will like, comment, click (if a link is included) and share. Most people have a handful of "go-to" sources, either in their favorites or subconscious – websites and social profiles that they routinely share from. This selection promises them consistently valuable content they can share with their friends and fans, and your aim should be to become one of these trusted sources.

That doesn't mean that every update that you publish has to be a world-beater. It's perfectly fine to make small talk or to build connections in a more relaxed way. You might even find that's often what works the best - sometimes a simple question like "What are your goals for today?" can get a big response, with small interactions from fans that might lead them to check out some of your weightier posts in the future. Overall, don't constantly fret about making it too light or too deep; strike a balance and make it *you* (see the 80/20 rule in the next chapter for more information).

The bottom line is that the more consistently engaged a customer is with your posts on social media content - liking, commenting, sharing - the more likely they are to continue to do so in the future, and the more exposure you will get. Increasingly (with sites including Facebook, Twitter, and Instagram), positive interaction like this will ensure that your posts will continue to appear in their News Feed for future engagement opportunities. Social networks' news feed algorithms filter content into individuals' feeds according to what they think is most relevant to them, so if a fan never sees posts from you (because you are inactive), ignores your posts for a prolonged period of time because they are not engaging enough, your posts may disappear from that person's News Feed and you may find it difficult to get them to re-appear without paying for the privilege.

Note: With organic reach on Facebook and other social networks at an all-time low, it might seem that the best solution to gain exposure for your content is to post *incredibly frequently*. However, in some ways this approach is actually counter-intuitive. Not even your most passionate fans will enjoy being constantly flooded by posts from you, and by decreasing the pressure of needing to produce a rapid stream of top quality content day in, day out, you leave more time to make sure that what you *do* publish is as good as it can be - stuff that will garner the most engagement from fans. In addition, if you substitute the time spent on "excess" content for supporting "core" content with a smattering of advertising dollars, you increase the number of unique fans who see these posts. And, if they engage with a like, comment, or share, they're more likely to see the next one, organically, in the News Feed.

Which types of posts get the most engagement?
One of the great debates among social media marketers is whether text, image, video, links, or other post types are the most effective in reaching fans and encouraging them to interact. The truth is that nobody can tell you for certain. - Social networks are forever tweaking their algorithms, forcing brands to play catch-up - and at the end of the day, it very much depends on what your individual data reveals to you is working best. For example, way back in 2012 Facebook was telling businesses that posts that include a photo album, picture or video generated about 180%, 120% and 100% more engagement, respectively, than text posts alone. But what use is that potential for engagement if you notice that *your text posts* at any given point in time happen to reach 5x more people than when you use images? My advice is to resist the temptation to blindly follow trends, fads, or tricks that promise to deliver high levels of engagement. Instead, use them as a guide but always focus on providing awesome, valuable content first and foremost. Continue to test and tweak with a close eye on your *own* stats, and keep adapting to push on with what is working best *for you* (not everybody else) at any given time.

Don't get hung up on reach; focus on creating loyal, passionate fans and meaningful relationships
As you now understand, fierce competition between individuals, brands *and* the way social networks' algorithms work means that not all of your fans will see your posts in their news feeds when you publish them. Therefore, you need to think less about chasing "likes", follower numbers, and post reach (the number of people who see a post) - as these metrics (although having some influence and merit, especially if they are reaching a targeted, high quality audience) can often be arbitrary. Instead, concentrate more on producing great content that will grow a loyal following of people who love what you do (showing it via post likes, comments, sharing your content, and eventually through sales), therein encouraging *more* people to invest in your cause. I'd say if you're getting anywhere near 5% reach to all of your fans without paid promotion, you're doing *extremely* well.

14

On the subject of building and maintaining a strong relationship with your fans, try as best you can to keep engagement with your audience timely and use @mentions as a means to be more personable. If someone comments on a status update you make or posts a public message on your profile, be sure to reply to it as soon as possible. Any chance to further the conversation, answer a query, or give thanks for a customer's support is all but lost if there is no reply – and it's something a lot of businesses on social media fail to do, to their detriment. If your profiles are really busy and you simply don't have the time to respond to every fan comment (or if it doesn't necessarily warrant a response), giving a "like" (rather than ignoring them) will at least show that you are listening to what they have to say.

Provide great customer service; handle complaints well

Unlike other forms of media, social media gives your company instant and effective exposure to your customers 24 hours a day, 7 days a week. Customers also have similar access to *you*, and this is no more apparent than in what can only be described as a revolution in customer service. In addition to making your customers feel good, answering complaints provides a useful insight into your target audience's personality, what your business is doing well, and what it could improve on. With the instantaneousness of a Facebook post or a tweet, people's expectation to receive a swift and effective response to their queries or problems is higher than ever. Many social media experts will advise you to *always* reply within an arbitrary time limit of something like 30 minutes. If you employ a dedicated social media community manager this may be possible, but for the vast majority of businesses it just isn't a realistic target. I'd still recommend that you deal with customer service issues as soon as possible after they arise, but suggest that a response time within 24 hours (on weekends, too, if you can manage it) is acceptable to most people. Furthermore, instead of constantly monitoring for problems, simply assign a few dedicated batches of time in a day to respond to customers and handle issues.

Of course, the best way to avoid customer service issues being played out publicly on social media is to prevent them from happening. To facilitate this, give people several options to solve problems themselves and for making contact - online FAQs, email, telephone, private message - and place them where people will see them easily, like in your main bio or About section. The simpler it is to contact you, the more likely a customer is to try that first to help resolve a problem, rather than spouting off angrily at you online. In addition, demonstrate your willingness to accept that problems do sometimes occur by using your social media profiles as a way to announce less-than-positive news about product or service issues. There will always be *some* fans who are upset when they read this, but they'll be a lot more aggrieved if they have to discover the issue on their own. If someone does post their angry grievances in public about you on social media, two of the most important pointers to remember when approaching such a situation are as follows:

Don't ignore it: The longer you leave a customer complaint to sit and fester, the angrier said customer will be, and by refusing to reply to negative feedback, it looks to *everyone* like you are unwilling to deal with problems and are simply hoping that ignoring them will make them go away. Look to respond as quickly as possible, as most customers expect a swift response.

Don't delete it: Just as bad (if not worse) than ignoring negative feedback is to delete a negative, critical or complaining post or review submitted on your profile. When the customer who complained notices that their comment has been deleted, they will only be *even more* upset and other fans who see what you have done (especially if the original criticism was screen-grabbed for evidence) will think negatively of you, too.

In short, always respond to complaints on social media in a professional and courteous manner, and in a time frame that matches the resources of your business. Be ready to acknowledge the customer's feedback (even if you don't think you were in the wrong, as going off on the defensive is a very bad tactic, too) and be willing to admit your mistakes. We're all human – customers realize this and will respect you a whole lot more for being open and honest about any errors instead of simply trying to sweep issues under the carpet. To sweeten instances like this, explain how you will work to fix or improve things if necessary, ask for input from your fans if the situation calls for it, and send a follow-up note a couple of days after the issue has been resolved as a way to make sure everything is still okay *and* to reaffirm a social connection between the customer and your company. Occasionally, consider going above and beyond the call of duty to remedy a customer's problem - in public – in order to harness a wave of respect and good karma. When a Citibike customer in New York City fell off one of its bicycles and ripped his jeans, instead of just apologizing, Citibike delivered the gentleman a voucher to buy a new pair of pants. Surprised and overjoyed, the customer shared the news (and a photo to prove it) on Twitter, to all of his followers.

Automation isn't a dirty word

With so much work involved in growing and maintaining a strong social media marketing strategy over a variety of channels, automation will allow you to save time, stay flexible, and plan your social media strategy down to the minute. Tools like Buffer (http://www.bufferapp.com) or Post Planner (http://www.postplanner.com) allow you to manage multiple social media accounts from a single dashboard (letting you to upload in bulk for the week's upcoming post, publishing content when you are asleep but your audience is not, or when you are on vacation, etc.). In fact, automation tools can help to successfully build a long-term social media strategy by scheduling new and "evergreen" blog posts for repeat exposure, i.e. sharing the same great content multiple times across several social networks, over a set period of time. This will allow more of your existing audience the chance to catch your great content *and* allow new followers to find it if they missed it the first time around. Pay close attention to the frequency that you automate such posts. It may be fine to post a blog post link to Twitter a couple of times in one day (where the flow of information is incredibly quick and dense), but for sites like Facebook and LinkedIn, a bigger delay between each share would be more appropriate. On that note, when you *do* prepare to share the same link multiple times, you're best off re-styling it to make each share as unique and engaging as you can. Check out the Blogging Tips section for more information about using this technique.

In spite of all of the help that automation tools provide, remember that building strong personal relationships with genuine one-to-one interaction should remain at the core of your work. You certainly should not try to automate that (i.e. automating replies to comments on your profiles is a bad idea!), as the results will not likely be good.

Note: On the topic of scheduling and automation, here's a nifty strategy for scheduling posts that you might not have thought of: schedule posts to publish *just before or after the hour* (rather than right on the dot) as a way to catch people who are checking social media at the start of their day, lunch break, after work, between meetings, etc.

Invest time to see results

Social media is now an essential marketing and PR tool, and should be taken seriously. If you ask an existing employee to take over responsibility for your social media output, do not expect them to be able to do it *as well* as their current job. If you're going all-in, expect it to take up *at least* 12-15 hours a week to plan, create, and schedule content, measure results, and engage with customers. Consider employing somebody as your Social Media Manager full time. Alternatively, outsource your activity to a local specialist marketing firm, experts who can help you hit the ground running. If you do, ensure that they understand your brand, marketing goals, and speak your customer's language.

Draw up a social media policy; make employees ambassadors

A clear, company-wide social media policy will clarify the objectives for staff mentions of your brand on social media and empower them to positively support your brand, helping to make you a more socially active business. To prepare the information you need, consult with the key influencers in your business, adhere to state and federal laws, gather feedback from your employees, and outline guidelines about use of social media (whether mentioning your brand or not), both inside and outside business hours. Try to summarize the most important points in a document no longer than one or two pages (otherwise it might not be read and leave you open to issues in the future), and highlight the benefits that responsible use of social media can bring to the company as a whole. Employees need to feel confident about social sharing guidelines to be good brand ambassadors, so make writing company-related statuses easy. For example, invent a hashtag related to life at your business, and encourage them to take pictures and share updates using it. The person in charge of social media content, of course, should know the policy inside out.

Social media marketing isn't free; experiment with paid ads

Many years ago, social media marketing was seen as the new digital gold rush, a way for pioneering brands to reach and promote to their customers for free. In certain aspects, this was true. Now, however, with competition greater than ever, algorithms that prioritize paid content over organic posts, *and* a more astute audience, paid promotion is all-but essential. That's not to say you *can't* still achieve excellent results without spending a penny, but it will be much more difficult, and even a nominal figure spent well (such as $5 per day on highly targeted Facebook ads) can noticeably compound a brand's success. The key to a lot of successful social media advertising is promotion that blend into a user's experience of the site or app on which they appear, mirroring the tone and publishing style of the audience - as with non-paid content, think *seamless* instead of *disruptive*. There's lots more about paid advertising for each specific social media platform to come, including best practices and strategy.

Reconsider return on investment (ROI) metrics

Social media return on investment is not like traditional marketing. For a variety of reasons, you may not always want to focus solely on monetary return within a fixed period. Consider metrics such as brand awareness, word-of-mouth promotion, traffic driven to your website via social media, and strengthening loyalty and engagement with existing customers. These can all be just as valuable in the long run - leading to plenty of sales over a longer period of time, rather than a short-term gain that dies off quickly.

Measuring performance with Google Analytics and other tools

Understanding the performance of your social media marketing is key to being able to succeed in the long run. One of the most cost-effective ways (read: free) to monitor social media conversions is through Google Analytics. Two of the most valuable reports for social media marketers feature under the "Social" section of the site: Network Referrals - shows the data on social media traffic referrals to your website from social networks; and Landing Pages - will show you which of your website pages are shared most often on social media. You can also use Google Analytics to setup and monitor goals, like completed sales, enquiries, and engagement. One of the simplest goals to setup is URL Destination - Google Analytics will mark a goal as met when a visitor lands on a particular page on your website, e.g., a "Thank you for your purchase" page.

Other useful tools for measuring the performance of your social strategy include social networks' native tools (Facebook Insights, Twitter and Pinterest Analytics, etc.) Bit.ly (to measure click-through rates on specified links), and Social Mention (to track mentions of your business name, competitor names, etc. In essence, use analytics tools to set goals, see where your social media strategy is working best, and work out how your customers are finding you so that you can fine tune and optimize your efforts going forward. It is unlikely that you will nail your social media strategy on the first attempt, so evaluate your progress often and don't be afraid to test the water with new ideas, tweak old ones and repeat what works for you.

Note: For an elegantly simple way to monitor the growth of your social media profiles, download my Social Media Progress Tracker spreadsheet. For more details, check out the *Premium Content Bundle* chapter of this book.

Slow and steady wins the race; be patient and ignore scams

Social media success does not happen overnight. Just like in real life, friendships and bonds between you and your audience can take a long time to build, and some people just take longer to warm to you and convert into paying customers than others. Sometimes the metrics that don't pay off instantly (increasing brand awareness and customer retention, or improving customer service) are the ones that will have the greatest impact on conversions later on. I have seen *so* many instances of businesses diving into social media marketing with gusto, only to give up shortly afterwards because they did not have 1.3 billion Facebook fans and a ton of sales after their first week of posting ten times a day (okay, that's an exaggeration but you understand what I mean!). If you're not serious about working at social media for not just weeks or months, but years, you are already setting yourself up for failure.

On a related noted, ignore 'get followers fast' scams. It might be tempting to use services offered all over the web to rack up fans and followers quickly, but you'll only end up with hundreds of random strangers - or bot accounts – won't care about you or your business. 50 interested, engaged, and loyal followers are insurmountably better than 5,000 who are not. The only real "secret" to growing an audience on social media is to be consistent and patient in your efforts.

Above all, enjoy the ride; build strong, meaningful relationships

The stronger someone acquaints with your brand on social media, the more likely they'll remember you and pass the positive word on to their friends and family. As I've hammered home throughout this chapter: be consistent, present, real and genuine in all of your content and communication if you want to foster genuine interaction with customers on a slow and steady path to creating loyalty, sales and brand advocates for life.

Explained: The Best Types of Content to Post on Social Media

With the foundations of social media marketing covered, let's get down to the nitty-gritty of social media content. In this chapter, we'll look at a variety of proven posting strategies to help your social media strategy thrive. The following content strategies are generalized in a way that applies to the majority of social networks covered in this book, but you'll find more *specific* advice about how to maximize its impact for each platform within each social network's individual chapter.

Note: What follows are some of the most popular content strategies for social media. If you'd like *tons* more ideas demonstrated alongside real life examples, check out my list of *101 Social Media Content Ideas for Business* at http://bit.ly/101smmideas

Ask questions and start discussions

Get to know your fans and give them a chance to get to know you by posing questions and starting discussions. These questions can be about a product or event related to your business, a quick trivia quiz, or just about the wider world. Often the types of questions that garner the most engagement are those that can be answered quickly, e.g. those about preference *("Do you prefer product A or product B?")*; Yes or No *(Are you a fan of X?")*; those that ask for opinions *("What's your favorite flavor of ice-cream we offer?")*; or ones that politely challenge *("Opening our second Canadian store this month - guess where?")*. Even just ending a status update with "do you agree?" or "what do you think?" is enough to encourage people to get involved. There is also a place for questions that trigger deeper discussion – especially in community groups – but you'll soon figure out what your customers respond to best. Even the simplest question can be useful in achieving impressive levels of engagement (and consumer insight!), provided that the subject captures the attention of your audience. Interestingly, *where* you ask the question in a status update also affects engagement rates. Posing a question at the end of a post - compared to somewhere in the middle where it can easily get ignored - can increase engagement by up to 15%, according to a study by Buddy Media.

Note: Similar to the above – and also commonly used – are 'fill in the blank' posts as a way to encourage engagement. They're successful because fans will only have to type one or two words at the most to respond, e.g., *"If you could live anywhere in the world, it would be_____."*

Tell your story and feature the stories of your customers

Every brand and individual has a story to tell, whether through text or (often better) through visuals; we're hard-wired to react and respond to a compelling tale. Use social media as a destination where fans can get to know you and your brand much better than they can through simply viewing the products or services that you sell; make it a place where your voice, personality, and authenticity can shine through. Interesting and engaging topics of conversation to cover include why you launched your company, your achievements and failures and what you learned from them, what motivates you, highlighting issues that you are passionate about, and the people and events that inspire you. In essence, show customers that you share their thoughts and ideals, and become a brand that they want to emotionally invest in, which will eventually lead to loyalty and, ultimately, sales. In addition to your own stories, your customers or clients will always have fun and interesting stories about how you and your product or service fits into their lives (and often it's going to be more interesting than content you could come up with yourself), so encourage them to share their tales with you (through text, photos, and videos), so that you can feature them as part of your content strategy – this is referred to in the industry as "user-generated content". Doing so will excite and please the customers in question, encourage them to spread the love about your brand, help to build a stronger community around your product or service, and also act as strong social proof to others about how your brand positively impacts people's lives.

Dig into problems you solve, share your expertise, and be valuable

One of the most effective ways to influence social media users into connecting with you on a social and emotional level is to position your brand as an authority - a source that they can trust and respect, and whom they can rely on for the information or experience they desire. One of the best ways to do this is to dig into the problems your brand can solve and demonstrate your expertise. By this, I don't mean you should start boasting about how good your product is at solving "Problem X" at every opportunity; instead, be a valuable beacon of information within your field or industry. For instance, if your company sells antique furniture polish, you might publish posts to explain why it is so important to keep aged items in good condition, share recent examples and statistics about antiques that have sold for high prices due to their pristine preservation, and provide hints and tips about how best to treat different kinds of wood. Great content – whether single posts or links to a blog article – will also be shared, further increasing brand awareness.

Use breaking news, holidays, and special events to inspire content ideas
If you are able to weave hot, newsworthy topics into your social media posts (not just for the sake of getting likes and views, but adding something to the discussion), it can add a relevance and credibility to your output that will endear you to fans by showing you as a brand that is at the forefront of new trends within your industry (*and* in the case of Facebook, its algorithm works to show timely, trending stories near to the top of the News Feed, possibly leading to higher engagement). Use tools like Google Alerts (http://www.google.com/alerts) and Feedly (http://feedly.com/) to be notified of breaking stories when they happen, or sites like BuzzSumo (http://www.buzzsumo.com) to hunt down trending tweets and topics related to almost any subject. The cookie company Oreo is an expert at using this tactic. For example, at the end of 2013, it posted a short video clip accompanied by the text *"We're officially counting down to the last dunk of the year,"* and to celebrate the USA's Mars Rover robot successfully landing on the Red Planet, it posted a photo of an Oreo cookie with a red-cream center imprinted with robot tracks, and paired it with the caption *"Now, to perfectly land an Oreo cookie in milk."*

In addition, some of the most viral posts on social media are linked to one-off dates or celebrations throughout the year. Holidays like Christmas, Thanksgiving, Easter, Mother's Day, Father's Day, Halloween, or special days like St. Patrick's Day, the night of the Oscars, etc. are feel-good occasions and easy to create content for, e.g., wishing your fans a happy time, sharing a fun fact, asking a holiday-related question, e.g., *"How many Easter bunnies can you see in this photo?"*, or suggesting how your product or service can best be utilized at the particular time of year. Beyond that, there are even more "niche" occasions that might resonate with your fans and will display your brand's relevance: things like the release day of a big movie, International Talk Like A Pirate Day, Movember, or International Coffee Day. Mark all of the most relevant dates in your calendar, and prepare content ahead of time in order to "celebrate" them with your audience.

Note: When you *do* use the above strategies, it is important to do so in the right manner, and with appropriate tact. Avoid hijacking popular cultural events for the sake of it (especially if you cannot make the associated content relevant to your business), and try to do it in a way that doesn't come across as blatantly opportunistic. Spagettio's learned this lesson the hard way (via a tirade of negative feedback) after it commemorated the anniversary Pearl Harbor with an image of a spaghetti hoop holding the flag of the United States.

Promote products and services (adopt the 80 / 20 rule)
Way too many brands are either all business or none when it comes to social media, but you have to find a balance that works for your audience. Although the majority of your social media marketing content should not be overtly promotional, selling your product or service is ultimately what you're there for, and customers do realize that. Assuming that your brand-to-customer relationship is good and the rest of the social media content you post is valuable, they will tolerate the odd post to tell them about a new product or service, or a sale or offer that you are starting - heck, they might even appreciate you letting them know! An easy way to balance out your social media output in a way that will keep you on the good side of your customers, and one a lot of brands already use, is the 80/20 rule. It states that you should post non-promotional content 80% of the time (your own valuable, helpful, or personable stuff, or related content linking to another source, with the sole aim of driving engagement) and reserve the other 20% for being more promotional. Even within this 20%, there is a broad spectrum of approaches, from subtle to more overt selling, depending on how you believe your audience will react.

Note: Where sales and offers are concerned, one approach to keep customers engaged is to make certain promotions exclusive to the people loyal enough to follow you on social media; e.g. extra 5% off for quoting a code posted on your Facebook Page, or a surprise flash sale for people who spot a tweet from you. Another involves giving fans early access to new products or services, preceded by a campaign of posts that build awareness and make people feel a sense that they are getting something special and exclusive. These messages can either be hosted exclusively on a social media channel *or* can be used to push people to your website where you have more freedom to present your brand and its offerings, collect e-mail addresses and visitor data, give away coupons, etc., in any way that you like.

Make effective use of visuals – both images and videos - to drive engagement

Images are *the* most popular type of content shared by social media users, so it stands to reason that you should give them a lot of attention in your own content strategy. Additionally, where brands are concerned, there are real benefits to creating unique visual posts. Research shows that social media images are much more likely to be associated with positive emotions than text posts, and brand promotion via images is much more accepted than if by text (done right, they don't really look like ads, slotting seamlessly into people's news feeds – remember, *non-jarring* is what you should be aiming for).

Online tools (mentions of which are dotted throughout this book) now make the creation of beautiful visual content easier than ever. If you wanted to, you could crank out dozens of visuals per day. With this in mind, try not to fall into the trap of creating snazzy visuals for the sake of it, or to the detriment of your central marketing message. Study the performance of your images to spot which ones trigger a response in your fans and which ones do not. When you find what works, replicate and scale it. Remember, too, that good written content that spells out your value proposition, compels fans to act, and builds a dialogue between you and your customers, (when accompanying an image, on its own, or in reply to comments) remains crucially important. Make sure your marketing and sales strategy defines how and when visuals will be used, and that they complement your brand while upholding the quality of your product or service.

Where to find images to post on social media

Physically shooting photos or building your own original graphic images is always the best option for visual content on social media, but time and budget constraints make this impossible for most brands to execute one hundred percent of the time. Luckily, there are a ton of online tools to find and edit photos and graphics, either completely free or for a small fee. Where free photos are concerned, some of my favorite sources for free images include Comp Fight (http://www.compfight.com) and Unsplash (https://unsplash.com). For reasonably priced stock images, Yay Micro (http://www.yaymicro.com) is my go-to destination. Be careful when choosing stock images – avoid cheesiness and cliché at all costs; go for natural, visceral shots. As for graphics and vectors, Freepik (http://www.freepik.com) is my first port of call to look for free stuff. If I can't find what I like there,

Vectorstock (http://www.vectorstock.com) is my preferred site. With all of the above - whether an image is free or paid for - always read and understand the terms of using an image, e.g., whether accreditation is required, if it can be used for commercial purposes, etc.

Note: Each social network has its own specific best practices for image sizes, but the general rule of thumb for any visual content is that bigger is always better. The social networks will automatically resize your images as needed: there is no quality loss when the image is scaled down, but there will most certainly be if an image needs to be blown up. For simplicity's sake, sticking to the following measurements should cover you for nearly all of your visual needs: 1280 x 720 pixels for landscape images, 735 x 1102 pixels for portrait images, and 900 × 900 pixels for square images. In addition, it's useful to name your image files thoughtfully for SEO (search engine optimization): include keywords separated by hyphens or underscores, and alt tags to sit in place of your image when an error prevents it from loading, or it is being interpreted by someone who is visually impaired.

Brand your images (but sometimes choose not to)
One of the fundamental building blocks of branding is consistency. In order to help your fans learn to instinctively recognize your visual content when it appears in their news feeds or is "stolen" from the social network you originally posted to, it is critical to brand your content effectively. This can be achieved in one or more ways combined, such as adding a logo (create guidelines addressing size and placement for neatness), website URL or Twitter handle, and using a consistent color palette, photo filter, and fonts to reflect your brand personality. The colors, filters and fonts used in your images will strongly affect how people perceive your brand on social media, so choose them with care, considering what kinds of feelings you want each piece of content to evoke, e.g., bright and cheery, serious, nostalgic, etc. For efficiency's sake (and to compound a sense of familiarity over time) you may even want to create a uniform template for certain types of visual content, e.g., promotions, industry insights, milestones. Research has shown that it takes people between 5-7 impressions for people to begin to recognize your brand, so the repetition of key brand ingredients like logo, colors and typeface is extremely important. So, if your social media post graphics look and feel cohesive, then users can form a clearer understanding of your brand in their minds.

Note: In most cases, a subtle approach to branding works best; your image not your brand - should take center stage, and sometimes no text overlay or filter is needed. This is particularly pertinent for content created to mark occasions with emotional or historical significance, e.g. Mother's Day, Martin Luther King Day, Memorial Day, etc., where foregoing all branding might actually work in your favor for two reasons: slapping your logo on such content just doesn't seem right, and people may be encouraged to share high quality, original, "brandless" images because they feel more ownership over them - the visual content is suddenly much more selfless, or more about the fan and their connections than it is your brand. Although there is a higher chance that the images in question might be stolen and used without attribution, if those images *do* get more shares on the social profile you originally published them to as a result of having no branding, some sort of built-in attribution should remain each time they are passed along, e.g. a Facebook link to your business' Page or a "retweeted by" link on Twitter.

Make images powerful and self-explanatory
The best images to use on social media are ones that catch the eye, inspire curiosity, entertain, spur emotion, or broadcast a gripping message. It doesn't really matter if the image shows an experience related to your brand or not; the important thing is to help reinforce the kinds of emotions you want customers to associate with your company. Research by Buffer found that self-explanatory, stand-alone images perform better than those that need explanation and clarification in the accompanying description. In essence, if your image needs a caption to make any sense at all (rather than to elaborate and provide more value), it might not be as effective as you want it to be.

Share a special offer, discount code, or upcoming event
People love special offers, and images are a great way to highlight them in a bold and imaginative way - whether it's the launch of a season-long promotion, a one-off event, or a week where each day brings a new deal (a great way to encourage people to visit your social profiles multiple times). Compound an image's impact with accompanying text that includes a link for fans to access the offer/get more information, a time limit that will add a sense of urgency, and a call to action that will drive click-throughs. Where upcoming events, products and services are concerned, make a point of regularly highlighting these moments on social channels, and to continually differentiate yourself from the competition. Where relevant, make a point of accompanying such

images with words like "new" and "limited time only" to convey your brand as fresh and forward-thinking and to pique the curiosity of your customers.

Note: As an extra way to drive engagement, design an image that tells fans that they'll gain access to a secret sale, discount code, etc. if said image receives a certain amount of shares. Set a realistic target based on your existing audience and predicted reach, because you do really want to hit it and reward those who were interested.

Show customers enjoying your products and services
There is no greater form of social proof than customers showing others how much they are enjoying your product or service. Doing so with an image is extremely powerful way of converting people into customers because it helps people associate positive emotions with your brand, whether the photo is snapped by you or - even better - user-submitted. Smartphones make it extremely easy for people to capture and share experiences with your brand as they happen, so encourage your customers and fans to do just that when they are at your premises (with signs or purpose-made "group photo/selfie spots" with an interesting background, for example.), out and about, or at home (e.g., "Post a photo in the comments to show us the view you see while listening to our podcast"). Actively encourage customers to tag or mention your profile in updates containing photos, so that when you are notified you can easily save and share the user-generated image on your brand's profile page (giving credit, of course, but also making the person feel special and eager to show their moment in the spotlight to their friends). Unify these types of posts with a hashtag that you can track across all platforms to hunt down more user-generated content, and even add a subtle link to the product or service in question, if you think your audience won't mind. For an additional layer of persuasion, you could experiment with adding a short customer testimonial in the form of a text overlay on top of an image of a happy customer, both to spread cheer about your brand and help convert others into willing buyers.

Note: As a quick and powerful aside to your social media efforts, include customer images on the product pages of your website for top notch social proof. Include instructions with your product (on the packaging, confirmation email, etc.) to let customers know how to tag you on Facebook, Instagram, etc., then use a website plugin to have the images automatically appear on your site.

Show off product features in images or infographics

People viewing and buying products online don't have the ability to examine them as they would in real life, so high-quality product images with added details (or a link to where they can be found) are extremely important to social media marketing. Add annotations to an image of a product or service to show off features that might not be immediately obvious, e.g. the special type of fabric used in a garment, how efficient your delivery times are, or the wondrous technology hidden inside a gadget. If size is an important part of your product, think about juxtaposing it next to a common household item (or your competitor's product!) so that customers can easily judge the scale.

Infographics also work well to display lots of information - especially numbers and other data related to your brand, often based on a seasonal theme - in an eye-catching, engaging and shareable way. If graphic design isn't your bag, sites like Piktochart (http://www.piktochart.com) and Easel.ly (http://www.easel.ly) will help you to create great-looking infographics in a simple, drag-and-drop manner. While infographics render well in Twitter and Pinterest feeds, do *not* upload and post a full infographic image to sites not designed for such images, like Facebook or Instagram, because it will be shrunk, squashed and be almost impossible to read. Instead, select a square portion of the infographic (either the top section where the title is or from its most interesting point), cut it out, and post *this* along with a link and a call to action to encourage people to click through to your website, Pinterest profile, etc. to view the infographic in full.

Share inspirational, aspirational, motivational and nostalgic images, and blog post quotes
Two types of image posts that often perform well on all social media are inspirational, aspirational, and motivational quotes. In addition to their tendency to stir a deep emotional response, they are also highly shareable, so target your quotes to relate to the mindset of your customer. Nostalgic photos with a text overlay work similarly in the way that they strike a chord of a shared experience within us, often from our childhood. Subjects for these might include historic images of your target audience's city or neighborhood, or dusty old snapshots that relay the heritage of your brand. And of course, everyone on social media loves a funny image - uplifting and shareable. The following are some very broad guidelines for creating strong examples of each type of image. With repetition and consistency, your fans will learn to tie the emotions they feel when viewing these images to your brand, product or service:

Motivational images: items or landscapes that inspire optimism and positivity; strong sans serif fonts that capture attention and reinforce authority (capitalize words to create emphasis); bright and vivid filters to compound impact of your words. Often, the best kind of inspirational content arrives in the form of case studies, customer testimonials and stories of your own failures and challenges.

Aspirational images: Aspirational content doesn't necessarily refer simply to that which appeals to customers who aspire to attain great wealth, social status or to own expensive possessions. An aspiration is defined as a hope or ambition of achieving *something*, so can describe any genuine desire - like improving a golf swing, taking care of pot plants better, or becoming more confident. Underlying these aspirations are deeper motivations: to connect with people, to impress our friends, to find a romantic partner, etc. Aspirations are linked to people's identities. Therefore, aspirational content speaks to feelings rather than needs, opening up the potential customer pool from those who are currently in the market for your product, to anybody who is capable of experiencing those feelings. As well as producing images that *show*, consider how they help to build a story to help your audience *feel* a certain way about your brand and products; one that will help them to reach their own personal goals.

Nostalgic images: Choose a retro, relatable, interesting photo of your company, your community, etc., ideally several years old; hand-written, narrow fonts are wistful and memory-laden; match your filter to the occasion or season, e.g. bright and over-exposed for summer. Tie nostalgic images to a popular hashtag like #tbt (Throwback Thursday) to add some extra clout and shareability.

Funny images: Images that are created to entertain don't have to be directly related to your products or services, but should appeal to your target audience in order to be successful. Match the font type to the tone of the humor, e.g. serif for playful, sans serif for dry; use warm tones and filters. Highly shareable, they can work by transforming your company into a relatable, more personable entity.

Note: A similar strategy to the above involves lifting a choice statistic or quote from a blog post and converting it into a powerful image that will motivate your readers to click over to read the article in full. Graphics and text overlays can be quickly and easily created in programs like Photoshop, PowerPoint or

Keynote, *or* through online tools like Canva (http://www.canva.com), or Adobe Spark (http://spark.adobe.com) *or* apps like A Beautiful Mess and Phonto (both available for iOS and Android devices).

Share hints, tips, and tutorials

Offering hints and tips to your customers is a great way to be consistently valuable, increase the potential virality of your posts, and to grow brand loyalty. One of the easiest ways to do this is to show simple, step-by-step instructions by composing a photo album or a single photo split into several frames (the Instagram-built Layout app, websites like Fotor (http://www.fotor.com) and Canva both offer free collage-making tools, while mobile apps like PicFrame and Diptic will help you to achieve a similar effect on iOS and Android devices). To take one example, Petsmart uses a single Instagram image split into multiple images to give simple pet training advice, like teaching a dog to sit and lay. The photo's visual instructions are complemented by further explanation in the text caption.

Show behind the scenes

To increase intimacy with your brand, show your human side, and to make customers feel that they are getting a special sneak peek at the inner workings of your company, use photos to snap photos of behind-the-scenes goings-on — either vague, but exciting teasers *or* documenting each stage of a project as you go along, showing fans your work in progress. For example, Tiffany & Co. once snapped a photo of an artist they had employed, right in the middle of him painting a new backdrop for its new Fifth Avenue store. Other examples might be as simple as showing off the treats bought for the office to celebrate the end of the working week, taking a snapshot of a special visitor, or posting a photo to welcome the newest member of your staff.

Highlight your charitable side

To help enhance your brand image, stand out as a brand that cares; use images to highlight your charitable side. Levis regularly promotes the good its company does, such as posting a photo of a t-shirt printed for the free day it gives all employees so that they can help projects in their local communities. Get your fans involved in the process, too. For example, you could create a poll ("Poll" or "Offerpop" are two handy Facebook apps for this purpose) and ask your audience to vote on the charity or cause that they want to see you support.

Share popular memes; adapt them to your audience
Memes (most often humorously-captioned images or GIFs) are hugely shareable and extremely popular on social media. If you're unfamiliar with memes (I'm sure you'll have seen one even if you didn't recognize the image as one), the best thing is to visit a site like Know Your Meme (https://knowyourmeme.com) to discover trending examples for use on your Page, or to create your own - you'll pick up the idea in no time. Humorous and cute memes and images also do well on social media - anything that will evoke an emotional reaction, particularly if it is a positive one. The "Funny", "Aww" and "Pics" subreddits of Reddit (http://www.reddit.com/r/funny, http://www.reddit.com/r/aww and http://www.reddit.com/r/pics respectively) are an almost infinite source of such content, but if you have your own original images, all the better. The unstoppable spread of many memes and funny images means that crediting the original source can be an almost impossible task, but it's always good to do so if you can. Despite the widespread popularity of memes and other viral images, do not rely on them heavily as a way to bulk out your social marketing strategy. Regardless of the high engagement rates they might get, this type of content can be regarded as not "high quality" (especially in the eyes of Facebook, as often the engagement it *does* get is not the most highbrow). So too much of it could hinder your reputation and reach more than it helps. But used once in a while, memes shouldn't do any harm.

Jump on fads in popular culture
Just as the popularity of a meme comes and goes, so do real-life photo trends. So-called "photobombing" and selfies are trends that look like they are here to stay, but others like "whaling" and "owling" (remember those? Me neither!) burned out as quickly as they arrived. Nevertheless, all of these trends can be taken advantage of in order to boost engagement in your own content strategy, whether you take the photos yourself or encourage your fans to so that you can share their efforts on your social profiles. For example, Currumbin Wildlife Sanctuary in Australia encourages visitors to take selfies with some of the animals within the park, which it then features on its Facebook and Instagram profiles.

Build Presentations for Slideshare
With over 60 million visitors a month, Slideshare (http://www.slideshare.net) is the web's biggest hub for hosting and sharing presentations on almost any topic. Some of the most popular slideshows are business-related, which makes

the site doubly important for B2B companies. The site's visual nature makes it one of the most efficient platforms from which to create or re-purpose work in order to generate high quality leads (paid membership even allows you to place contact forms within the presentation itself). The most successful Slideshare presentations are laser-focused in their subject, turning individual aspects of written content (blogs, e-books, speeches, and even infographics) into highly visual content, using strong and emotive photos or graphics, a consistent color scheme and fonts, and keeping text to an absolute minimum - often just a single sentence (or even half of one!) per slide. Check out the Explore and Popular pages on Slideshare for examples of featured content, and mirror this style in your own uploads. Slideshare decks can be created, saved, and uploaded via software like PowerPoint and Keynote, online tools like Canva or apps like SlideIdea (http://slideidea.com/). Once published, Slideshare presentations can be shared onto Facebook, Twitter, Pinterest, LinkedIn, and more, *and* embedded into websites.

Other image types: word clouds, screenshots, and snack size data
Word clouds are a fun and inventive way to represent a piece of content when sharing it to social media, whether using the words from a blog post, the transcript of a video, or the opinions of people commenting on a particular status update. Sites like Wordle (http://www.wordle.net/) ask you to paste in a body of text, which it will then use to generate a word cloud – customizable by font, layout, and color scheme. The more times a word appears, the more prominence it is given in the cloud. If you want to direct people to a specific part of your website or show them a quick step-by-step process, then screenshot images are one effective way to go about it - show people, don't tell. Creating them is as simple as using a snipping tool like Skitch (https://evernote.com/skitch/) (or even the Print Screen key) to grab a snapshot, then adding text and arrow annotations before sharing. Or if you want to add a bit of visual flair, check out a service like PlaceIt (http://www.placeit.net), which allows you to insert a screenshot onto professional stock photos of devices captured in real-life settings. Screenshots are also useful if you simply cannot find a suitable image: grabbing block quotes, ordered lists, or short paragraphs (stuff that can be easily digested) is the best option here. Infographic-style images needn't be big, full pieces of work. Sharing a snippet of fascinating or impressive data in the form of a graphic with a text overlay or a chart can be just as powerful. Examples might include the number of hours it takes to manufacture a single pair of bespoke

shoes, how the amount you've given to charity has increased over the years, or how many cups of coffee your team goes through during a busy week!

Experiment with animated GIFs

While the popularity of animated GIFs has prevailed for many years, their usage has boomed thanks to more accessible creation tools and faster Internet connections. Animated GIFs are currently supported on Twitter, Facebook and Pinterest (and, of course, make create additions to blog posts) and they are an easy way for brands to add a fun, engaging element to content. A few methods for their use include: demonstrating a tricky step in a how-to guide; replaying a hilarious moment from a recent event, ad campaign, or behind the scenes at your business; flashing up the benefits of a product or service; making an announcement, thanking a customer, relaying a reaction or emotion like happiness, surprise, or fear; or simply creating a cool effect like a seamless loop, in a much more dynamic way than text or static emoticons. Check out Giphy (http://www.giphy.com) to search for and discover a massive archive of animated GIFs, create your own using software like Photoshop or simple web tools like Make A GIF (http://www.makeagif.com), and use Loop Findr (http://loopfindr.tumblr.com/) to build animated GIFs that contain seamless loops.

Video Content Strategies

Video content (pre-recorded or live streaming) is a *huge* part of the social media mix, and many of the strategies above can very easily be adapted to work in video form for multiple social channels. Later chapters will include *specific* advice on maximizing the impact of video for the social networks in question. In the past, the focus on social video was mostly about achieving viral success. However, virality doesn't always do much for your brand in the long term. Short, authentic, raw, entertaining, and valuable videos go much further than forcing an idea in the hope that it will become a one-hit wonder. With attention spans being so small on social media, short-form videos give you more freedom to produce emotive, relatable videos that get to the point quickly, without the overhead of creating more in-depth content.

Develop compelling video content for social media
Make sure that your videos reward people's attention and tells a story, even if only the first few seconds are watched. Use mobile native tools, and techniques and styles that mirror the organic content your fans like to see. Even though

people's attention spans are now sporadic and short, consumers are more focused on their phones than ever. As a result, your job is to build new ways to tell meaningful, emotional stories in short form. Make your video more visually engaging by using a format unique to mobile, such as a vertical or square video. It's easiest to just build for mobile right from the start, as you'll avoid the time and cost of editing for mobile. Otherwise, check out Animoto (www.animoto.com) Animatron Wave (www.animatron.com) for an easy way to create three versions of the same video: landscape, square, and portrait, all at once. My recommendation is when you broadcast solo, is to use portrait mode. And when you go live with a guest or show a view, use landscape. Square videos work well for almost any content - so stick with that if you want to keep things simple!

Experiment with live broadcasting tools
Tools like Facebook Live have brought the ability to easily live stream video to the web well into mainstream consciousness, and for brands and businesses, instant web video - complimenting some of the content strategies listed above, e.g., product demonstrations, a look behind the scenes, Q&As, etc., can be used as a highly engaging way to connect with, and expand your audience. I'll get into the particulars of different live broadcast tools later on in the book, but if it's an avenue you are interested in, the following basics will ensure that your live streams leave audiences wanting more. Just because live video is raw and unedited, doesn't mean the need to prepare falls completely by the wayside. You still need a structure, consistent brand voice, and smooth production values, including:

Decent connectivity: Nothing will annoy your audience more than a stream that constantly pauses, drops, or stutters. So wherever possible, ensure that you maintain a good Wi-fi or 4G connection. If you think there might be issues, make your audience aware so that their expectations are managed effectively.

Appropriate setting: If you are broadcasting from your home or office, record a test clip to ensure that what your audience sees will be an adequately lit and well-composed setting without a distracting or unprofessional background (i.e. dirty dishes, messy storage cupboard) - think about the image that you want to portray! Obviously, your power to control this out on location might be different, but always try to do so.

Steady camera: Okay, this isn't going to be possible at all times, especially if you're outside filming a dynamic scene, but if you're filming yourself or something static, then a tripod or selfie stick can work wonders.

Good sound: Poor quality audio or distracting background noises can be the bane of audiences tuning into live broadcasts. So, if streaming in a quiet spot isn't an option and you don't want to rely on your phone's built-in mic, look into buying a cheap, clip-on mic. If it has a fluffy cover to block wind noises, all the better.

Live broadcast structure: keeping fans engaged

One of the most important things to consider about live video is that people who watch the very beginning of your stream are most likely watching a replay (the logic here is that the chances of *everyone* that watches tuning in right at time the broadcast goes live, is slim). Keep these viewers in mind and plan to start talking immediately - the first 60 seconds can make or break your stream. Welcome live viewers and those watching the replay, introduce yourself and then talk about what viewers can expect from the broadcast. Keeps viewers' attention early on by asking an easy-to-answer question like, "Where are you from?" This approach is especially useful on Facebook because when more people comment and like, it will show your engaging broadcasts to more people in the News Feed. Go on to share valuable insight and ideas with viewers, then ask if they are enjoying what you're sharing. If they are, encourage them to ask questions and invite their friends to join the live broadcast. As your broadcast is coming to an end, recap the most important points and share a little about what viewers can expect in your next broadcast. Tell them when it's going to happen and ask fans to follow so that they can tune in live.

Host contests on social media

Contests (promotions, sweepstakes and prize draws) are a staple strategy for many brands on social media, and they're a great way to increase awareness of your company, generate buzz for a new product, encourage engagement, and build communities on your profiles. The goal of a social media contest should be to attract highly engaged fans who will stick with you after the promotion ends, slowly converting them into loyal regular customers. To this end, offer a prize that targets your audience's wants and needs (e.g. free coffee for a week if you own a coffee shop, a free pampering session if you own a spa, a store-specific voucher, etc.). Contests with generic prizes (Amazon gift cards, iPads, etc.) will attract low-value fans who aren't necessarily interested in your brand offering, and unlikely to convert to loyal fans and customers in the future. To further prevent unwanted entrants, make your contest last for a long time to discourage those people only looking for the chance of a quick win (perhaps weeks or even months depending on the prize), and also make the barrier to entry something that only true fans would take the time to do. Other simple ideas for contest success include making it easy for people to share news of the contest with their friends, hosting a joint contest with a related business to share audiences, and considering paid promotion to encourage entries in the campaign's infancy.

Work with influencers

One of the biggest trends to emerge in social media over the last several years is influencer marketing. Essentially, it involves building partnerships with individuals that already have a large social media following, and who would be interested in promoting what you have to offer. Crucially, that individual should also already love what you do (or be open to trying it out), and be willing to share it with their audience – ideally, a crowd who match your target demographic. Having an influencer mention your brand or your products can provide your brand with oodles of exposure and credibility, and it is a relationship that can nurture and grow over time.

It is now common for popular influencers to receive many requests from brands to mention their products, and for those with a huge following (hundreds of thousands, millions even), a not-unsubstantial fee is usually involved. However, for smaller influencers, building a budding relationship needn't cost a fortune. You could start simply by commenting on their photos, sending a tweet, or tagging them in your posts. They'll receive a notification, and after a few mentions, they might be open to connect. Alternatively, an inexpensive way to tempt influencers to work with you is to offer free samples of your product or services. If your offering matches the influencer's style of content, they'll often be more than happy to write a blog post, share a photo, give you a shout out, etc., in return for a freebie.

Note: To improve your chances of success, be selective about who you send offers to. Do your research and select influencers who have a history of getting their followers to take action. If you're just starting out, aim for influencers with smaller follower counts who might be more receptive to your offer, e.g., someone with a couple of thousand followers who lives locally vs. a worldwide social media megastar with millions of fans.

Tie everything together with a strong hashtag strategy

Hashtags on social media help to group conversations, give context to your posts, and because using the"#" symbol in front of a word turns it into a clickable link – a sound hashtag strategy can help you and your content get discovered by your target audience. In most cases, clicking on a hashtag included in a post will take a person to a list of posts containing the same hashtag. Many brands use hashtags because "that's the thing to do" but adding them without purpose can one can weaken the impact of a post, or even have the power to turn people off your brand completely. Hashtags for business use normally fit into one of three types: branded, community, or campaign. Branded and community hashtags work best as part of a long-term strategy, while campaign hashtags are best for short-term goals:

- A branded hashtag is one that's unique to your business; it can be as simple as your company name, slogan, or the name of a product, e.g. #traderjoes. Getting fans to use your branded hashtag is key to getting discovered on certain social networks, particularly Instagram. When fans use it, it means they enjoy your product or service and want to share the experience with others. Even better, when fans post images or videos using a branded hashtag, it can be a great source for curating influential user-generated content for use in your own future content.

- Community hashtags also enable brands to connect like-minded people around a specific topic, but unlike branded hashtags, community hashtags don't have be directly related to a business — they often focus on a theme, feeling, or idea. For example, Levis uses the hashtag #LevisPride to show its support for the LGBT community. You can also use community hashtags as a way to express an emotion or sentiment relating to your brand, e.g., #ShopSmarterChicago or #SparkYourHappy.

- Campaign hashtags usually last for a few days, weeks, or months, because campaign hashtags are most often associated with specific campaigns, like a new product launch or a contest. For this reason, brands promote a campaign hashtag heavily when a campaign is live to generate as much activity as possible, then stop promoting it once the campaign has ended. For example, Whole Earth Foods used the hashtag #ManvHorse2018 to promote the fact that it was sponsoring the Man Versus Horse event in 2018, and to encourage fans to get take part.

General hashtags best strategies

I'll be covering hashtag strategy for specific social networks in later chapters, but these tips will be useful for wherever your hashtags appear:

- *Identify your hashtag goals* to give you the direction you need to successfully implement them as part of your social media strategy. Goals can range from creating buzz around a product, to driving contest entries, to encouraging user-generated content.
- *Research your hashtag:* Search and listen to see what hashtags people are already using when talking about your brand, and capitalize by using those. Also check to ensure your desired hashtag isn't already being used by another company. For inspiration, tools such as Hashtagify (Hashtagify.me) can help you to discover relevant or trending hashtags.
- *Make hashtags easy to remember* – and to spell. Don't leave room for possible typos, which will make hashtags hard for people to use.
- *Short hashtags work best.* #ilovechocolatecakeandeatiteveryday - a hashtag like this is difficult to read. In addition, use legible formatting. Symbols don't work too well, and capitalizing words helps make hashtags a bit more readable, e.g., #BigSale rather than #bigsale.
- *Educate your audience.* Make sure you clearly communicate the hashtag to them in your own posts and more importantly, explain why you want them to include it in their own posts.
- *Be patient.* If you've rolled out a hashtag, chances are that your audience won't take to using it "organically" straight away, especially if you're using a brand slogan or other one-sided hashtag. The best hashtags are inclusive, shareable, and discoverable. If it doesn't organically fit within a post, it will come across as forced and lose its impact.
- *Give people a reason to use your hashtag.* The best hashtags draw people in and invoke curiosity to explore and become part of a conversation. Whether it's as part of contest entry or the fact you recognize hashtag users with a like or a comment, your audience will be more likely to use your hashtag when the relationship benefits you both.
- *Measure your results and adapt your strategy.* Measuring your results and adapting your campaigns as needed is the best way to make sure you

stay on track and deliver on the goals you set out to reach or improve through the use of hashtags. More than ever, social media users are tagging their updates with "emotion" hashtags, too, e.g., "Had an awesome meal at Betty's Grill today! #stuffed #bestburgersever." Whether the sentiments are good or bad, they can often give you a deeper insight into your brand image than you imagined. Hashtag search tools like Tagboard (https://www.tagboard.com) provide a way to find top recent tweets related to any given hashtag, conduct competitive hashtag analysis, and track hashtag use across different platforms.

Facebook Tips:
Marketing Strategy You'll Like and Share

Facebook is the most visited social network in the world, with well over one billion users across desktop and mobile. As the king of social networks, your target audience is almost guaranteed to be there.

Years ago, Facebook was a veritable goldmine for brands looking for a large captive audience and lots of web traffic, but this unfettered potential has slowly declined over the years as competition has increased, paid promotion introduced, and as Facebook tries to re-balance the site's stream of personal vs branded content. In its latest big News Feed updates in 2018, Facebook made clear more than ever that the News Feed will favor showing updates posted or shared by friends and family over that of business Pages and that content that encourages communities to gather and interact in meaningful ways, is what the site's algorithm will prioritize. It makes sense, given that Facebook users primarily visit the site to interact with their friends and family and they want to see their posts, but they *also* visit Facebook to be informed, inspired, to converse amongst likeminded people, and be entertained - which is where you come in. So, while Facebook marketing isn't as straightforward as it used to be, the site is still a must-use resource for nearly every brand interested in social media marketing. If you're smart about your approach, there is still *ample* opportunity to reach your target audience and reach your business goals. Use the tips in this chapter to build, brand and market your business on Facebook, as well as amass a following of highly engaged customers.

Facebook Business Page Setup Strategy

Pages are no longer just a home for your brand's Facebook posts. As a lot of content from Pages gets overshadowed in the News Feed (or doesn't appear in it at all), Facebook has moved to create additional value for businesses by making Pages a *destination*; a place where people can find all the information they need about your business: opening hours, to read or write reviews, to make a purchase, book a reservation, submit customer service queries, and more, *as well* as a place to engage with content that resonates with them.

Small and local businesses in particular should think of Facebook as they would other platforms such as TripAdvisor, Yelp, and Google. Even just doing the

41

simple things such as keeping business hours up to date, completing profile information completely are critical for discoverability on Facebook. So, before you dive in and start posting on Facebook, it pays to take some time to lay solid foundations to help get your brand presence set up properly and in a position to impress fans when they visit your Page.

Create a Facebook Page, not a personal profile

When you sign up to Facebook, you are assigned a Personal Timeline by default. Personal Timelines, often referred to as profiles, are designed for individual, non-commercial use. For your business to take advantage of everything Facebook marketing has to offer, you must create a separate Facebook Page. Facebook Pages look similar to personal Timelines, but provide unique tools for brands like analytics, custom tabs to host business-related information, and advertising tools. Pages do not require separate Facebook accounts and do not have separate login information from Timelines. You can create a Facebook Page in one of three ways: by searching 'Create A Page' in the search bar at the top of the site, by clicking the 'Create A Page' button at the top of any existing Facebook Page, or by visiting https://www.facebook.com/pages/create.

Note: If you are currently using a personal profile for business purposes, there is a possibility that Facebook will find and shut your account down without notice. If you are in this situation, this is what to do: compose a status on the profile you created that explains that you have created a new Facebook Page for your business and ask people to go and like the Page to continue receiving updates and information from you. Share your Page and the same message to your personal timeline and ask friends if they'll like and share it to help grow your audience back. Once you've built momentum, deactivate your initial profile, group or event. While building a Facebook Page is essential for businesses on Facebook, there are also several ways to utilize a personal profile - in a non-commercial. For now, we're going to concentrate on Pages, but look out for Timeline-based tips in the *Using Your Personal Facebook Profile to Boost Business* section at the end of this chapter.

Keep your Facebook Page name short; get it right the first time!

If at all possible, try to keep your Facebook Page name short, as this will help if you go on to create Facebook ads, where the headline space in the advert (often the name of your Page) is limited to just 25 characters. If you are *not* happy with your Page name at any time, go to the "About" section of your

Page, click "Edit Page Info" and type the amendment into the Name section. Changing your Page's name does not affect its username or Page web address (explained below).

Get a custom Facebook username and URL for your Facebook Page
Set up a vanity username and URL for your Facebook Page (available when you gain 25 likes), ideally named after your brand, e.g. @yourcompanyname / www.facebook.com/yourcompanyname. To reach the 25-fan threshold quickly, invite your e-mail contacts and current Facebook friends – a community of people who already care about you and your brand - to visit and "Like" your Page. To create a username for your Page, click Create Page @username on the left side of your Page. Enter your desired username, and the username is available, click Create. Your Page's username will appear below your Page's name, in search results and in your Page's URL to help people find and remember your Page.

Fill in business info accurately and in detail
Fill in as much of your business' details as possible in the About section of your Facebook Page, including address, brand story, contact details, product information, website (add multiple URLs by separating them with commas in the website box), and links to other social profiles. Putting the effort into populating these sections makes your Page helpful to customers who can see all of your essential information in one place, and the keyword-rich blurb is also good for search engine optimization (SEO), as the text in your About section is indexed by Google. Restaurant owner and selected Restaurant/Cafe as your Page's category? Make sure you include the types of foods you serve, and also upload your menu as a PDF for customers to browse, or if you're in the U.S. or Canada, you can also add a menu through SinglePlatform.

Note: In November 2016, Facebook rolled out an easy to optimize your Page based on type, by offering pre-made templates. They include quick setups for Shopping, Venues, Professional Services, Restaurants, and more. Each option gives different defaults for the tabs along the side of your Facebook Page and for the buttons under your cover photo. So, if you want to update your Page's look and feel instantly to match your business type, do so via the Templates section under Settings > Edit Page.

One more benefit of a full and thorough Facebook Page setup is related to Facebook Professional Services (https://www.facebook.com/services/), the social network's answer to Yelp - a directory for customers to find, research, and contact local businesses. Search results return a link to your Page (with "Like" button), contact details, opening hours, star rating, and customer reviews - so it's in your best interest to make sure everything in the About section of your Page is populated and up-to-date!

Verify your Page and get an official check mark on your cover photo

If your Page's category is Local Business, Company or Organization, Facebook may make it eligible for a gray verification check mark - similar to the blue check mark given to celebrities and other public figures. Verified Pages appear higher in search results and show people at a glance that you are the official brand Page for your company on Facebook, so it's well worth doing if you have the option to. To verify your Page, visit your Page Settings and choose Page Verification under the General menu. You'll need to confirm your business-representative status via a telephone call to a publicly listed number for your business, or otherwise upload an official document, e.g. business phone or utility bill, business license, business tax file, etc.

Create an awesome cover photo and add a call-to-action button

Use your Facebook Page's cover photo to effectively communicate your brand or message in one simple, high quality, image. Facebook's guidelines say that the ideal size for a cover photo image is 820 × 312 pixels - any smaller and Facebook will automatically stretch the image, making it appear blurry. However, Facebook displays Page cover photos at 640 x 360 pixels on smartphones. This means, rather confusingly, that cover photos can appear differently on desktop and mobile. To ensure any text on your cover photo also displays on mobile (i.e. is not obscured or cropped), create an invisible buffer of 134 pixels either side, and feature the text in the middle - the remaining 560 pixels. Ideas for cover photos include one powerful image that communicates who you are and what you do, a collage of your products, highlighting an ongoing offer, or featuring a photo or testimonial submitted by one of your own fans - the latter will really "wow" your customer and hopefully they'll spread the word to their friends. Keep users engaged by periodically updating your cover photo and profile pic – once per month is a good target to aim for, but a seasonal change is popular among brands, too.

When you upload a cover photo, click on it and you will be able to edit it to add a text description. Here, type a short, relevant blurb, then add in a call to action and related links to your website, a product, an offer, a Page tab, or feature a discount code as a reward for clicking. Many Facebook Page visitors click on cover photos for a closer look, so use the description as a way to anchor the photo and encourage them to take action. To encourage more clicks on your cover photo, you can try experimenting with a "button" as part of your cover design with its own call to action, e.g., *"Get 10% off your next purchase with us - Click Here!"* Alternatively, (and to tempt the people who won't click on your Page's cover photo - call to action or not), you might want to use it to let non-fans know what value there is to them in "liking" your Page, e.g., Free DIY tips, daily dessert recipes, regular parenting advice, etc. Every time a Facebook user "likes" your Page, a large part of your cover image (along with your profile photo) will show in the News Feed of that person's friends, inviting them to "like" the Page too, so do your best to make the design as compelling and visually representative of your brand as possible, even at a smaller size.

Facebook most recently amended its rules about cover photos in July 2016. They read: *"Covers can't be deceptive, misleading or infringe on anyone else's copyright. You may not encourage people to upload your cover to their personal timelines."* Facebook has been known to remove the cover photos of Pages that don't follow along, so stick to its rules in order to avoid any nasty surprises. Once upon a time, Facebook also told Page owners that their cover photo could not feature text that covered more than 20% of its entire area. This restriction no longer applies, which means that you can include contact details and pricing and purchasing information about a product in your cover image to whatever extent you like. While this is mostly good news for marketers, I would still advise caution. Too much text can make a cover photo look spammy and unprofessional, so I would recommend at least some restraint, as the importance of the instant visual impact of a great cover photo cannot be overstated.

Add a call to action, offers and links in the cover design and description
In December 2014, Facebook announced the roll out of solid, clickable call-to-action buttons that can be added to cover photos, including "Book Now", "Contact Us," and "Use App." Designed as a way to bring your business' most important objective to the forefront of your Facebook presence, call-to-action buttons can be linked to any destination on or off Facebook. In late 2016, Facebook's CTA buttons were enhanced - with the "Get Quote", "Request Time" call-to-action buttons, and more since. When a person takes an action on your Page, such as asking when they can schedule an appointment, a Messenger (Facebook's instant chat service) conversation is automatically

created between your business and that person, allowing you to chat and confirm the appointment.

Upload a Facebook profile photo recognizable at a small size
While the cover photo dominates your Facebook Page, arguably, it's the profile photo you choose that can have the most influence overall, as it is seen all over the site: in the News Feed of followers, in posts on your Page's timeline, in all comment replies, and of course, next to your Page's cover photo. The recommended upload size for a profile photo is 180 x 180 pixels, but it is displayed at 170 x 170 on your main profile on desktop, 128 x 128 on smartphones, and as small as 43 x 43 pixels next to comments. Ideally, the image you choose should be recognizable (or at least distinct) at this smallest size. While your profile photo will display as a square on your Page, it will be cropped to a circular shape next to posts, in Messenger, and on ads. Think about how your profile photo will look when cropped into a circle, and upload a design that will look great whether a square or circle. With design in mind, upload a profile photo that complements your cover image designs, and vice versa. Don't be afraid to tweak the colors of your profile photo to help the hues match, but do ensure that your brand logo is still recognizable.

Note: As with the cover photo, edit the description of your profile photo to add some relevant blurb and a link to your website or an offer, as a way to reward those curious enough to click it.

Add Business-specific Shop, Service, Events, etc. tabs to your Page
Facebook allows businesses to add and arrange a variety of tabs to Pages, depending on your business and what you provide. These tabs can be a great way to promote your products, services, events, offers, etc. more prominently – the most popular of which I detail below. To add any of the following tabs, visit Page Settings > Edit Page, and scroll down to the Tabs section.

Services tab
As a way to showcase what services your business provides, and to give customers an easy way to enquire about them, use the Services tab. When you setup a service, you'll be asked to add in information like its name, a photo, price, and duration. When customers enquire through your Services tab, you'll receive a notification through Messenger and be able to arrange and confirm the appointment through a private conversation.

Shop tab

Use the Shop tab to list products you sell and connect with more customers on Facebook, who can buy and enquire about your items directly through the site or app. Although any business Page can add a Shop tab, it will have different features depending on your location. For any Shop, you can:

- Add products and product information.
- Curate your shop's product inventory.
- Receive insights (such as views or clicks) about your product listings.
- For US-based Shops, you can sell and manage orders directly from your Page, marking orders as shipped or canceling and refunding orders right from your Page. Elsewhere in the world, you can specify a link (outside of Facebook, like to your website) where customers can purchase an item).
- When you add a Shop, your products may also appear in Facebook's Marketplace, allowing more people to discover them.

When you upload a new product to your Shop, consider sharing it on your Page to make customers more aware of it – you can even tag them with the "Tag product" option in the status update box. To make posts about your products stand out, add content and context to them. For example, explain if the product is brand new, on sale, limited edition, etc.

After you add a Shop section to your Page, you can also create a collection to categorize your products. Dividing your products into collections will make it easier for customers to find what they're looking for when they're browsing your products. To add a collection:

1. On your Page, click the Shop section
2. Click the "cog" dropdown menu and select Manage Shop.
3. In the menu under Shop, click Collections.
4. Enter the name of the collection and decide if this collection will be the featured collection that appears at the top of the Shop section. You can add as many products to a featured collection as you like, but Facebook will only display the first ten on your Page.
5. To finish, check the boxes next to the products you want to add to the collection and click Save.

Events tab

Use the Events tab to promote upcoming events hosted by your business. Once an event has been created, it will be published to your Page as a post, and appear in the Events tab on your Page. Here, Facebook users can register their interest and discuss the occasion. Get involved in the conversation, generating buzz for the event before, during, and after it has happened. Use the Events tab discussion to thank people for coming and reminding them when your next one will be.

Consider Facebook Page custom apps to promote your brand offering

Custom tabs – one-page sub-menus of your Facebook Page - display in a column on the left-hand side of your Facebook Page. They're great little hubs for things like hosting contests, or encouraging people to sign up to your e-mail list. Just search for a particular kind of app in Facebook's search bar, e.g., "contest app" and chances are it will be automatically suggested to you and can be installed in just a few clicks. Apps can also be used to cross- promote your other social profiles like Pinterest, Instagram, YouTube, Twitter, etc. One of the best ways to populate custom tabs to appear exactly as you desire (with branded design, links, etc.) is with the free Static HTML iframe app. To get started, simply find and install the Static HTML iframe app via the Facebook search bar. If the relatively basic coding required by the Static HTML iframe app is beyond your knowledge (and you don't have a developer to help you), check out "freemium" services like Pagemodo (http://www.pagemodo.com) and Woobox (http://www.woobox.com) that, through a simple step-by-step process, will allow you to build customized custom tabs.

Add a Facebook Page Plugin and share buttons to your website

To promote your Facebook Page on your website, grab the code for a Facebook Page Plugin (formerly the "Like Box" at https://developers.facebook.com/docs/plugins/page-plugin and embed it into a suitable spot on your website. When you set up the plugin, make sure to check the options to "Show Friends' Faces" and "Show Page Posts, as this will ensure that the plugin shows viewers the profile photos of any of their friends who already like your Page, as well as a scrollable, clickable preview of your most recent status updates. Although most Facebook Page Plugins are placed in website sidebars, some people have had success by inserting the widget *underneath* blog posts. In this position, the plugin works as part of a call to action, e.g. *"Did you enjoy reading my blog post? Yes? Then, click "Like" to stay updated on Facebook..."*

In addition to the Facebook Page Plugin, embed the Facebook "Like" and "Share" buttons on top of, beside, or underneath the blog posts and products on your website. Doing this encourages people to broadcast their love for your work to their friends and also lets them choose how they want to do it: "Like" posts links to Facebook with one click, while "Share" allows them to add a personalized message before posting. Grab the code for these buttons by searching the web for 'Facebook Like button' (Google 'Facebook Like button') or by visiting the Facebook Developers' page at https://developers.facebook.com/docs/plugins/like-button/, or automatically via a service like AddThis (http://www.addthis.com).

Note: For access to all kinds of official Facebook brand assets for you to use online and offline (including Facebook logos and "Find Us on Facebook" badges) simply visit https://www.facebookbrand.com/

Get set up for customer service via Facebook Page and Messenger
As explained in a previous chapter, the role of social networks as a customer service portal is growing all the time, and if you're active on your Page, then Facebook fans will expect you to respond to their queries, either direct on the Page, via private message or via Messenger.
Many people prefer instant messaging as it can resolve issues easier and faster. First, enable people to message you directly in the Messages section of your Facebook Page settings. Visitors to your Page will see a "Message" button, which they can use to start a conversation with you on Messenger. The other huge benefit of conducting customer support via Messenger is that it can vastly expand your reach to target Messenger-based ads - the more people interested in your products who chat with you, the more you can target in the future - more on this below. Facebook's unified inbox, accessed via the Inbox link on your Facebook Page, will help you seamlessly manage all of your conversations across Facebook and Instagram.

How customers can connect via the Messenger app
- To make it easier for people to identify and contact you, your Page has a unique username (e.g. @500socialmediatips) that can be set and edited. Your username will appear directly on your Page, underneath your Page title with an @ symbol before it, and in the search of the Messenger app. Pages that already have a vanity URL already have a username, because a Page's username and vanity URL are the same.

- Messenger Links and Messenger Codes prompt direct communication with your business. Messenger Links use a Page's username to create a short and memorable link (m.me/500socialmediatips) that, when clicked, opens a conversation with the business in Messenger. Messenger Codes work in the same way. They're unique codes that people can scan in Messenger using the camera in their phones to open a thread with your business. You can use Messenger Links and Messenger Codes in ads, on your website or in any other marketing channel to prompt people to reach out to you directly. Messenger Code images are available to download from your Page's inbox.

Manage customer service introductions and expectations with Greetings and Instant Replies; set up Saved Replies for quick response times.

Messenger Greetings are customizable notes from your business that appear in a new message thread before messages are sent. You can use this text to greet people and set a friendly tone while letting people know what types of messages are expected. Set and edit your greeting in your Page's Message Settings:

- Create and show the answers to frequently asked questions to make it easier for people to start a conversation with your business.
- Instant Replies send a one-time, automatic response to the first message a customer sends to your Page, e.g. Thanking them for their message, reassuring them that you will respond soon, pointing them to an online FAQ to help answer their query, etc. Instant Replies will not be sent if your status for responding messages is set to "Away" – which can be toggled on (for a maximum of 12 hours) or off via the Messages (inbox) of your Page.
- If your Page receives the same query often, set up Saved Replies in order to be able to fire back a quick response. To create or select a new Saved Reply, click the speech bubble icon in the message reply box and choose "Create New Reply". Enter a title (for selecting it later), add the message body and images, then add personalization's that will be pre-populated when the message is sent, such as the person's first and last name. Saved Replies won't only save you time, but will impress customers (especially those eager and impatiently waiting for your reply!) *and* help to maintain your Page's response rate.

- Any time you're away from your computer or phone, turn on Away Messages to let customers know that you'll get back to them as soon as possible. This helps you keep your responsiveness rating and set expectations with your customers.

Note: Another way to manage and serve your customers more efficiently is by providing an easy way to see basic information about them, and tag them with custom labels "frequent customer," "high priority," etc. Within the Messenger app, tap the person's name to see their publicly available profile, as well as their previous interactions with your business. Use this information to help personalize your communications. Facebook also makes it easy for businesses to view people's feedback so you can and improve upon their Messenger experience, simply clicking on Page Settings > Messenger; a feature that aggregates all feedback in one place.

Explore using chatbots in Facebook Messenger
In addition to manual Messenger chat, chatbots are fast-becoming a gamechanger. Chatbots allow you to scale the number of people you can communicate with and give you the ability to reach more people, helping them purchase more products through an automated process. Best of all, tools like ManyChat (https://manychat.com/) and ChatFuel (https://chatfuel.com/) mean that anybody can quickly and easily create powerful chatbots for business. Here are several ways chatbots can be used to boost your Messenger game:

- *Deliver your content:* Rather than sharing your content via email, use a Chatbot to share it directly with users in Messenger. They can ignore an email much more easily than they can a chat notification.
- *Help fans find the most relevant content:* you can also use Facebook Messenger to help your followers "pull" content to themselves. This turns things around for content marketing. You now have a non-intrusive way to deliver personalized content to your target audience.
- *Engage event attendees:* Provide attendees information before (reminder of the event schedule), during (key information, video replays), and after (follow-up asking for feedback) an event to keep them in the know.
- *Re-engage your potential customers with ads:* Facebook ads are an effective way to get people chatting with you. There are two types of Facebook Messenger ads: click-to-Messenger ads allows you to direct people

from the Facebook News Feed to a Messenger conversation with you. Meanwhile, Sponsored Messages allows you to initiate a Messenger conversation with anyone who has messaged your Facebook Page in the past. A great way to use these Facebook Messenger ads is to re-engage potential customers, like people who have visited your product page but didn't purchase, or people who have asked you questions via Facebook Messenger before. For example, you can use click-to-Messenger ads to offer to encourage them to ask questions or Sponsored Messages to send relevant content and offers to them.

- *Generate sales leads:* Run click-to-Messenger ads to target your audience on Facebook. When a person clicks on the ad to learn more, they will be taken to a Messenger conversation with a chatbot that would ask a series of questions.

- *Reach your target audience one-to-one:* The Facebook News Feed is saturated with ads; Messenger allows you to divert away from all of that noise. Customers will see your ad in the home tab of their Messenger mobile app, which is hard to miss compared to News Feed ads. When they tap on the ad, they will be brought to your website or a Messenger conversation.

Facebook Marketing Strategy

Now that your Facebook Page is looking great and you're encouraging people to visit it, let's explore some ways that you can make the most effective use of the platform, in conjunction with the content strategy ideas described in the previous chapter. But first, some very important considerations:

Pin important posts
Facebook allows you to pin a single post to the top of your Page's timeline for up to a week. Use this to feature important content and make it more visible to fans who visit your Page. All new status updates will appear below the pinned post until it is unpinned (or a week elapses), whereupon it will fall into its original chronological position. After creating a post, hover over it until the pencil icon appears, click it and choose 'Pin to Top'. In particular, posts to consider pinning include special announcements, contents, promotions, etc.

Boost interaction with Facebook-embedded posts
In August 2013, Facebook rolled out the ability to embed personal profile or Page posts into an external website. Use embedded posts to lift conversations from your Facebook Page to help encourage and boost interaction with your

statuses in places away from the site, such as part of a blog post, or even in an e-mail newsletter as a way to drive readers to your Page. As long as the status update you post is public, *anybody* can embed it from your Facebook Page or embed it from wherever else it appears, which - if your status is really shareable - could give your Page and content a lot of exposure. Embedded posts even include buttons for viewers to "Like", comment, and Share the post, *and* a button to "Like" your page.

How to embed a Facebook post
1. Hover over the post you want to embed, left-click on the arrow that appears, and choose "Embed Post".
2. Copy the code that appears and paste it as HTML on your website or blog.

Re-post top notch content, but don't be spammy about it
Since not everyone checks their Facebook News Feed all day every day, and only a small proportion of your fans will see your content first time around, if you have a killer article or link to share, post it several times as a way for as many of your fans to see it as possible. However, make a concerted effort to share the information under different guises, e.g., different wording in the text, an image with a link, a link share post, etc. Facebook will penalize your reach if you publish the exact same status over and over, as it has found people react negatively to "copy and paste" posts.

Increase organic engagement with Facebook Audience Optimization
Facebook Audience Optimization is a tool that lets you target or restrict organic (i.e. non-paid) Page posts to specific fans, based on information such as their age, gender, location and interests. Depending on your business and content strategy goals, not ALL of your fans will be interested in ALL of your posts, so the ability to focus certain posts towards a subset of your audience (rather than a random percentage of them as a whole) could increase your engagement rates. What's more, if these people engage with your posts because they match their interests, your posts should start to appear in their News Feeds more often as a result, giving your content a boost in organic reach over time. If you haven't already enabled this feature, click on the Settings tab of your Page. From here, click on General and switch on the 'News Feed Audience and Visibility for Posts' option. To use Audience Optimization, click on the crosshairs symbol within the Facebook status update box. Choose between Preferred Audience (targeting people based on up to 16 interests),

along with the potential reach based on your audience). Vary the interests you choose: try some broad, some narrow, and remember to keep them tailored to your post. The Audience Restrictions (limiting who can see the post, based on age, gender, location, and languages) is optional, but well worth considering. When you're done, click Save. Analytics data for Audience Optimization posts can be identified by the crosshairs symbol within the Targeting column of Facebook Insights. It is well worth running tests to see how non-targeted posts perform against those that are.

Encourage clicks through calls-to-action but avoid "click-baiting"
To encourage higher click-through rates from Facebook and other social media to your website and blog, being specific about what you want your customers to do using a clear call to action is often a good bet, e.g., *"Click here for more information [your link]"*. Sometimes that little push can make all the difference between a successful status and one that sinks without a trace.

Note: In relation to the above, it is worth pointing out that Facebook periodically updates its News Feed algorithm to crack down on so-called "click bait" article-sharing. These are typically articles with vague and over-promising headlines like *"You'll never believe who puked on the red carpet last night... CLICK to see our exclusive pic!"* that do not make it plainly clear what the post will entail. Facebook wants you to share valuable content that people will read and share with their friends, so if it spots that your fans are clicking on these types of links and returning straight to Facebook (because the content is poor) and *not* sharing, similar posts will receive less visibility – appearing lower down in the News Feed. Conversely, high quality links that get shared many times over will benefit from higher reach.

Guarantee views with "Get All Notifications" and "See First" strategy
One tactic that can be used to all-but guarantee that fans see all of your Page's content is to train them to select the "Get Notifications" and "See First" options, found in a drop-down menu when hovering their cursor over the "Liked" and "Following" button underneath your Page's cover photo. With this selected, every time you post a new status update, the fans in question will be informed with a notification under the blue "globe" icon in the status bar of their Facebook account *and* your new content will appear at the top of that users' News Feed. These requests are best communicated through a status update with a screen grab of the menu to demonstrate the exact action that you wish them to take. Whether or not you are comfortable with asking at the risk

of appearing pushy is up to you; you should make this judgment based on the strength of the relationship you have with your audience. If you do decide to do it, I wouldn't force it upon fans very often, particularly as they are unlikely to be right on your Page when they see your instructions appear, and even more unlikely to click through and carry out the instructions.

Optimize blog images to make an impact on Facebook

In September 2013, Facebook introduced a significant increase to the size that thumbnail images from linked articles appear in the News Feed. When you post a status update including a link, Facebook will automatically pull an image from the article, and as long as it is of sufficient size, that image will display at full width on your Page and in News Feeds with the blog title and blurb below it. In exact terms, for a linked article's image to display at full width on Facebook, the width of the image needs to be 1.91 times its height. Facebook recommends an image that is at least 1200 × 630 pixels, which, truthfully, isn't realistic for most bloggers. Instead, aim to produce blog posts that include at least one image that is 600 × 315 pixels (even if it is an image that is uploaded large, but shrunk to fit your blog's formatting style), as this is the minimum size that Facebook requires for any linked article's image to display at full width in any position on all devices - desktop, mobile, or tablet. If your linked article's chosen image is below 600 × 315 pixels, Facebook will automatically shrink it much smaller.

Note: Somewhat related to the previous tip regarding the popularity of images and quotes in particular, why not try the following: Pick out a blog post's most quotable, shareable snippet and turn that into an image either as a quote on its own or coupled with an appealing photo. Then, link back to the blog post from the text box in a status update and monitor how well the post is received.

Maximize the impact of pre-recorded video on Facebook

The emergence of video content on Facebook has changed the landscape of the social network, and it's only going to keep getting bigger. In many cases it pays to upload engaging video content directly to the site, rather than, for example, sharing a YouTube link. This is because native Facebook video is given a more favorable treatment in terms of reach (but keep an eye on your analytics to see how things go). If the video is "evergreen" in nature (i.e., it's still as relevant in the future as it is now), why not post the video twice - once by uploading directly to Facebook and at a later date via a shared YouTube link?

- Videos uploaded to Facebook play automatically and *with* audio on (unless a user's phone is on silent) - when a user pauses on it while scrolling through their News Feed. With that in mind, consider how you will hook your fans into watching your clip (and turn the sound on if it is off) from the very first frame – catching someone's eye with movement in the first 2-3 seconds is one way to do this, or if a person is seen talking in front of the camera, fans who are interested will click to hear what's being said. Alternatively, publishing videos (with captions if necessary) that do not require sound to be understood, is another popular strategy – especially for mobile viewers for who playing audio (in a public setting, for example) is not an option. As well as creating captions within the video file yourself, another option is to upload an SRT file, which adds captions to your videos. There's an added benefit to SRT files: Facebook favors videos that include them because it can analyze the content, which helps the site show it to the right people, which can in turn benefit you.

- Organize videos into playlists via the Video tab on your Page (to encourage increased watch time) and choose one video to Feature. The Featured video will appear in prime position below the "About" section of your Page - a great opportunity for an introductory video to your business, or to highlight a current promotion.

- Add descriptive tags to make your video more discoverable, tag people featured in your videos, and select the best thumbnail available from the menus that appears after the file has been uploaded (or upload your own custom image – 1920 x 1200 pixels will fit fine). Choose a high-quality image containing less than 20% text. If text on the thumbnail features more than 20% text – and you later choose to boost the video's reach with ads – Facebook may not favor as much as videos with cleaner thumbnail images. Don't forget to grab the video embed code to include in a blog post on your website to encourage more exposure and interaction – choose between embedding the whole status update, or just the video player itself for a cleaner look.

Note: If you're looking for free music and sound effects for videos you share to Facebook or Instagram, check out the Facebook Sound Collection (https://www.facebook.com/sound/collection/). Browse sounds by genre, mood, length, and vocals to find just the right tracks.

The video content you choose to post should reflect the same types of stuff referred to in the *"Explained: The Best Type of Content to Post on Social Media"* chapter of this book.

Experiment with Stories on Facebook

In August 2018, Facebook gave Page owners the ability to share Page Stories with their fans. Page Stories almost identical to Instagram Stories, which has been a feature of that app for several years, allowing you to share photos and videos - short, relatable, and fleeting moments that represent your brand or business - directly from your mobile device. Often peppered with colorful text and stickers, Page Stories are a way to engage your audience in a more frequent, authentic and casual way in order to develop deeper connections, and can be a key strategy to increasing the humanized and community-driven appeal of the site that Facebook encourages. Their "rough around the edges" and quick creation makes Stories a compelling accompaniment to your more polished, ordinary Page posts. What's more, people can view your Page story by tapping on your mobile page's profile picture, and they also appear to followers of your Page at the very top of the News Feed in a highly visible area - separate from the intense competition and crowded nature the main News Feed.

To create and share Stories to Facebook:
1. Visit your Page on the Facebook app and tap "..." in the top-right corner.
2. Tap "Open Camera" and create your Story.
3. When you're finished, tap the "+Page Story" icon to share it with your audience.

For much more information on Stories strategy, please see the appropriate section in the Instagram Tips chapter.

Utilizing Live Video on Facebook

In February 2016, Facebook rolled out its "Live" feature worldwide. Facebook Live is a function that allows people to record and (after the fact) publish live video streams to Facebook via its mobile app or via your desktop webcam. To record live video (for up to 30 minutes at a time), tap on Update Status and choose the Live Video icon. You can write a quick description and choose the audience that you want to share with (your Page, Event, or group) before going live. During your broadcast, you'll see the number of live viewers, the names of friends who are tuning in and a real-time stream of comments and reactions. When your live video session ends, you'll get immediate insights into how many people watched your broadcast (including the number of concurrent watchers, repeat viewers, and how many stayed until the end). Your live video can then be published onto your Timeline, where it can be watched again by anyone who missed it (use a description to tell people why they should click play), or paid- promoted for added exposure.

Strategies to improve your Facebook Live strategy

- With the spontaneity of live video, many viewers will miss your stream without proper notice. Pre-schedule your live stream video within Video Manager to build anticipation and allow viewers the option to mark their calendars so that they can be reminded to tune in. With the spontaneity of Facebook Live, some people found it hard to participate without proper notice. Scheduling not only creates a post on your Facebook page that alerts your fans, but if you click the time stamp on the post, you'll also get a unique URL you can share anywhere to help spread the word.

- If your Facebook Page has a Product Shop, think about combining the two to broadcast your own infomercial-style broadcast. When you mention your products in a live broadcast, you can tag them in your video, allowing viewers to watch your livestream and access a link directly from the stream, where they can purchase your product right within Facebook. After your video has uploaded, click the Tag Products icon, enter the names of the products featured in your video, and click Publish when you're done.

- Bringing in a contributor to chat with live? Two-person split-screen broadcasts are available to all on all Pages, via the Facebook mobile app. Called "Live With", if you start your Live video in landscape, you and your guests will be side-by-side. When you start your live video in portrait, guests are picture-in-picture.

- Add a descriptive title. Facebook recommends crafting a descriptive title that will make the video easily searchable. With Facebook seeing billions of searches every day, it's worth the little extra effort.

- Use the caption to provide a preview. Briefly describe your video using your post's copy. Taking out the time to watch a video can be a stretch for some, so it helps to provide a little information about your video so that people can quickly decide if it's worth their time. Facebook recommends "pulling out a key quote or moment from the video as the text component of your post" in order to set up the expectations of what the viewer will see.

- Another method by which you can spread the reach of your Facebook video is by tagging other Pages that either contributed to it, or that you would like to make aware of the video.
- Include a call-to-action. While Facebook has removed the call-to-action functionality for videos, there are still several free ways to add a CTA to your Facebook video. In your post copy, you could include a link to a blog post or website and invite viewers to find out more information by clicking on the link. You could also simply ask your audience to share their thoughts as comments. During the video, you could mention a CTA if you are talking in the video or use a text overlay (e.g. Learn more social media tips at blog.buffer.com). Wistia found that such mid-roll CTAs have the highest conversion rates. At the end of the video, you could have a text overlay or a static image with a CTA and let the video play for a few seconds after the actual content ends.
- You may not have time to respond to every comment and question from viewers during a broadcast (and some people may join as you're about to finish) so make sure to respond to comments just after the show has gone off the air. Also check in regularly to address comments made on the replay, especially if you asked your audience to share the link with their friends while you were live.
- If you regularly live-stream from a business Page, organize your replays into video playlists to make it easy for people to find episodes on specific themes after the event. Navigate to the Videos tab and you to create a playlist from there.

For more ideas and insights into the benefits of using live video on Facebook and other platforms, check out the *"Explained: The Best Types of Content to Post on Social Media"* chapter of this book.

Use hashtags to encourage engagement and conversation
In June 2013, Facebook joined sites like Twitter and Pinterest by rolling out the use of hashtags, which appear as clickable links in Page and personal profile updates and in posts on the News Feed. People can use hashtags in Facebook search to discover posts related to specific topics or interests. Billions of pieces of content are shared on Facebook every day - peaking in the 8-11pm primetime slot - so hashtags provide a huge opportunity for brands and

marketers to participate in conversations in a meaningful, relevant and timely way. While the use of hashtags hasn't blown up in the way Facebook imagined it might, used sparingly they still can be of benefit.

Several ways to use hashtags effectively on Facebook
- Since most brands will be trying to keep the length of Facebook copy to a minimum (most research shows that shorter post captions deliver better engagement than long ones), using just one or two hashtags per post is a good idea. Research by Track Maven found that using a single hashtag in a Facebook post generated more engagement than using several.
- As well as your own branded hashtags, so-called news-jacking hashtags can be a powerful way to piggyback on widespread events that are popular amongst your fans - and a way for people who haven't discovered your brand yet, to perhaps stumble across it.
- Discover new Pages and partners by scouring for specific hashtags in Facebook search and track your own hashtags to monitor what people are saying about you and your brand, then join the conversation.

Ask for Likes and Shares – and invite Likers to Like your Page
Ask users to 'Like' and Share your content when you post, so that it will be shared on their walls and in their News Feeds, therefore increasing exposure for your Page. Don't appear desperate by doing it too often (Facebook will limit the reach on these types of posts if you do, especially if the content associated with the post is poor) and word your request in a way that endears you to your fans. Buddy Media found that action keywords like "post," "comment," "take," "submit," "like" or "tell us" are the most effective. Be direct in your request and fans will listen and take action. Enhance the experience by creating a community that encourages your fans to discuss topics and interact with each other within the comments. Did you know, too, that you can invite people who liked a post but *haven't* liked your Page, to do so? When a post has had more than a handful of likes, the message below it will read "[name], [name], [name], and [number] of others liked this." Click on the "others liked this" bit for a list of everyone who liked that post and a notice of whether they have liked your Page or not (chances are that many people will only see your post as a result of someone else engaging with it and their being notified). If they haven't liked your Page, you can click "Invite" next to their name to send them a notification asking them if they'd like to. If they've

enjoyed your content once, there's a greater chance they'll be open to seeing it again.

Note: On a somewhat related point - and here's an opportunity to create common bonds and emotional ties between your brand and fans - did you know you can humanize your Facebook Page updates by sharing what your business is feeling, watching, reading, listening to, drinking, eating, playing, traveling to, looking for or exercising? Just click on the smiley face in the status update box and select one of the options.

Encourage your fans to react to posts to boost reach

Facebook offers five reactions on every published post - Love, Haha, Wow, Sad, and Angry. In the spring of 2017, a Facebook spokesperson revealed that the site's News Feed algorithm judges reactions to be *more* valuable than just likes. A reaction, they say, is an even stronger signal that a person wants to see more of that type of post. For businesses, that means getting people to use them is more important than ever. So, how do you make people express an emotion stronger than a like? Make them feel it! If you're already regularly share content that makes people feel a strong emotion, then keep it up! Otherwise, encourage people to react by dropping hints in what you post, e.g. placing a "wow" or "angry" face on top of an image that you post. Use this strategy when sharing links, too. A lot of people share, comment on, and react to Facebook links without actually clicking on them first. In addition, asking fans to respond to an informal poll is an effective way to solicit reactions. Ask them to match their reaction to a particular answer choice.

Note: Facebook has laid out two of important of rules regarding the use of reactions. First, the reaction you ask for should match the emotional intent of the post, e.g. "Choose "love" if you think this puppy is cute!". Second, don't use reactions to conduct polls via a video, where the whole thing consists of static or looping graphics or images. Fail to follow them and you could see your post reach negatively impacted.

Encourage reviews and Recommendations

Local business Pages have always been able to feature ratings and reviews on their Page, but in the summer of 2018, Facebook updated Reviews and Ratings to Recommendations. Recommendations allow customers to share richer feedback about your business to help you become more visible in your local areas:

- Facebook users can indicate whether they recommend your business with a simple "Yes" or "No" option, and can explain their opinion with tags, text and photos.
- Recommendations can be created from directly on a Page, as a comment on a friend's post asking for Recommendations, or via a prompt after tagging a Page in a photo or post.
- Recommendations given publicly across appear on the Reviews tab.

As mentioned, Recommendations appear on your Page and are discoverable across Facebook when people are searching for or talking about your business. The opinions of the people they know and trust - their friends and family - will be surfaced most prominently. So, as a way to spread awareness of your business, after their purchase from you, encourage customers to post a Recommendation or review of your business.

Encourage check-ins and use Place Tips

When a user views your Page and business information on the Facebook mobile app, they'll also be shown information like which of their friends have visited and checked in and whether they or the wider Facebook community have recommended you with photos, star ratings and reviews on show. Knowing this, it pays to encourage people to "check-in" if you have a real-life location. Display notices in prominent areas of your establishment, such as the entrance, receipts and point of sale, to prompt customers to get out their smartphones, check-in and inform their friends of where they are, encouraging them to visit too. When a review is left for a business, a status update is created that goes out to the News Feed of that customers' friends, along with the business' cover and profile photo and its star rating. If a customer is already at your location and opens the Facebook app, Place Tips come into play. Place Tips uses Wi-Fi, GPS, and Bluetooth (for the latter, you can apply for a Bluetooth "beacon" to beam your information via http://bit.ly/facebookbeaconinfo) to *automatically* show visitors more information about your business, including the aforementioned reviews, photos, check-ins, etc. In addition, it will encourage people to check-in and like your Page and, visit the About section of your profile, you can specify a custom Welcome Message to greet customers to your establishment - perhaps give them a heads-up on offers and discounts too!

Add Timeline milestones; use as marketing opportunities

Facebook allows you to add Milestones in the history of your business (past and present) on your Page by scrolling through and marking dates on your timeline (e.g. when the business was established, your 1000th sale, etc.). These help flesh out your company history and can give customers a fascinating insight into your growth over the months and years (particularly if you were in business way before Facebook came on the scene). You can even use upcoming milestones as a way to connect with customers and provide them with an incentive to remain engaged, e.g., *"Here's to each and every one of you for helping us reach 20,000 fans! Check back tomorrow at 6pm for a special promotion to say thanks!"*

As a twist on this strategy, and as a way to really make your customers feel a sense of ownership over your Page, why not highlight them and their stories as milestones on your Timeline? Ask fans to submit stories that explain how your product or service has affected their lives for the better, then add them - with images - as milestones that show just how much a part of your brand your customers are, and as encouragement for other people to invest in you just as much.

Create Facebook Offers

If at least 50 people have liked your Page, you can create an Offer on your Facebook Page. When a fan claims an offer, they'll receive an email that they can show at your business' physical location or a code to enter online so that they can get the discount. Offers aren't free to run (there is a minimum spend of around $5 - $10), but they are useful in promoting special deals, rewarding loyal fans, and encouraging them to spread the word about your business to their friends. To create an offer from your Page, click Offer, Event + and click Offer from the top of the status update box. Fill out the details to make your offer shine, including Headline, Image, redemption link, start date, and expiration date. Preview your offer in the top left and make any changes, then click Post Offer.

Some pointers to help run a successful offer include:
- Make offer discounts substantial (at least 20% off a product or service, or the opportunity to get something else free when purchasing is recommended for the best results) and ensure that they are exclusive to Facebook fans.

- Keep your offer and its terms and conditions simple and give people a reasonable amount of time in which to claim it (this also allows them time to spread the word about your great deal to their friends).
- Use simple and direct language in your headline to reduce any confusion, and showcase the value of the deal your fans will get, rather than just using a slogan.
- Use a clear and engaging image to represent your offer, but *not* your profile photo, as that will often be displayed next to the promotion around the site.
- Pin the offer to the top of your Page for added visibility and train your staff so that they are prepared when a customer wants to redeem their offer.

Facebook contest strategy for success

As of August 2013, Facebook re-allowed contests to be administered *on Page Timelines*, not just through third-party apps like Woobox, Shortstack, and Heyo. Businesses can:

Collect entries by having users post on the Page or comment/like a Page post (e.g., *"Like this post for a chance to win one of our new sandwich toasters - releasing March 21!"* or *"Comment with a funny caption for this photo - the one that makes us laugh the most / gets the most likes wins X prize."* or *"Post a photo in the comments of you using our product - our favorite will win X prize."* or *"Suggest a new menu item in the comments below - our favorite will go into production and the inventor will win X prize!"* Another spin on this entry method is to ask viewers to comment and tag a friend to enter. Your fans will tag friends who would be interested in winning the prize and this will drive interest in your Page and product or service. This route works best if you can reward the winning commenter and their tagged friend with a prize, e.g., dinner for two at your restaurant, or two free gifts of your product. Collect entries by having users message the Page (e.g., *"For your chance to win this fantastic sweat band, message us using the button above and tell us why you deserve to win!"*) Utilize 'Likes' as a voting mechanism, e.g., *"Help us choose our next smoothie flavor. Click 'like' to vote on your favorite pic and we'll choose one lucky person to win a $20 gift card with us!"*

Note: Free tools like Agorapulse's Timeline Contest page (http://contest.agorapulse.com/) give an easy way to host and select winners from Timeline sweepstakes, quizzes, or photo contests.

While creating a promotion on a Page Timeline is faster, easier and cheaper (great for a spontaneous giveaway for example, but more likely to attract poor quality entrants), third-party apps - while requiring a small fee - still do have many advantages. I would certainly recommend them over Timeline-only contests for bigger and more serious campaigns. Advantages of apps include:

- A more professional and customizable campaign, more in line with your branding strategy.
- More space and flexibility for content than a Page post alone, as they are hosted on a Page tab.
- The ability to collect data (such as e-mail addresses) in a secure and structured manner.
- Easy to add "share" buttons to increase virality of contest once someone has submitted their entry.

Whichever type of contest you run on Facebook, there are still important legal guidelines to follow, including offering terms of eligibility and releasing Facebook of any association. I urge you to read the Promotions section of Facebook's Page Guidelines for a full rundown: https://www.facebook.com/page_guidelines.php

Publish and Promote Events on Facebook
Publicizing an event on Facebook is a popular method for generating buzz and discussion about a brand, and a way to funnel potential customers to your Page or Group to engage with you further - whether the occasion will occur offline (like a store's grand opening) or online (like a live webinar or the start of a sale). Facebook Events appear can be shared on Pages, in the News Feed, in Messenger, and appear in the site's main Events section. Keep reading for essential tips and best practices for getting your Event seen by as many people as possible and attracting new customers as a result!

Creating an event
You can create a Facebook Event using your personal profile, a Page, or a Group. The exact instructions below relate to Pages, but the general strategies will work for all Events in general. To create an event, click on the Create Event option in the status update box, where you'll be presented with a pop-up window in which to fill out all the Event details.

Event cover image

The recommended size for an Event cover image is 1200 x 628 pixels, or you can upload a video between 30 seconds to 5 minutes long. Your Event cover image acts like a marketing banner for your event, so design it to catch people's attention with a bold image and color pallet - whether they see it on desktop or mobile.

Event name

Keep the Event name clear and short, as long names can get cut off on certain displays.

Event location and time

Add a location for the event and Facebook will generate a map to show people where to go. A location will also mean that your event appears in Facebook's Events Near Me section for users - free advertising, essentially. If your event's start and end date is longer than two weeks apart, create two separate events with their own time and location.

Event Details

Utilize the space in the Details section to help secure the attendance of people curious enough to view your Event page. After the first 10 or so lines, users will have to tap or click to see the event's full details, so keep critical information - like a reminder of the event name and location; a link to where tickets can be bought; and one snappy sentence that sums the event up and why people can't afford to miss it - "above the fold." Use the rest of the Details section to include a bulleted list of things people can expect to do and see at the event, a call-to-action to encourage their attendance (with another link to tickets), and to share the event with friends. Use @mentions to tag the names of the venue, sponsors, people or Pages appearing at the event, so people can learn more about them. You can also use the Details section to let people know that they can comment in the discussion section with any further questions they might have, and that you'll get back to them with an answer ASAP.

Keywords, co-hosts, and ticket URL

- Before publishing your Event, you'll see options to add keywords, co-hosts, and ticket link URL.
- Adding relevant keywords allows Facebook share your event to the people who will most likely be interested in attending.

- When you add Pages as a Co-host to your event, they will be able to invite all of their friends and followers and the event will be added to their Facebook calendars, so it's a great way to build awareness.
- If you're selling tickets to your event, add your ticketing website link to the Ticket URL field. This makes it easy for people to buy tickets and unlocks the ability to create ads that can help drive ticket sales.

Promoting the Event

When your Event is published, Facebook will create a post on your Page to let your fans know it's coming up and also add an Events section to your Page where its listing will remain even when the initial post is long gone. Both options give people the chance to select an option to indicate their interest or intention to attend. To give your event even more exposure, you could:

- Update your Page's cover photo to promote it, as well as update the cover photo call-to-action button to feature your ticket site link.
- Pin your event post to the top of your Page to make sure it's the first thing visitors to your Page see.
- Re-order your Page sections (via Settings -> Edit Page) to bring the Events section to the top in the run-up to it.

Events can also be promoted via paid ads, through the form of Boosting your Event post - which converts it into an ad - or by creating custom ads via Facebook's Ad Manager. While the former method is the quickest and easiest, Facebook's main ads tool will offer you more targeting options, which often means a more effective ad, and more bang for your buck. These include being able to target people who have attended your events in the past, or those that have simply shown interest. Both allow you to help you increase awareness, RSVPs and ticket sales for your event on Facebook.

In addition to using ads to promote an event events created via a Facebook Page, you can use Facebook event frames to build awareness - and encourage fans to do the same. Event frames are profile and page photo overlays that your attendees can use to promote the event to their friends, followers, and fans. To begin creating an event frame, use Facebook Frame Studio in the Camera Effects Platform (https://www.facebook.com/fbcameraeffects/)

Gather leads and build brand awareness through Facebook Events:
- If your event is ticketed, you can offer tickets (including free ones) through a service like Eventbrite to register attendees for your online

or offline event. Anyone who purchases a ticket becomes a part of an exportable list of contacts that you can use as a lead. An additional way to capture leads using your Facebook events is to create lead ads and ads for the lead generation pages on your website. Target your ads to an audience of people who responded to your Facebook event.

- Stream live from your Facebook event to encourage viewers to attend or to show them what they're missing out on. In the Facebook mobile app, go to your Facebook event. Tap the status update box and look for the Go Live option.
- Keep the magic of your event alive until the next one arrives. After it's over, thank attendees on the event page and remind them when the next event will take place. Encourage attendees to share their favorite stories, photos, and videos on the Facebook Event page and their own profiles. Of course, you can do the same on your own Page.
- Use the Event's page to promote your Facebook group, so that event attendees can join to network with other event attendees, organizers, speakers, and sponsors in a more permanent location.
- Facebook event attendees (or those who engaged with your event page) can be used as part of a target audiences in future Facebook ad campaigns, meaning that you can promote your business' products, services, or future events to those who engaged with your Event page.

Note: Page admins can easily repeat a Facebook event with the Create Repeat Event option in the drop-down box on your Event page. In addition, to prevent the need to invite fans to events within their area, you can invite them to subscribe. When a fan subscribes they will automatically be notified when your event is in their locality – ask them to subscribe by clicking on "Events" below your Page's cover photo and hitting Subscribe.

Thank your newest fans and have a fan of the month
Post a special 'Thank You' message about once a week to welcome new fans, even listing them by name if there aren't too many - find them via the "See Likes" link in your Page's Admin Panel. Doing so adds a personal touch to your communication and reflects well on your image as a brand that cares about its audience. To encourage further engagement on your Page, launch a "Fan of the Month" initiative. By highlighting one of your most loyal fans in this way, you indirectly encourage other fans to engage more, so that they can win the coveted title the next month. For an added incentive, offer a little prize to the winner. There are several free "Fan of the Month" apps available via the

Facebook search bar and paid versions with additional options if you're interested in delving deeper.

Cross-promote with (and on) other Facebook Pages

One of the most powerful ways to increase the number of genuinely interested eyes that come across your Facebook Page is to work with other Page managers within your niche or businesses in your same locale. Get in touch to discuss ways in which you can occasionally cross-promote each other's Pages, share posts, conjure up offers and increase exposure for your businesses. For example, a kids' clothes store owner might get in touch with a local ice-cream parlor - places that share the same clientele - to work a cross-promotion arrangement on Facebook. Additionally, you might want to communicate with other businesses to encourage them to add your Page to the Featured "Likes" section of their Page and agree to do the same in return. This works great with complementary products and services and helps spread the word of your business, as Featured Pages sit prominently on your Page and display on rotation depending how many are set up. *To add a featured Like on your Facebook Page:*

1. Visit and "Like" a complementary business while using Facebook as your Page (or by clicking the three dots underneath its cover photo, choosing "Like as Your Page..." and selecting your company's Page if you're browsing under a personal account).
2. Return to your Page and click "Settings" and then "Featured" on the next page. Under the "Likes" section, click "Add Featured Likes" and choose the Pages that you would like to showcase on your Page.

A more covert way of making your brand known (especially to the audience of rivals in your business niche) is to engage and post relevant, friendly, and useful (not spammy or self-promotional!) comments on statuses of their Facebook Pages, posting under your Page's username (make sure you are posting as your Page by clicking on the flag icon beneath the post you want to comment on, and choosing "Liking and commenting as [your page]".). Your profile photo and link to your Page will be visible with every comment you make, hopefully encouraging people to visit and check you out. Again, make your comments interesting, helpful, insightful, funny, witty, charming, etc., to increase the chances of a click-through! The last thing you want to do is come across as shady or desperate, especially like those *"It's Andrew from Andrew's Aardvark*

Farm - just dropping in to give you a Like! Check us out!" kind of posts that commonly occur. If I ever see any type of blatant self-promotion on my Page, it gets instantly deleted!

Track your progress

Use Facebook Insights (click "Insights" at the top of your Page) to track how your Facebook Page is performing day by day and over a longer period of time. The Likes tab displays your overall Page growth and where your audience is finding you, while the Reach, Visits, and Post tabs will show you which types of updates - text, links, video, etc. - are preferred by your audience (click on individual posts for more detailed stats about engagement) and at what times they are most likely to be on Facebook to digest your activity. On the People tab, you'll be able to learn about the demographics of your audience, including gender, age, language, and location. All of this data is extremely useful in helping you to tweak and tailor your ongoing content strategy and to deliver the kind of stuff that you know your fans will love.

Note: In February 2016, Facebook introduced Reactions - an extension of the Like button, that allows people to choose one of five additional emoticons to communicate their feelings about a post (ordinary or a sponsored ad) – Love, Haha, Wow, Sad, or Angry. You'll find a breakdown of reactions to each post in Insights; this extra sentiment-focused data will allow you to better tell, in a quantitate manner, whether your audience is responding to your content in the way you hope, especially those who in the past – without Reactions – would not choose comment or found "Like" inappropriate.

Another notable section of Facebook Insights is Pages to Watch, a feature that allows you to track a variety of metrics relating to your rivals' Facebook activity, including the number of posts, engagement rates, and new Page likes. Adding the competition to this list will enable you to keep an eye on their performance to see what is (and what isn't) working for them, and you can use this knowledge to influence and improve your own strategy. In addition to direct competitors, it is often useful to pay attention to other companies in a similar, but not identical, field, e.g., another retail or B2B venture in your vicinity, as well brands that are unrelated to yours but which your audience like and engage with. When researching others' Page content to build upon within your watch list, look for stuff that gets high engagement (likes, comments, and shares), low engagement but potential to improve (that *you* can improve on for your Page), and specific trends within your industry to capitalize upon.

Utilizing Facebook Groups to build your business

Facebook Groups are a convenient way to network with peers, strengthen relationships with current customers, or attract new ones - whether you create your own or join one of the millions that already exist – and can act as a powerful partner to an existing Facebook Page. Your own custom-made group can exist as a place to provide customer support, promote upcoming events, get feedback on upcoming products, and for customers to connect, collaborate, and share (valuable consumer insight for you!). To get the most benefit from groups which focus on discussions concerning your chosen industry, your aim should be to position yourself as an authority figure: be active, give help, and be genuine, i.e., no focus on selling. Over time, your knowledge and influence will be recognized and this will help to pique people's interest, perhaps enough to make them want to consider your product or service. As brands battle for precious organic reach, Groups provide a fresh avenue to cultivate a loyal community who can interact with you and each other, to boost engagement, and could help to fill the gap lost in organic reach over the years. To start, click on "Group" under the 'Create' section at the bottom of the left-hand sidebar on Facebook.

Optimize your Group in 8 simple steps:

1. Give your group a name and select a group type to help people understand what the group is about.
2. Add a cover photo (the ideal photo size is 820 x 462 pixels); check how it looks on desktop and mobile.
3. Write a description to tell people what the group is all about and what it can be used for. It is not uncommon for group admins to use this space to share information that they want the entire group, especially new members, to know such as rules and community guidelines.
4. Add five tags to help people find your group; a mix of generic and specific tags will work best.
5. If you are a local group, add your location so that people who are looking for Facebook Groups in your area can find it more easily.
6. Customize your group URL. An easy-to-remember group URL makes it simple for you to share a link to your Facebook group in online communication and real-life marketing material.
7. Link your Group to your Facebook Page to make it existence more visible and encourage fans to take a look, and hopefully join. To link

your Facebook Group to your Facebook Page, choose the option within the Groups section of your Page settings.

8. Promote your new group and encourage people to join. Hit the Share button below your cover photo for you to share your Facebook Group to different parts of Facebook: timeline, Messenger, and Page. You can also create a handy short link for your Facebook group and include it where people will see it, like in your email signature, in blog posts, marketing material, or product receipts.

Building an effective group: essential strategy

Fostering an engaged Group community will strengthen your customers' relationship with your brand, and this equity can then influence their future purchasing decisions. Here are three strategies to help build a strong and loyal group audience:

Setup Membership Requests to ask up to three questions of group members upon joining. You'll find the option on your group under More > Edit Group Settings > Setup Membership Requests. For example, you could ask questions including how they found the group, what their biggest struggles are in relation to your brand's mission, etc. This is a fantastic way to instantly see what your future group members desire, and an opportunity for you to create and publish posts that serve their needs - which they'll love!

Engage with your group members regularly: When your group is new, there might only be a few members and not a lot of posts from them. To help kickstart discussion, take it upon yourself to introduce conversations on a consistent basis, a couple of times per week. For example, you could welcome new members every Monday, initiate a topical discussion on every Wednesday, and invite members to share their weekend plans on a Friday. At least in the initial few months, I would recommend that you comment on every post and answer every question in your Facebook group to ensure your members feel heard and that they feel like they are getting value from being an active member of the community.

Feature popular and/ or active group members outside of the group, on your Facebook Page and in other locations. You can find out who these people are from the More Member Details section of your Group Analytics. Compliment the individual, explaining what they bring to the group as a way to encourage new members to join.

At least once per week, thank your most engaged members as a way to keep them motivated to post regularly. Like Facebook Pages, Groups include analytics for you to monitor your group's performance (those with 250 members, at least) and you can use these to develop your group-building strategy. You can find monitor insights like your Facebook Group is growing, when your members are most engaged, and who your most engaged members are. With this data, you can learn to post on days and at times when engagement is high, track active membership growth, and thank your most active group members.

Note: If you trust someone enough and want to bestow more prestige upon them (thus increasing their brand loyalty), promote them to become an admin or moderator of the group. The latter will, as well, give you some extra eyes on helping to police any spam or other unwanted posts that might appear and free your time up to focus on building your business in other ways.

A lot of group content can reflect what you might post on your Page, but with a little tweak or a twist to make it exclusive and worthwhile the group members' time. Tried and tested content like running a poll, starting a debate, quizzing members or asking them to join a discussion in a live video, or sharing an actionable, "quick win" tip will always go down well.

Host regular events. Hosting events is a great way to get community members involved (and maybe even attract inactive members back to the community). Examples of events that you can old include Q&As with an expert from your company, panel discussions about a particular topic, and where possible, real life get-togethers to re-enforce relationships made online. When you have planned an event, create an event in your Facebook Group and invite members to attend. Asking people to show their interest will help generate buzz and they'll receive a notification closer to the time as well.

Crowdsource from your group: Use your group as a place to gather information that you can use as content and marketing elsewhere, like testimonials, product reviews, or a personal story connected to your brand that you can use as the basis for a blog post or video.

Host a Watch Party with group members:
Watch Party is a feature that lets a group owner share video streaming sessions, with everyone in the group being able to see and comment on the same videos

at the same time - a fun and interactive way to foster engagement in your community around videos that you or others have uploaded. Starting a Watch Party is just like posting anything else to a group's wall - just choose the Watch Party button under the status update box. Write a catchy description to encourage group members to participate, search for Facebook-hosted videos to add to a playlist you want to view, then send out invites. Once a few people have joined the party, the stream will begin. Once the Watch Party is over, a post will be available in your group for members to comment upon and discuss what was watched. Use this post as a way to initiate post-viewing conversations and remind people when the next Watch Party will happen.

Utilize similar groups for exposure: If a search on Facebook (or LinkedIn) shows that there are other groups in your business niche, full of people who you think would like what you do, here's a way to bring them to your attention. It's simple: reach out to the group administrator and ask them nicely if you can feature them and their group in an interview for your blog, podcast, etc. Once the (very flattering!) interview is live, provide the link to the group admin and ask if they'd share it with their group. In the likely event that they do, you've just earned your brand some priceless promotion in front of an untapped audience.

Get fans to turn on notifications: Like Pages, not all group posts will necessarily show in a member's News Feed, but they can be notified when they appear. If they want to do so, ask them to turn on notifications (in a video or image post showing them where to go) - specifically the All Posts option - from the Notifications drop-down at the top of the group (blue checkmark > Edit Notification Settings on mobile).

Remain open, honest and authentic with your group members. Refrain from talking down to group members, talk to them on their level and it will go a long way to making you stand out as a leader.

Paid Advertising Strategy on Facebook

Facebook marketing success is as much about distribution as it is content - getting your content in front of not just any old people, but the right people. A budget for Facebook advertising is an extremely important consideration as part of your marketing strategy, particularly because the competition for eyeballs on the site's content is ever-increasing and the continued throttling of organic (non-paid) reach. In fact, Facebook now deliberately limits the appearance in the News Feed of Page Post content that features only promotional messages - asking people to buy something, encouraging them to enter a sweepstakes, etc., which makes paid promotion even more crucial. You wouldn't launch a real-world business and expect people to just turn up and continue to maintain their interest without promotion, and a Facebook Page is really no different. Luckily, you don't need to spend a fortune: Facebook ads can be a cheap and effective way to gain new fans, keep existing fans engaged, direct people to your website, or get them to do whatever you please on the way to reaching your marketing goals. Consider this: if you allocate just $1 of marketing spend per day on Facebook ads, your content will be exposed to several thousand people per month that would not otherwise have seen it. If you are doing this and your competitors aren't, you'll be way ahead in the awareness game for your business niche.

Before you start with any type of advertising on Facebook, having a clear measurement of success in mind before you start will help you to understand the performance of your ads and make any adjustments to ensure you're delivering maximum value for your business.

The most basic Facebook advertising: boosting posts
To increase the ordinary reach of your most important posts - like special offers, big events, or a company milestone, Facebook encourages you to use its "Boost Post" tool, located via a button underneath each and every status update. Boosted posts last for three days and will increase the reach of your content beyond the people who see it organically. In basic terms, boosted posts create a set of instant Facebook ads without any of the detailed customization options available through the main Facebook ads tool. Boosted posts do the following:

1. Promote your post within mobile and desktop News Feeds of Fans, and on Instagram.
2. Promote your post within mobile and desktop News Feeds of Fans, their friends, and via a limited set of variants like age, gender, interests, and location.
3. Generate a Sponsored Story ad within mobile and desktop News Feeds.

The eventual cost of a boosted post depends on the number of people you want Facebook to try to expose to that specific piece of content. Costs range from a maximum budget of just a dollar or two for a few thousand people, to hundreds of dollars if your aim is to reach many thousands of users. Once Facebook approves your boosted post, which doesn't normally take very long, the promotion will begin. The amount you are charged rises as your boosted post reaches more people, but if you don't feel like you are getting value for money, you can stop the promotion at any time. On a similar note, you can add to your initial maximum budget if the promotion is going better than expected. If your boosted post does not reach the number of people Facebook estimated it would reach, based on your budget over the three-day window, you will only be charged according to the number that it did reach.

To get the most out of boosted posts, remember the following:
- Wait at least 5-6 hours before boosting a post - let its organic reach take hold and settle first.
- Once a post is boosted, it may take some time until it reaches the full breadth of your target audience. Will it still be relevant as much as a few days away from when it was first promoted?
- Don't boost every post. Spend money on increasing exposure to content that will drive meaningful engagement or make an impact on your bottom line, e.g., eyes on a new product or service, or clicks through to a valuable blog post.
- Pin your boosted post to create additional visibility for the promotion.
- Measure the success of your boosted post through Facebook Insights and other analytics tools.

If you're a small business owner that wants a quick and easy way to increase the visibility of standout posts a couple of times a week, then boosting posts should be a very strong consideration. If you are want a bit more control and customization *or* aim to build complex advertising campaigns on Facebook, utilizing the main ads tool makes more sense - see below for more information on this.

Note: The Boost Post button is also available in Facebook Groups, which you may also want to consider if you would prefer to target fans and customers if you're the owner of burgeoning or already-thriving group. With it, group admins can use three targeting options for promoting link posts inside the group: generate more clicks; attract more engagement with likes, shares, and comments; or prioritize potential customers. Group admins also have the option to integrate a WhatsApp number, edit the call-to-action button, gather insights on post reach, and more.

Beyond the Boost: Facebook Ads Strategy

If you decide that boosting posts is too simplistic for your needs, the Facebook Ads tool at https://www.facebook.com/advertising is a significant advancement over boosting posts, with many more customization options and, crucially, it's pretty user-friendly. Some of the options available in the Facebook Ads tool include:

Choosing what the ad promotes depending on your goal (your Facebook Page, a particular post, a Facebook event, a custom tab with a newsletter sign-up form, an external website, etc.).

Choosing where on Facebook the ad appears (e.g., desktop and mobile News Feeds, Ad Network, on Instagram, right-hand column).

Adding a call to action button to ads to increase click-through rates, (e.g., Shop Now, Read More, for web-based targets, or Call Now, Get Directions for local, mobile customers).

Choosing who the ad targets (based on location, age, gender, interests, and connections). Before targeting non-fans, I would suggest honing in on existing fans (many of whom won't have already seen your content or promotion organically, as well as your email list - both of which Facebook enables you to do). Facebook's Audience Insights tool will break down all sorts of information about your current audience on Facebook to help you target your ads to people with similar attributes including age, gender, relationship status, job, education, and more. All this can be used as a way to help tailor your ad design and reach an even more targeted audience. To see the Audience Insights for your Page, go to www.facebook.com/ads/audience-insights/ and choose the "People connected to your Page" option. Use the options on the left-hand side to filter the results.

Tracking conversions like registrations, checkouts, and views of key pages on your website.

When creating Facebook ads from scratch, you can choose from two options: Guided Creation (this option walks you through the whole process step-by-step and is best if you're new to Facebook ads) and Quick Creation (allows you to set up the ad campaign and then create ad sets and ads later; best if you're already familiar with Facebook ads and the previous Power Editor tool). Switch between either option at any time by clicking the Switch button at the top of the window while creating ads.

Tips for Facebook ad creation
Successful Facebook Ads all have three things in common: they are specific, targeted and compelling. The ad has one job: to get the customer to click on it, and you'll need to marry every element of the ad just right to generate optimum results. Whether you stick to Facebook's main ad-creation tool or bravely dive into Power Editor, the following pointers will help maximize the success of your promotional campaigns.

- When writing ad copy, speak to your ideal prospect in a tone that will resonate with them. Tell your customers what makes you unique and why investing time in (and clicking) your ad is worth their time. Your message should be to the point; no long or confusing sentences. Always end your ads with a call to action, either in text or with a built-in button. Don't assume that the audience knows what to do. Tell them outright what action they should take. It's obvious, but make sure the CTA matches the ad and the intent of the customer.
- Craft a headline that addresses the "you" to make the person reading feel like you're speaking directly to them.
- The image is just as important, if not more so than your copy as it's what gets people to stop scrolling and engage with your ad. In general, you should avoid generic stock photos, even though Facebook has millions available for you for free - people are desensitized to them. Choose an image that's bright, colorful and grabs people's attention in contrast to the dominant blue and white of Facebook's News Feed. Show people what life looks like as a result of using your product (like happy or relieved faces) or demonstrate its benefits.
- Create at least four versions of each ad per campaign so you can experiment with different images (both promotional and more natural/lifestyle in focus), calls to action and copy so that you can clearly understand which ones are performing the best.
- Test a variety of ad types (lead ads, slideshows, a product ads carousel, canvas, video, etc.) in a variety of placements (News Feed, mobile, and sidebar) to see how the results vary. News Feed and mobile ads should (as much as possible) blend naturally into the ordinary stream of Facebook content, while for the smaller sidebar ads in particular,

subtle calls to action and images with human faces or simple color combinations, seem to work best.

- Facebook's own research found that when mobile video ads play loudly when people aren't expecting it, 80% of people react negatively, both toward the platform and the advertiser. You might take this as a notice to create video ads that do not require any sound at all to be understood. However, in cases where this isn't possible, you can add captions manually, or let Facebook create them automatically. Automated captions are currently only available through Power Editor. When creating video ads in Power Editor, your video captions will be generated after uploading your video (it may take several minutes for them to appear). After your video ad has finished uploading, click Select. Below Video Captions, use the dropdown that says "Generate Automatically".

- Test a variety of target groups, based on criteria such as age, gender, Pages liked, interests, location, etc. If your advertising budget is small, hyper-target your audience - around 100,000 people is a decent sample. To target specific individuals and those most likely to be interested in your offering, get savvy with advanced targeting options such as lookalike audiences, custom audiences, partner audiences, re-targeting, website custom audiences, and conversion pixels, in order to get the most bang for your buck (look out for these terms during the ad setup process and use the "?" button next to each for a fuller explanation). In fact, if there is one Facebook ads-related task all businesses should do, it is to install the Facebook tracking pixel on their website. A small piece of code placed in the header of your website, the Facebook's tracking pixel has two major functions: tracking users who took action outside of Facebook because of your Facebook Ad (signing up for your newsletter, purchasing a product from your website, etc.), and tracking activity on your website for retargeting purposes.

- Utilize Facebook's Custom Audiences tool to reach new and existing customers through Facebook and make the most of those relationships. For example, Retargeting is a powerful way of winning new customers and tempting people who've shown an interest in your product back to your website, by reminding them of products they have shown an interest in. Meanwhile, Lookalike Audiences targets people similar to those who already know and like your brand, and this can be especially useful when you're aiming to use your ads to boost growth.

- Use a structured naming convention for your ad campaigns, ad names, and ad sets to make identifying and tracking them easy. With campaigns, for example, I like the format *"[Business/Client Name] - [Page Name] - [Item Promoted] - [Objective]."* The Business/Client Name qualifier may or may not be necessary, depending on your circumstances.

- When budgeting and bidding, don't sweat too much over terms like cost CPC, CTR, CPM, etc. Instead, focus on your business' cost per desired action, e.g., clicking a link and signing up to your email newsletter. This method will allow you to calculate your return on investment, i.e., how many conversions you drove per dollar spent, much more easily.

Checking that your ad image adheres to the 20% text rule

In the past, Facebook rejected any ad where text made up more than 20% of the ad image. As of Spring 2016, this rule has been abolished, and Facebook now categorizes the amount of text in an ad by density: OK (little to no text), Low (around 20%), Medium, and High (text covering a considerable portion of the image). Sounds okay, but there's a catch: *"...ads with text overlay around or above the 20% [Low] limit will receive reduced to no delivery instead of being disapproved."* Basically, the more text in your image, the less distribution you will receive – ad images with medium and high-density text will see their reach severely limited, and therefore you will incur higher costs for reaching your target audience. There are exceptions, including book covers, album covers, full product images, text-based businesses, app screenshots, infographics, and more. My advice? To prevent your ad performance from being affected, pretend that the 20% text rule still exists and, if possible, reduce the amount of text in ad images as much as possible. If you want to check that your photos meet the text rule guidelines, there are a number of handy tools to help you do just that, including Facebook's own Text in Images compliance tool at https://www.facebook.com/ads/tools/text_overlay. Simply upload a file and click the boxes to highlight the areas where text appears. The tool will count up the percentage and let you know if your image is Facebook-ready.

Monitoring Facebook ad performance strategy

One of the biggest mistakes people new to Facebook Ads make is to set ad campaigns to go live and then come back to check performance once the campaign is completed. But by doing this, you're missing out on huge opportunities to enhance the performance of each of your ads. Frequently monitoring your Facebook Ads campaigns enables you to know whether or not your ads are resonating well with your audience and allows you to make adjustments as you go along. For example, if your engagement isn't great you can create a new ad set with a fresh design. Or if your clicks are low, perhaps you need to tweak your call to action. Or if you aren't reaching as many people as you thought, maybe your audience parameters or ad placements need tweaking. Keep in mind that it can take a few days until you have enough data to start really measuring ad performance, so I'd recommend waiting until your ad has reached at least a few thousand people before making changes. The strategy outlined here is best used if a set of ads in a campaign are at least performing moderately well. f all ads in a campaign are performing poorly, Facebook's algorithm might decide none of your ads (tweaked or not) are worth giving a second chance, so it might be best to scrap them and start again.

Note: If you want to gauge early on if your ad is hitting the nail on the head, look for its Relevance Score in your ad reporting - a rating of 1-10 based on how your audience is responding to your ad through likes, clicks, comments, etc. It appears after the ad has received at least 500 impressions. One simple strategy is to keep your budget low, tweaking your ad until you achieve a relevance score of 8/10 or higher. At this point, you can think about promoting the ad more heavily, but always keep an eye on the ad in case the score (which updates in real time) starts dipping.

Unless you're very lucky, you won't create the perfect ad first time around. Expect to experiment and learn a lot in order to produce Facebook ads that will deliver the results you are looking for. As a simple example, you might start with 3 ad variants, one of which is clearly outperforming the others. You can then stop running the underperforming ads, giving more of your budget over to the one that is driving results. You might even want to create a new ad variant, based on this ad, to see if that helps deliver even better results. Ideally, you want to create several ad sets and ads before you start your campaign and then eliminate under-performing ads as your campaign progresses.

Note: When you are testing with Facebook ads, it's important to change only one element each time, keeping everything else the same. If you don't, you won't be able to tell what actually changed the result! I recommend that for each element you test, you start with wildly different changes to get a better overall sense of what's resonating with your audience. Check your ad report at least once per 24 hours so that you can get a good overview of how it's performing.

I could write a whole other book on Facebook ads - much more than I have the space to include here, unfortunately. Until I do, a quick web search will return plenty of detailed step-by-step guides for making the most of Facebook ads, and I definitely recommend you do this before jumping in, getting bogged down and lost in the options available, and simply wasting your money! Be smart, start small, and remember that there is no one guaranteed formula for Facebook ad success; experimentation is the key, as too is playing the long game. For example, after one successful campaign, you could use the Facebook Pixel to create a new ad to re-target those who engaged positively with a that promotion, or to have another shot at persuading people who might have visited your website but left without making a purchase.

Advertising aside, your main focus should always be on producing top-quality content that gains maximum traction organically. Typically, I only spend "big" on any ad campaign (whether it be a Boosted post or properly-planned ads) if I have a product or contest to launch, a coupon code or offer to give away, or if an organic (non-paid) post does surprisingly well and I think it has strong potential to go viral. The rest of the time, I rely on a small, but regular ad budget solely used to help new fans find my Page.

Using Your Personal Facebook Profile for Business

As explained at the beginning of this chapter, using your personal Facebook Timeline specifically for commercial purposes is against the site's rules. However, there are a number of useful little strategies that you can implement via your individual profile that can help support your overall business marketing.

Add a Follow button to your personal profile

If you are the figurehead of your company and happy to share your personal profile's updates with customers as a way to help them feel more closely connected to you, but don't want them all to be added as friends, consider adding a Follow button to your profile via https://www.facebook.com/about/follow. Anyone who chooses to become a follower will see posts you mark as Public (toggle this option via the drop-down menu underneath the status update box) in their News Feeds. Use this ability to filter updates about your family to Friends and updates pertinent to your business or things that you're comfortable sharing with a wider audience to the public.

Note: Visit your Timeline settings ("..." button on your profile > Timeline Settings), then click on the "Followers" link in the left-hand menu. From here, you can adjust your Follower settings and also grab code that you can use to embed a "Follow" button on your website, too.

Create custom lists to target business-y posts to friends
Related to the tactic above, Facebook's custom lists feature allows you to target status updates to customized groups of people who are also connected to you as friends. Again, these shouldn't be promotional or commercial in nature, but perhaps stuff like news and events occurring within your industry that only a specific portion of your friend list would be interested in:

To create a new custom list:
1. From your home page, hover over the Friends section in the menu on the left and click "More."
2. Click Create List.
3. Write in the list's name, e.g., "Current Customers". Enter the names of the people you want to add to this list in the Members section.
4. Click Create.

By clicking on the links that now appear in the sidebar of your Facebook account, you can easily see, comment, like, and interact with activity from people in your lists. Remember to peruse your custom lists often for opportunities to more deeply connect with your peers, building relationships that will eventually pay off as part of your business strategy.

Change your personal profile 'Work' to your business page
If people search for your business on Facebook and come across your personal profile, you'll want to make it as easy as possible for them to find your business Page too. Click on the 'Update Info' button at the top of your profile and search for your Facebook Page in the 'Where have you worked?' box and choose it when it appears in the drop-down menu. If you *don't* see your Page appear when you type its name into the box, try typing its username instead, i.e., the bit that comes after the 'www.facebook.com/' of the Page's address. If

you're still having no luck, insert your exact Page name, click the drop-down that appears and enter the additional details (Position, City/Town, etc). When you click 'Add job', it *should* populate correctly.

Note: Here are two more soft-sell Facebook Page promotion opportunities: add the URL to your Facebook Page under the 'Website' area of the Contact Info section of your personal Facebook profile. In addition, add your personal profile as a Featured Page owner on your Facebook Page. When you add a featured page owner, your personal information will be displayed in the About section of the Page and the Page will be shown on your personal profile.

Learn about (and capitalize on) the ad strategies of your competition

If you're your company's ideal customer, then you're going to be your competitor's ideal customer, too. As such, chances are that you are going to be exposed to ads from your competitors in your personal News Feed. Keep an eye out for them. You may discover that your main rival seems to advertise mostly on Wednesday evenings, that they appear on mobile and not desktops, and that certain types of images seem to get more attention than others. It's far from scientific, of course, but by grabbing screenshots and making notes, you'll have some broad information that you can use quite effectively when it comes to running your own paid ads.

Twitter Tips: Tweet Your Way to the Top

Twitter is used by millions of businesses as a way to monitor conversations about their brand, interact with customers, manage customer service issues, promote offers, share rich and engaging content like images and videos - all within 280 characters per tweet (originally and famously 140 characters, but doubled in 2017). A 2013 study by analytics company KISSmetric even found that Twitter users were more likely to buy from brands they follow on the site by a margin of 64 percent, and that's just one statistic about a site that has the power, arguably greater than any other social network, to connect with customers and to create loyal brand advocates. In this chapter, we'll explore some of the ways to make this a reality for you.

Twitter Profile Setup Strategy

No stellar Twitter strategy is complete without a profile built to knock the socks off your customers, so let's get started with some indispensable setup and optimization tips.

Top Twitter username and a tip for the "Name" box

Your Twitter username is extremely important, as it will make up part of your Twitter profile URL - the address you'll put on all of your marketing material to direct people to follow you on the social network. Try to keep your username short, simple and memorable. Most companies use their brand name as their username, so that their address reads www.twitter.com/yourbusinessname. Unlike most other sites, Twitter will allow you to change your username as many times as you like via its Settings menu, but it's worth remembering that if you've publicized one username for a while, unexpectedly switching to a new one would not make good business sense.

Write an engaging Twitter Bio, use real names

Your Twitter profile is likely to appear high up in web search results for your individual or business name, so it's crucial that you use its 160-character bio right (the bio text is used as the search link's description and, of course, appears on your Twitter profile itself). Use the space to accurately and succinctly tell people who you are, what you do, and why they should follow you; use an upbeat tone to reflect Twitter's fun and conversational nature, and if you're an individual, single "descriptor" words separated by commas, lines, or hyphens (e.g. globetrotter | entrepreneur | wine lover..." are commonly used space-savers. If you're a company, it's a good idea to include the real name of the person handling your Twitter account so that customers feel more like they're talking to a person rather than a faceless brand. If you have room, you might also want to throw in a URL, or @mentions to link to other accounts you are associated with, and even brand or industry-related hashtag, too - but be careful that the latter doesn't mess up the readability and balance of the bio as a whole.

Upload an effective Twitter profile image
Ditch the default Twitter avatar and use a headshot photo of yourself or your brand logo – text works too, if the name is short enough. Twitter's one-to- one interactions mean that people will identify much more closely with a profile that displays a person's smiling face rather than the dreaded default 'egg' image or something similarly anonymous. Twitter recommends that your profile image be uploaded at 400 x 400 pixels.

Create a custom Twitter header image
In April 2014, Twitter rolled out a new version of its desktop profiles, complete with a big 1500 x 500 pixel Facebook-esque header image - a large banner that spans the whole width of the profile, ripe for customizing with your own design. How you choose to fill the header image is up to you, but tactics similar to Facebook - simple branding, highlighting promotions, featuring customers, spelling out your mission statement, etc., are a few of the most common strategies.

Note: Download a Twitter header template optimized for desktop and mobile screens (and lots of other great stuff) via the *Premium Content Bundle* chapter of this book.

Consider applying to be verified on Twitter
Getting verified on Twitter - earning a blue check mark next atop your profile – is highly sought after, and often tricky to earn. Once reserved for celebrities and other high-ranking users in specific fields like journalism or government, anyone (or business) can now apply. Although not at all essential to make a success of yourself on Twitter, verification is a sign of high authority and authenticity, so it might well be worth applying if you feel like your brand would significantly benefit - but it might be worth biding your time, especially if you're new to Twitter. Twitter only rewards consistently active accounts with a verified check mark, so if you aren't tweeting often, you aren't helping Twitter reach its goal of directing people to accounts that people will want to follow

and engage with, and they're unlikely to approve your request. If you're ready to go ahead, here's what you need to do:

1. Visit Twitter's verification request form page to start the process https://verification.twitter.com/welcome. In order for your account to be considered, you'll need to have the following elements present and correct within your profile: a verified phone number, confirmed email address (@yourcompany.com, not a free web account like Gmail), an accurate bio (the bio should specify an area of expertise or a company mission, a professional profile photo and header image, your website, and all tweets set to Public.

2. Twitter will ask you to enter up to five websites that can be used to identify you, and associate you with your Twitter account. As your bio lists your official website, there's no need to add this again. Instead, link to other websites that showcase your influence, such as appearances in the news or other high-traffic sites.

3. Lastly, you'll see a section where you can freely state our case; a space to tell Twitter why you think your account should be verified. If you're applying as an individual, explain your public reach and specific instances where you've made headlines within your field. For brands, highlight your vision, what steps you have taken to achieve it, and the successes along the way. Twitter will email you when a decision has been made, and you'll know that you've been verified once the @verified Twitter account follows you.

Using Twitter for Customer Service: Essential Strategy
In addition to providing an effective platform for pushing your business and its products or service, Twitter also provides a great way to handle customer service issues. Here is a selection of tips to help you optimize your approach to handling customer queries via the medium of tweets:

Consider a profile dedicated to customer service
Depending on your company's resources and levels of Twitter interaction, you may want to consider opening a Twitter account dedicated only to responding to queries from customers. The idea here is that you can use your brand's main Twitter handle to focus on positive engagement, sharing valuable content, and posting the odd marketing message - leaving your secondary account available

to host conversations with unhappy customers. If this is something you intend to do, be sure to make clear which account customers should tweet to with complaints by placing the @username and an explanation on your website, pamphlets, and in your main Twitter account's Bio or header design.

Handle acute problems with direct messages
If lots of people are asking the same question on Twitter in a short amount of time, due to an acute problem, use direct messaging (DMs) to reply to them and prevent clogging your news feed with @replies. To prevent further negative tweets flying in your direction, post one public tweet to explain the situation and pin the tweet, so that it can be seen prominently on your news feed.

Switch to a personal Twitter account for pressing matters
For the most pressing matters, switch to your personal Twitter account to deal with customers who require special treatment to keep them happy. It will show the customer that you really care about them and, perhaps more importantly, it will protect your brand image from a storm of controversy away from your company's Twitter account.

Measuring Twitter customer service success
Measuring the success of customer service on Twitter requires a different approach to ordinary Twitter activity (covered later in this chapter). Some of the metrics that you might want to consider analyzing include the number of @mentions requiring customer service, the response time (how long it takes you to reply to customer queries) and response rate (the number of tweets actually replied to).

Enable Twitter's Essential Customer Service Tools
In November 2016 Twitter introduced three great new tools to help businesses handle customer service queries more smoothly. To setup these new features, you need to enable them from the Customer Support menu of your Twitter Dashboard: https://dashboard.twitter.com/i/settings/support

Show people your account provides support
When you check this box, the phrase "Provides support" will appear next to your Twitter name in search, and a message button will also be added to your profile. This option is particularly useful if your brand has multiple accounts, e.g. one for marketing and another specifically for support; a way to direct customers where to get help quickest.

Add your support hours

In the past, brands would usually add their available hours of support within the text of their bio. That space is now freed up, as you can let people know the best time to tweet or DM you with a dedicated line at the top of your profile. Tap the "Support hours" button in Settings and enter the hours and days that best suit your business. Don't forget to select your time zone from the drop-down box.

Add a Welcome message for DMs

When you add a welcome message, it will appear automatically when people select to DM you from your profile. A welcome message can be used as a quick way to greet customers and let them know how you can help.

Twitter Marketing and Content Strategy

How's that Twitter profile looking? Pretty good? Great! Now let's look at some content strategies to help your brand presence on Twitter shine...

Concoct the perfect tweet, add a sign off

Spelling, punctuation and grammar all count, especially when you only have 280 characters to communicate your point in a single tweet. Practice writing the perfect tweet, and always double-check for errors. While it might be tempting to use text speak to cram as much as you can into Twitter's 280-character limit, doing so is at best unprofessional, and at worst makes your tweets unreadable. If you have multiple tweeters on the same account, be sure to allow space to add a 'sign off' at the end of each tweet, e.g., initials like "^AM", so customers are clear who they are corresponding with. And as consumers want to know who they're interacting with, why not include a photo of the people responding to users' inquiries in your Twitter cover design too?

Don't exceed the tweet limit

Wherever possible, do not allow your Twitter statuses to spill over into multiple tweets, as this makes it confusing for your followers to keep track of what you are trying to say, especially if they have a really busy Twitter feed (likely), where your updates may appear sandwiched between tweets appearing from other people that they follow. If there is no way that you can keep a Twitter update to 280 characters or fewer, consider using a service like TwitLonger (http://www.twitlonger.com/) as a workaround. This site allows you to type as long a message as you like. When you submit the message, it will be sent out to your followers using your Twitter account. The first portion will be visible, then a URL will be displayed to allow followers to click through to read the full message at the TwitLonger website. Alternatively, write your long message in the Notes on your phone or in Word, then screengrab the message and upload it as an image.

Tweets: aim for quality and consistency; don't spam

Don't post tweets every minute of the day, spamming your followers' feeds and annoying them enough to unfollow you - be sparing. Independent research has shown that posting more than two or three tweets an hour can result in a decrease in engagement, while Twitter's own research found that brands that tweet two to three times a day can usually reach an audience that is equal to 30% of their follower base during any given week. Of course, a lot of factors can affect this estimation (e.g., if one particular tweet goes viral and the rest do not) and you can measure this with the site's analytics tool, but the principal stands - quality always trumps quantity.

Tweet your top content several times; schedule for ease

Given the comparatively high number of people an average Twitter user follows and the amount of tweets people post, the main news feed of a user (without segmentation – see Twitter Lists info a bit later on) can become unfathomably busy. Twitter's algorithm *does* periodically show users a small selection of tweets they may be interested in (and might otherwise has missed) towards the top of their timeline (ranked by relevancy – the tweet's popularity, connection to the user, etc.) but otherwise, in theory, it then will show *all* of the tweets from all accounts that they follow thereafter in chronological order. With this in mind, you realize how fleeting, without Twitter's algorithm favoring your content for a user or opting for paid promotion, the appearance (and disappearance) of one single tweet could be.

To give your tweets the best chance of being seen, don't be afraid to post the same content under different guises, several times (i.e., experiment with unique wording and different headlines for the same article one or two days apart, then note which wording performed best). If you produce a lot of valuable "evergreen" blog content, i.e., that which will remain useful no matter its age, use a service like Buffer (www.bufferapp.com) to schedule and automatically post tweets linking to this cache of content periodically. In February 2018, Twitter updated its rules to prohibit the sharing of tweets that are identical or substantially similar to one another across multiple accounts, so if you're in this situation, it's always best to re-jig your copy.

Note: On Twitter, many people simply share the title of a blog post followed by the link. There's nothing wrong with this approach, but you might also want to experiment with other methods to lead into the content and to see if they garner more clicks and engagement. These include sharing a short quote from the article, giving a brief opinion, or asking a question about it – particularly through Twitter's simple two-question Poll function (click the poll icon in the tweet box to set one up).

Another method to get your content that little bit more time and attention is to *sparingly* retweet your own top tweets a few days on from their original posting date. Allowing this duration of time ensures that your fans aren't bombarded with identical tweets, and gives the room for you to truly discover which tweets have performed best, and therefore which are the best candidates for retweeting. You can either perform this strategy manually through Twitter (use Analytics to discover your most popular tweets ranked by impressions and engagement and click their timestamp to retweet), or through a scheduling tool such as Buffer. One advantage of the latter method is that you'll be able to schedule the retweets, whereas through Twitter you'll have to perform the retweets right away.

Share engaging content, use past success to shape future content

One of the best things about Twitter is that it is an open platform, meaning that even people who don't follow you can still stumble across one of your tweets if one of your followers' favorites or retweets it. So, with the right content, you can potentially reach many more people than just the group that actively follow you. To help attract new attention and build relationships with customers, share the types of selfless, newsworthy, and engaging content we talked about in the "*The Best Types of Content to Post on Social Media*" chapter of this book, including links to useful and interesting content (whether your own or that of others). Use Google Alerts to be notified of fun, fresh, and relevant content for your Twitter feed and followers – a single tweet with an interesting take on a current event could garner you lots of extra attention. If you will be including a link to your own content within a tweet, consider shortening it beforehand using a site like bit.ly. Twitter will shorten links automatically, but using bit.ly also allows you to customize them for neatness and analyze the click-through rate, which is great for seeing what kind of content resonates best with your followers. To compound the impact of a tweet containing a link, upload an image with it to help it stand out within people's news feeds.

Use hashtags to group tweets, drive engagement, and research
Use hashtags to group tweets of the same kind and to highlight your message. Top-trending hashtags appear on Twitter's home page, and can easily be found via Twitter search. Tweets that include hashtags have been proven to receive twice as much engagement as those without, so their usage is vital. Don't include more than one or two hashtags per tweet, as it can get confusing for followers; engagement with tweets that include more than two hashtags tails off considerably, research shows.

In the same way as you would use keywords in Twitter search to find ongoing conversations related to your business), use the hashtags and comments that you find associated with them to reach out to people: be helpful, offer suggestions and recommendations, etc., as a way to build trust and authority. Don't be pushy or self-promotional. Be tactful with this approach, using your discretion to decide when it looks like someone wants to receive a reply, and when they might not.

One of the most useful features of Twitter analytics – found under the Events section - is the ability to view data on recurring trends. Recurring trends gives you access to valuable stats on Tweet volume for commonly used hashtags – hashtags you can take advantage of to boost your brand awareness on Twitter. When you're looking for the kind of regularly popular hashtag that can inspire action and engagement, instead of guesswork, Twitter's recurring trends breaks down each top hashtag by gender, age, and location. Using this information, you can accurately target your hashtag use based on the make-up of your followers.

Pin important Twitter posts, use as marketing opportunity
If you want to spotlight a particular tweet, you can pin it to the top of your feed for extra visibility, especially to reach those who visit your profile directly - all subsequent posts will appear below it. On the desktop version of Twitter, click on the three little dots underneath a tweet and choose "pin to your profile page." Use a pinned tweet to highlight one of your most engaged-with tweets, an important announcement, an upcoming event, a tweet that summarizes your brand and its mission, to sell, or broadcast a message that spurs emotion and

encourages people to share and spread brand awareness through retweeting, e.g., something funny or inspirational. A pinned tweet performs best when it includes an eye-catching image (to help it stand out), a strong call-to-action (with trackable link), and a relevant hashtag (your own, or existing popular one).

Promote and sell with the Twitter widget and Tweet button
Twitter has its own equivalent of the Facebook "Like" box, which shows a live preview of your Twitter stream's latest activity, along with a "Follow" button and a box for users to tweet to you. Create yours at https://twitter.com/settings/widgets and embed it prominently on your website to attract new followers. To increase website page views and to drive sales, you can also grab an official Twitter "Tweet" button to place above or below each of your blog posts, or next to products on your website (when someone tweets from the button, it will be seen by many of their followers who will be encouraged to take a look). Set one up at this link: https://about.twitter.com/resources/buttons. When you set up your "Tweet" button make sure to check the box to show the tweet count (the more times a post or product link has been tweeted, the more likely someone else is to share it too) and include a hashtag relevant to your brand that will automatically be added to the auto-generated tweet. However, you'll want to switch up the "Share URL" and "Tweet text" options depending whether the button will sit on a blog post or product page.

For blog posts: Set the Share URL option to use the page URL, use the title of the page for the tweet text, then enter your username into the via box. An example might read: *"How to Use Snapchat Stories to Captivate Fans http://www.andrewmacarthy.com/-captivate-fans-with-snapchat-stories #snapchatmarketing via @andrewmacarthy."* The long URL will automatically be shortened by Twitter.

For product pages: Set the Share URL option to use the page URL, but customize the tweet text to read like the sharer is tweeting about the item personally and not in over-promotional manner, e.g., "I love these stripy Craesa sneakers from Aldo #aldoshoes http://www.aldoshoes.com/women/shoes/trainers/30189991-craesa/16." Again, the long URL will be automatically shortened upon tweeting.

Encourage retweets and social sharing using Tweet This

Short, helpful, and inspirational quotes are a brilliant way to market you and your business on Twitter. One of the coolest ways to implement this strategy is via the free Tweet This website at https://clicktotweet.com/

Here's how it works:

1. Enter a quote from your blog or website that you want others to tweet.
2. Click the "Generate Tweet Link" button to create a custom link URL and embed code.
3. Share the link and/or get the embed code.

If you imagine the following quote is a part of one of my blog posts or a page on my website, the final result from Click to Tweet might look something like: *"Consistency is one of the key strategies to rocking your social media strategy via @500socialmedia [Tweet This]"*, where ["Tweet This"] is a clickable link that opens up the user's Twitter account, pre-populates the status update box with my chosen quote, and is ready for them to share with all of their followers instantly. Notice how I included my @username to add an element of attribution, which might also gain me some interest. Another strategy for Click to Tweet involves using it on the "Confirmation" page that loads after a purchase on your website has taken place, as an opportunity to encourage someone who has just purchased to share their excitement about the transaction, e.g., *"I just bought a copy of 500 Social Media Marketing Tips - I'll be a pro in no time! #socialmediamarketing [product link]."*

Respond to @mentions and DMs in a timely manner, and with personality

Whenever you receive notification of an @mention of your brand, be sure to respond as soon as possible. Replying to a customer or fan with a mention is a quick, easy, and hugely powerful way to make someone feel like you're really paying attention; it makes them feel happy and appreciated and, in turn, promotes positive connotations towards your business. Just think how good (and sometimes unexpected!) it feels to receive a quick thanks or comment from a brand or personality that you admire and you'll begin to realize the value in this approach. A lot of the bigger businesses don't reply to a large proportion of brand mentions, and it hits their credibility hard. As I've harped on plenty already in this book, people on social media like to connect with other people. So, try to fit in some brand personality to your replies where you can, using your tone of voice and mentioning the person by name. It's a great way to bring business accounts to life and truly connect with the customer. To go that extra mile where the situation calls for it, a follow-up tweet like a simple "Everything still good?" is a fantastic way to ensure that a customer's issue is truly resolved.

As well as mentions, keep a close eye on any direct messages (DMs) you receive and use them to respond to customers quickly and efficiently, too. As of April 2015, you can opt-in to receive Direct Messages (DMs) on Twitter from anyone, whether you follow them or not. In the past, Twitter users could only send a DM to someone if they followed them first, and both would need to follow each other for a two-way chat to occur. By opting in to receive DMs from anyone, you make it easier for customers to initiate a private conversation with you - great for customer service issues that demand it and stopping some negative interactions from being broadcast in the public Twitter feed, where everyone can see them. To opt-in, check the "Receive Direct Messages from anyone" box in the Privacy and Safety portion of your Twitter Settings.

Use Twitter Search to discover and connect with customers
Aside from direct @mentions of your brand (those which you'll receive a notification about), use Twitter Search to find people who have indirectly mentioned your business name, website address, area of interest or expertise, etc., and interact with them to begin building a meaningful connection – in many cases, they'll be even more surprised and delighted that you have made the extra effort to reach out to them. Don't jump in all sales-y (even if it looks like the opportunity is there). Start a conversation, get to know your customer a little, and then, maybe a few tweets down the line, start to move the conversation towards your end goal. Target your search by location and date in the Advanced Twitter search (https://twitter.com/search-advanced) for more localized and time-specific results and use keywords within quotation marks and the minus symbol (-) to omit results with unwanted keywords, e.g., "'Paula's Prom Dresses -tiara'" - any other Boolean search technique will also work. One cool strategy is to use keywords associated with your business to find the problems which people are tweeting about and target the issues that your business can solve. Pair your company's name or related ideas with words like "bad" or "sucks" to find people spouting negative feedback, and do the same using common misspellings of your brand name, @mentions, and a search for your domain name, e.g., "andrewmacarthy.com" to catch instances of people tweeting about your content. In addition, search using the question

mark symbol ("?") to look for questions related to your brand or industry. On a similar note, make sure to filter search results to "Show All", not just the "Top Tweets." You never know, one single helpful tweet could lead to customer loyalty that lasts for years. Warble Alerts (http://warble.co) is a nifty tool that checks Twitter for the keywords and phrases you select.

Twitter search won't display every tweet mentioning your keywords or hashtag that has ever existed, but it will look at a variety of types of engagement, such as favorites, retweets and clicks, to determine which Tweets to show. Although some mentions might be weeks or months old, it is still worth retweeting or engaging with them, as you never know where a dormant mention may lead.

Note: Upon searching and finding a Twitter user that you think your service can help, do not be overly aggressive in your attempts to connect or constantly tout your product or service as a solution - you risk doing more harm than good with this approach. Instead, your first few interactions should be sincere and helpful. Play the slow game; add value and your expertise to the conversation by passing along a helpful blog post or simply asking questions and showing sympathy for the person's predicament. Make it the *beginning* of your sales funnel, not the last step. This strategy has been shown to be much more successful in building trust with potential customers, especially as your approach is essentially "cold calling."

Save Twitter searches
Use the 'Save search' feature on Twitter to quickly access regular searches that you make, such as those searching for mentions of your brand name and keywords related to it.

To save a Twitter search on desktop:
1. Type your search query into the search box at the top of the page and hit return.
2. Click on the "three-vertical-dots" icon that appears at the top of the page and select 'Save search' from the drop-down menu.

To revisit a saved search:
1. Click anywhere in the search box at the top of the page. A list of your saved searches will appear below the search box.
2. Click on the saved search to revisit results for that query.

Search and 'steal' customers from the competition

If you have a local competitor, search for tweets mentioning their business name as well as your own. I wouldn't wholeheartedly recommend replying to the tweets you find, because it could come across as too being too desperate or forward. But just knowing what is being said about your competition can be enough to give you ideas to help you up your own game and give you a competitive edge. If you *do* decide to respond to tweets mentioning your competitors (if the rival firm doesn't ever reply, for example), be helpful and conversational with no put-downs and no hard selling. Hopefully your good grace will get the customer in question to switch allegiances.

Show appreciation with favorites

For a subtler way to thank your followers for their kind words about your business, "Like" a tweet by clicking the heart icon next to it. Not only is "Liking" tweets an easy way to collate customer testimonials - or 'save' a tweet that you want to think about or investigate before replying to (they appear in the Likes menu of your Twitter profile for easy reference) - but a user is also notified when one of their tweets is Liked. Different to retweeting, however, is that this notification is not shared publicly – only with the individual to whom it applies – so it looks a little less like you are tooting your own horn... not that that's a bad thing to do occasionally! Some Twitter users Like any tweet that happens to mention them, but as your Favorites are publicly visible via a link at the top of your profile, you may want to use it to collate messages in a more strategic way, such as a way to "wow!" anyone who happens to take a peek at the slew of amazing feedback you have received.

Use images to drive engagement, as a text replacement, and to tease offers

Research shows that tweets that include photos are significantly more likely to be retweeted than those without. Twitter also supports animated GIFs, which loop continuously within the news feed. While images uploaded to Twitter appear within the feed, they do not always display in their entirety. In December 2015, Twitter announced a change in the way that single images uploaded within a tweet display on its desktop website. Rather than cropping all images to be the same horizontally formatted size (as in the past, thus forcing viewers to click a button to see the full image while scrolling through the news feed), it has increased the height limit (before cropping occurs) to be the same as the width of the main news feed column – 550 pixels. Handily, this now ensures that you can upload "widescreen" *and* square format images to Twitter and know that they will display without cropping. If you upload a portrait-like pic to Twitter and you want the full image to be visible with cropping, make sure the image is no taller than 505 pixels. It won't fill the width of the column but at least viewers won't need to click it to see the full image.

Upload multiple images and tag them to boost engagement
In April 2014, Twitter rolled out the ability to attach up to four images to a tweet (previously limited to just one). Multiple images display as a collage: one main image and three smaller ones. Brands take advantage of these collages in many ways: to spell out a single message across the four separate images, provide simple step-by-step tutorials, or using multiple photos to tell the story of an event in the life of their company. Along with this feature, you can tag up to 10 people, e.g., customers, contest winners, business associates, etc. in each image. The people who are tagged will receive a notification to let them know, so do take advantage of this as a way to encourage engagement and start conversations centered on your posts. To top it all off, the characters used to tag usernames in Twitter images will not deplete any of the original 280-character space for the accompanying text. To tag people in a photo, select it once uploaded and type their name or username into the "Who's in this photo?" box. When the tweet is published, the usernames of the tagged people will appear next to it as live, clickable links.

Video marketing on Twitter – short clips and live streaming with Periscope
The Twitter mobile app provides an easy way to film (or import), edit, and share clips direct to your profile. The maximum length of a Twitter video is 140 seconds and (like on Facebook), videos posted to Twitter play automatically within users' feeds. While text is going to be your predominant method of communication on Twitter, occasionally replying to tweets via video such as answering a question in a Twitter chat - is a fun and engaging way to let your fans get to know the people behind your brand. Video replies is one specific way to use Twitter video for business, but please refer to the *"Explained: The Best Types of Content to Post on Social Media"* chapter of this book for plenty of ideas for making the most of video marketing, whatever the platform.

If you want an even *more* dynamic way to interact with your Twitter followers (and beyond), the Twitter app includes a live streaming video option. With one tap, you'll be able to broadcast instantly with your fans – to show them behind the scenes, to answer questions, to support the launch of a product, or whatever you like! Here are a few quick tips to ensure that your Twitter live stream is a hit:

- Your live video can appear anywhere that a Tweet can go. This means that it will be searchable on Twitter, and it can be embedded on other websites. It will also exist and be searchable on the Periscope app, which powers live videos on Twitter.

- Promote your stream in advance – through Twitter and other avenues, to encourage as many viewers as possible. Maybe make the stream's content a one-off so it becomes a "not-to-be-missed" occasion. To automatically notify Twitter followers each time you go live, hit Edit profile on desktop and check the "Show when I'm LIVE" box beneath your bio.

- Host it at the right time: use Twitter analytics to see when your audience is most often online and host your stream at a time when they are going to be around to watch!

- Add a clear and compelling message to help people identify your live stream just before you go live. People who follow and who have opted in to notifications will be notified when you go live (for the current broadcast and those in the future – make sure you check the " Show when I'm LIVE" option under the "Edit Profile" menu) and the associated tweet will make up part of an automated tweet and push notification used to promote your broadcast.

- Join in with the live conversation - acknowledge viewers and their questions and ask for likes and shares as a way to help build your audience for the next stream.

- For additional exposure, embed your live stream anywhere on the web by simply using the embed code from the tweet that your broadcast generates.

- Analyze your performance within the app – number of likes, views, and replays, to see how you can improve your live streaming for next time.

For ideas and insights into the benefits of using live video on Twitter and other platforms, check out the *"Explained: The Best Types of Content to Post on Social Media"* chapter of this book.

Experiment with Twitter Moments

Twitter Moments is a tool that allows you to curate slideshows using tweets from different users - you or others - which anyone viewing that Moment can quickly scroll through. To start building a Moment, choose Create A Moment from the Moments tab of your Twitter profile page and search by account, tweets you've liked, tweet link, or search. Here are some tips to make the most of your Moments:

Write a short headline to spark curiosity and choose an eye-catching cover image.
Both the description and cover photo of your Moment will be what people see of your Moment in their feed, so they're important to get right. Give people a taste of what to expect by summing up the content of your Moment in its description. Think of the description as a summary, whereas the tweets in the Moment itself give a more detailed explanation with links, reactions, and insights from different sources. Twitter describes the cover photo of a Moment like the cover of a book. You can either choose an image from one of the tweets in your Moment or upload one of your own. You can even use a GIF, so find something that represents the tone and message of your Moment.

Keep it short and sweet with plenty of variety
Twitter Moments are designed to be consumed quickly, so try to keep the number of tweets to a sensible number - around 10 is a good target. To keep viewers engaged, incorporate different types of tweets throughout a single Moment - text, images, GIFs, and videos, to best engage your readers.

Twitter contest strategy

Twitter is a great platform to hold a competition on, to encourage views and interaction with your profile, or link to an external source. Entry requirements can be as simple as asking your followers to retweet something that you have written or @replying to answer a question. If you run a competition, don't ask users to DM you the answer to a question: it shuts off promotion of the competition to vast numbers of users who won't see others tweeting to you in Twitter's search.

Real-time offers and Twitter-specific codes

Many people follow brands on Twitter specifically to hear about promotions and discounts, so give them what they want! Offer your Twitter followers special coupons, exclusive discounts, and free samples, to help build your brand's reputation. Create a striking image to help the offer stand out, and post it several times to make sure it is seen by as many of your followers as possible. If you want to measure sales and conversions made specifically through Twitter, tweet a tracking code only to your followers and be sure to ask for it during the transaction. e.g., TWEET20. It is good practice to place a time limit on your Twitter coupons as a way to drive short-term sales by increasing the sense of urgency; between 1 and 2 weeks is a decent time for people to both see and redeem the promotion. For businesses looking to engage and strengthen relationships with their customers, asking people to @message or DM you to receive an offer is one powerful strategy - just make sure you have the means to handle all of the messages you expect to receive!

Take orders over Twitter

Why not try taking orders or bookings over Twitter? If you want to give it a go but are worried it will clutter up your main profile, you can just as easily create a separate Twitter account and dedicate that one for taking orders.

Host Twitter chats for engagement and authority building

Twitter chats - live, structured conversations between users on Twitter - are an effective way to engage with and build stronger relationships with your audience, and also encourage new people to follow you. The reason why Twitter chats are so effective is because the people who participate in them are the ones that enjoy actively engaging on the social network. Many brands host weekly Twitter chats as a way to build authority within their niche, promote their products and services, and to grow their professional network by interacting with peers. Before you jump in and start your own, I'd recommend searching for and observing a couple of existing Twitter chats within your industry to familiarize yourself with how they work and to get a feel for whether they might be suitable for your own business objectives. Sites like Twubs (http://twubs.com/twitter-chats) feature tons of examples for you to choose from (or you could simply search the web for "[your keyword] + twitter chat), while http://www.tchat.io/ allows you to easily follow and reply in real-time to tweets that include a specific hashtag, i.e., the one used for your chat! If you want to host your own chat, set a date and time, a unique hashtag (so that others can follow along and join in more easily), and encourage interaction by promoting the event well in advance. Whether you host or join a Twitter chat, remember to contribute valuable tweets to the conversation using the relevant hashtag and retweet others' great responses to praise their input.

Use Embeddable tweets

Use embeddable tweets to take a tweet or a conversation and post it on your website or in a blog post. You can use this feature to share your Twitter content with a larger audience, e.g., re-capping Twitter chats, or adding positive product reviews or testimonials.

1. Locate a tweet on Twitter.com that you want to embed.
2. Hover your mouse over the tweet and click the "down" arrow next to it. Click 'Embed Tweet.'
3. Click inside the HTML code box to highlight the code. Copy the HTML code and paste it as an HTML element into your website or blog.

Creative uses for Embedded tweets

- Tweets can be a great source of customer testimonials for your business, particularly if you embed them onto your website or blog.
- Do you host business events? Embed the invitation tweet in a list of upcoming events on your website.
- Embed tweets from other people into your blog posts. Embedded tweets allow your readers to connect with new people and jump into the Twitter conversation right from your blog.
- Embed part of a Twitter conversation (one that has inspired a blog post) into your blog and reach more people than the original Twitter conversation.
- Embed a tweet of a glowing customer comment or add a tweet about an upcoming event in your email signature, to help seal deals and promote your activity.

Utilize Twitter Cards

Twitter Cards allow you to automatically attach rich information (photos, video, sign-up forms, additional product details, and more) to tweets that are created when someone shares something to Twitter from your website. As they stand out from ordinary text-only tweets within the site's feed, i.e., the feeds of the tweeter and their followers, they can be a powerful way to boost the number of click-throughs to your original content. Twitter Cards come in a number of different varieties, including:

- *Summary Card:* The default option, featuring a title, description, thumbnail, and your Twitter handle. There is also a similar option, but with a larger image.
- *Photo Card:* A Twitter Card that features only a photo. A Gallery Card option also exists; these highlight a collection of four photos.
- *App Card:* A Card to promote mobile apps. On mobile views, it will provide a direct download button, e.g., "Download in the App Store."
- *Player Card:* If your brand uses video or audio for promotion, a player card will allow you to embed a piece of media within your tweet.
- *Product Card:* Allows you to include a title, description, thumbnail image and Twitter username attributed to the product, along with details like as price, location, availability, and more.
- *Lead Generation Card and Website Card:* Cards used to collect email addresses or drive website traffic (see section on Paid Twitter Advertising for more info).
- *Offer Card:* A way for users to add an offer to their credit or debit card and redeem in store instantly, without a coupon (US testing only at present).

Implementing Twitter Cards is as easy as inserting a few lines of code onto your website (the code you use will depend on the type of card). To get started, visit the following page and scroll down to the "Get started in 4 simple steps" section. From here, click a link to the Twitter Card of your choice, and track the success of them via your Twitter Analytics account (more info on this later): http://bit.ly/twittercardsetup

Create Twitter Lists to segment tweets and organize prospects
Twitter Lists are perhaps one of the most underutilized functions of the site; they allow you to easily organize and view the content most worth reading from the people you follow and can also be used as a networking tool, i.e., to interact and engage with the people who you choose to add to lists. Tweets from people in your Twitter lists appear in a separate feed, which can allow you to filter out a lot of the 'noise' on the platform. Examples of groups of people you can sort into Twitter lists include customers, potential customers, your most passionate fans, people with whom you interact most, professional

contacts and people who inspire you. By checking in on the activity in your lists, you can more easily pick and choose the most opportune time to reach out with a conversational message and begin to foster potential relationships.

How to create and add people to a Twitter List:
1. Click on your profile icon at the top of your Twitter profile, choose 'Lists' and click the 'Create list' button.
2. Give your list a name and description, e.g., Business Influencers, and choose whether you want to make it public or private.
3. Search for people to add to your list by username, real name, or business or brand name, and insert them via the cog menu in search results or at the top of their profile. You can also use the same method to add people to a list from your own or anyone else's list of followers.

Note: Joining public lists is a useful way to discover interesting, themed content to share; these lists also act as ready-made group of people you might want to connect with. To follow a public list, go to a profile, click "lists" and choose the list you'd like to subscribe to. You don't have to follow a person's profile to follow one of their public lists.

Explore the business potential of Twitter Group DMs
Twitter's group direct messages – setup via the normal DM option, then adding names or usernames via a search - enable you to you to invite up to 20 users who follow you to join you in a group conversation. When someone joins the chat, they can invite people who follow them, even if those users don't follow you or others within the group - a fantastic opportunity to introduce yourself or be introduced to others. Some other notable benefits of group DMs on Twitter include making private, one-to-one introductions and connections with influencers and brand advocates, holding group discussions with fellow team members, and resolving a pressing customer service issue involving multiple parties.

Paid Advertising on Twitter Strategy

While Twitter advertising doesn't have the same extraordinary breadth and depth as Facebook's tools, it can still be a very powerful strategy in helping you reach an expanded audience through your tweets. To begin setting up a Twitter ad campaign, click Twitter Ads from the drop-down menu on your profile or visit https://ads.twitter.com/ and click the "Create new campaign" button. There are a number of Twitter ad products to choose from, depending on what goal you want to achieve. Some of the most popular are as follows:

Followers (Promoted Account): Use simple copy that clearly tells people what you want them to do (follow you!) and spells out the benefits - receiving deals and discounts, exclusive news, etc. Refrain from adding links or images that will detract from that all-important "Follow" button. With promoted accounts, your Twitter username, profile photo and a Follow button will also appear as a suggestion in strategic spots across Twitter on desktop and mobile, such as the Who to Follow box and Home timelines. If using this option, ensure that your profile picture, name, and bio are in tip-top shape, as this, in addition to your copy, is what people will be acting upon.

Website clicks or conversions: Combine this option with a Website Card for greater impact. Unlike an ordinary tweet that may just display a plain link, Website Cards show a preview photo and additional information about your site. The idea is that the eye-catching format of these tweets (complete with image, text caption, story headline and call to action button, e.g., "Read more...") will allow you to easily display website content within a tweet and drive relevant traffic to your home page, product page, or an important blog post.

Tweet engagements: Use this option to drive higher levels of engagement on your Twitter posts; particularly relevant to generating buzz around something like a product launch, upcoming event, or seasonal occasion.

Twitter Ads targeting advice

Use the knowledge you have of your audience to help Twitter define how best to target them with your ads. The targeting options may differ depending on your goal, but include:

Interests: As a way to broadly target an audience, picking out interests from hundreds of categories and sub-categories is a good way to go about it.

Followers: This option – more niche than the last - allows you to reach people with specific interests or who are similar to followers of accounts other than your own – like competitors, influencers in your industry, and businesses that *aren't* competitors, but do target a similar audience. Use Twitter's search to find usernames to add, and then use the 'expand your reach' link to find more. Adding around 10-25 usernames per campaign will ensure that you're reaching a large enough audience.

Tailored Audiences: If you already have a CRM (customer relationship management) list, Twitter can use this to target this audience on the social network based on data like email addresses, Twitter IDs, web browsing behavior.

Keywords: A way to reach people that engage with or search Twitter using specific keywords.
Device: Reach an audience based on what device they use to access Twitter.

Geography, Language, and Gender: Target an audience by country, state, zip, language, or their gender in order to increase relevance.

Once your targeting option is chosen, you'll be able to manually select the tweets you want to promote or let Twitter automatically select your five most engaging recent tweets for further exposure.

Twitter ad budgeting and campaign measurement advice
How much is one Twitter follower, website conversion, app install, email subscriber, etc. worth to you? Consider this and then set a daily and total budget for your campaign accordingly, either CPC (cost-per-click), CPF (cost-per-follow), CPL (cost-per-lead) or CPE (cost-per-engagement). All campaigns end once the budget has been used, so you'll never be overcharged. Use an A/B testing approach to Twitter advertising to see which combination of text and images is driving the most engagement at the cheapest price, and use this knowledge to optimize future campaigns. To help you figure all this out, the Campaigns Dashboard will show you a number of metrics related to your paid marketing on Twitter. You may also choose to setup Conversion Tracking within the Twitter advertising dashboard as a way to measure return on investment.

Monitor all activity via Twitter's Activity dashboard
Twitter's Activity Dashboard - available via http://analytics.twitter.com - gives detailed insight into how your tweets – both paid and organic - are performing. The dashboard will tell you how many times any individual tweet has been viewed on mobile and desktops, how many link clicks it has received, the

favorites and retweets it has attracted, and a month-to-month overview of your activity to show if your progress is on an upward trend. You'll also find data about your followers (the amount, location, gender, and their top interests), which can be used to work on content more tailored to them. Finally, you'll find the option to measure your return on investment by tracking the actions people take after interacting with your ads on Twitter, i.e., visiting your website and purchasing a product. Use the combined power of Twitter's analytics to track the progress of your Twitter strategy, to see what works and what doesn't, and to tweak your approach accordingly.

Note: On the move? In the Twitter mobile app, check out the Engagement feature for a quick glance at the performance of any tweet you send. From the tweet's detail page, tap "View Tweet activity" to see statistics for its views, engagement, and interactions.

Pinterest Tips: Pin Your Way to Marketing Perfection

The Pinterest website and app lets users create and organize virtual pinboards on almost any topic, then share these pins (which are most commonly images, but can also be in video form) to other Pinterest users and across the Internet via websites, blogs, and other social networks. Pins can either be uploaded directly from your computer or mobile device or shared from a website. Since launching in March 2010, Pinterest's popularity has rocketed. When you consider that Pinterest is the second biggest driver of web traffic among social media sites (beaten only by Facebook), it is no surprise that thousands of businesses, including the biggest in the world use it as a place to showcase their brand to an audience of over 200 million active users per month. Pinterest users visit the site to search for, browse, and collate the things that they love and that inspire them - and this is where the huge potential for businesses on Pinterest comes into play – plenty of these people are shoppers.

Pinterest success in a nutshell

The most successful pins on Pinterest pair captivating images with content that solves a problem, inspires a user, offers something desirable or appeals to a hobby or an activity. In short, the best pins represent the best ideas – they're inspirational and actionable. Your aim should be to create pins that have a clear audience, and are engaging for that audience. Think about how these pinnable traits can be applied to your brand as a way for people to discover content about the things they love that have been pinned by you - to encourage engagement and conversation about your company culture, products and services, and to drive click-through rates to your content outside of Pinterest.

While *some* Pinterest users visit the site with the explicit desire to find a product to purchase, others don't, or are at a different stage of the buying journey. Therefore, the mix of content you provide should appeal to and positively influence both types. In short, if the content you post makes someone want to buy from you, that's great (Pinterest users often create "wish list boards" as a stepping stone to purchasing products so you'll want to encourage them to add your products to these while browsing). But if it makes them laugh, smile, daydream, or think positively about you, that's a really good sign too. Pins that aren't solely promotional, but lifestyle-based and influential by positive association with your business can be just as effective in the long run. Whether your content offers a helpful tip or motivates a user to take an action, that's just more reason for them to repin it to one of their boards for safe keeping and to show off to their followers via their Home screens.

Even if your brand isn't very visual and you don't think the site would be a very good fit, it pays to remember that Pinterest is as much (if not more) about collating and sharing images by others, as pinning your own. For example, a coffee shop may have a board about their drinks and food, but also about the latest trends in coffee culture - gadgets, music, interior design, etc. People re-pin and follow accounts on Pinterest because they appeal to their passions and needs, not because they love your latest marketing campaign! Be a resource for pinners and pin with a service mindset, not one obsessed with profit.

Pinterest Profile Optimization Strategy

Pinterest's current layout doesn't give a whole lot of scope for customizing the look of your profile, but there are still a few key things you must to do maximize the impact of your account.

Sign up as a business (or convert your personal Pinterest account)
In November 2012, Pinterest ramped up its support for brands by allowing them to sign up specifically as businesses and also allowed those brands that already had a Pinterest presence to convert their personal accounts to ones for business. To do either, visit http://business.pinterest.com, and select the option that applies to you. Once you're signed up as a business, you'll gain access to a selection of business-specific resources, including Pinterest analytics tools, successful case studies and links to Pinterest buttons and widgets you can place on your website or blog to promote your activity on the site.

Craft an effective username
The first thing you'll want to get right when signing up for Pinterest is your username, which will form the basis of your Pinterest profile's URL (e.g., www.pinterest.com/yourcompanyname). You will want to publicize this URL both online and in the real world, so try to keep it short, simple and memorable. The obvious choice is your brand name, but if you have a keyword or slogan related to your company that could work better (especially if your brand's name is longer than the 15-character limit), then consider that instead.

Use the 'About' section to your advantage

The description you write in the About section of Pinterest appears at the top of your profile page, and acts to describe your brand and what you do. Crucially, however, it will also appear under your Pinterest URL in Google search results, so make sure to include two or three of your business' most relevant keywords. Don't overdo the length - 160 characters should be plenty. For example, mine reads: "Andrew Macarthy, author of the #1 Amazon Web *Marketing Bestseller, 500 Social Media Marketing Tips. Follow for social media tutorials and infographics!*"

Add your website and verify it for trustworthiness

Pinterest will display a little 'globe' icon at the top of your profile, which will lead to your website when clicked. It isn't hugely prominent on the Pinterest profile page, but every little bit helps, so don't leave it blank. To show people that you are a trusted source of information, Pinterest allows you to verify your website. Once verified, you'll earn a tick next to its URL on your profile and you'll also gain access to Pinterest web analytics. To verify your website on Pinterest, click the "Verify website" button next to the box in which you entered your URL. On the next page, follow the instructions to complete the verification process. You can verify using an HTML file or a meta tag.

Upload a great profile image

The two most popular types of Pinterest profile images for brands are your company's logo or, if you are the figurehead of your business, a head and shoulders shot - smiling and happy, of course. Pinterest profile images display within a rounded square on your profile page, and within circles next to pinned content and comments. To ensure your logo looks great wherever it appears on the site, upload a square 200 x 200 pixel image, but keep your business logo or face within the central "safe area," away from the corners. Download a template to help you do this (and lots of other great stuff) via the *Premium Content Bundle* chapter of this book.

Customize your profile cover image

Pinterest rolled out an update to the layout of its business profiles in spring 2018, which now include a profile cover photo that can be used to show visitors a selection of your best Pins. It's not customizable in the same way as other social networks, i.e. you can't upload a ready-made banner image like on Facebook, but you do have some authority over it. Click the pencil icon next to your cover photo to choose which selection of Pins you want to appear there.

Options include the most recent Pins saved to your profile, the most recent Pins people have saved from your site and linked accounts, or a selection of Pins from any existing board of your choosing. If utilizing this last option, you could choose a board filled with your most-shared pins to highlight those, or pick a board filled with pins that showcase a particular product or sale. Or you could make up a custom board filled with images that reflect your brand image (logo, colors, fonts, etc.), and select that to add a striking layer of branding to your profile.

Note: Just below your name at the very top of your profile, you'll see a helpful stat — monthly viewers. This tells you the total number of people who saw your Pins in the last 30 days, so you and the people who visit your profile can see how far your influence extends on Pinterest.

Customize the showcase at top of your Pinterest profile, setup Buyable Pins

As a business user, Pinterest allows you to feature up to five of your most important pinboards in a looping carousel, which sits at the top of your profile - it's the first thing visitors to your Pinterest account will see, so the perfect way to introduce yourself and show what you can offer - a collection of your latest products, popular pins from the past, or anything else that fits your business. To start building your brand's showcase, visit your profile on the web and click the edit pencil button in the bottom-right corner of your showcase placeholder, or visit the profile section of account settings.

If you want to use Pinterest to sell products *and* you use Shopify, BigCommerce or Salesforce Commerce Cloud to do so, you will be able to setup Buyable Pins. These special Pins let people buy your products without ever leaving Pinterest and are visible in search results, in related Pins and on your business profile, creating a seamless buying experience for your customers. And despite offering a potentially lucrative sales portal for your brand, Pinterest won't take a cut from your sales. With Pinterest being a hub for consumers' wishlists and a destination to window shop, Buyable Pins offer a fantastic opportunity to businesses, especially those open to impulse buying. For more information on setting up Buyable Pins, visit the relevant link below:
https://www.demandware.com/pages/pinterest
https://www.bigcommerce.com/pinterest
https://www.shopify.com/pinterest

Once your application has been approved and Buyable Pins have been activated (which can take several days), you will be able to pin products from your web store (the Pinterest browser extension makes this a breeze) to an automatically-created products board on your Pinterest account. This board will be hidden, visible only to you, but the pins you save there – as mentioned above – will be discoverable within Pinterest's search and explore features. Once Buyable Pins are live in your secret product board, repin them to your relevant public boards to make them more visible to customers.

Pinterest Marketing and Content Strategy

As discussed above, people visit Pinterest to find ideas from brands and businesses, and they actively seek out ideas and inspiration from great accounts. As a brand (and as is the case with most social networks), focusing on a niche group of highly-engaged users will produce far better results than targeting a broad, unspecified audience. If you focus on sharing consistent content within your niche, people will start to look to you as a trusted source of inspiration and information. Focusing on a niche audience will also produce favorable results within the Pinterest algorithm, which will show your content to more people who might also be interested in your Pins. What's more, unlike sites like Facebook, Instagram, and Twitter where the majority of a post's engagement and reach usually occurs within the first 24 to 48 hours of it being published, content on Pinterest will continue to be discovered over the course of days, weeks, months, and even years. As such, Pinterest is one of the most powerful social networks for long-term growth and driving consistent traffic to your website.

Note: Pinterest employs what it calls a "smart feed" algorithm, which measures the quality of a pin based on the attractiveness of its image and the authority of the source website from which it is pinned. Pins that combine these two elements are given preferential treatment within the site's feed. Of course, it's all-but impossible to tell if your pins are being picked out for special treatment by the smart feed algorithm, but knowledge of this back-end process should encourage you to consistently share only the most awesome stuff.

Optimum Pinterest pin image sizes and design
Research shows taller images encourage more re-pins on Pinterest as they work better in the way the site stacks pieces of content on top of another in its infinitely-scrolling, narrow-blocked grid. So, if you want the images on your

Pinterest account and blog to be shared more on Pinterest, focus on creating taller images. This isn't always possible, of course, but with image types such as infographics and step-by-step "how to" posts (both discussed below), there are several easy ways to implement this strategy into your Pinterest activity.

Pinterest doesn't limit the vertical size of images pinned to its boards, but the horizontal width of pictures does max out at 735 pixels. Any image width will work, but it will be resized and displayed at a max of 735 pixels. Pinterest explains that the ideal aspect ratio for a vertical pin is 2:3 - 600px wide x 900px high. Square images that are 600px wide x 600px tall can work well, too. Also keep this in mind: Pinterest only lets users pin from web pages where there is at least one image, and these images need to be a minimum size of 110 × 110 pixels big. So, to encourage pinning from your own website and blog, be sure to add at least one pinnable image to every page or blog post.

As for color and design, lifestyle images are often more effective than product shots on Pinterest. Much of what works with traditional print advertising will work on Pinterest, too (angles, graphic backgrounds, color, use of space, etc.)" In addition, a year-long analysis of some half a million pins by Philadelphia-based startup, Curalate, showed that images (particularly of products) taken against a plain and minimalist background tended to do better on Pinterest (in contrast to most other social networks) than those with too much in the frame. In addition, very light and very dark images were seen not to perform well - somewhere in the middle, then, is best. Pins that contained multiple dominant colors (rather than just one) were seen to receive more attention, while bold and warm colors like orange and red were seen to be repinned more than "colder" colors like blue. Lastly (and somewhat surprisingly), it found that images *without* human faces worked best on Pinterest - theorizing the reason behind this is that the site is a social network of "things," where faces are only a distraction, whereas a site like Facebook is a social network of people. While these trends may work as a starting point for formulating a Pinterest strategy, I recommend taking them with a pinch of salt and keeping a close eye on which content best works for you and your audience.

When and what to pin - be consistent and original

In order to stay in the good books of the Pinterest algorithm and to ensure the maximum level of exposure for your content, pin regularly and consistently – a few times a day is a good target - but keep the stream going steadily, instead of weeks with nothing followed by huge bursts of activity. Pinterest's algorithm

113

also prioritizes pins that are new to the web and to the site, so as soon as you create new content for your website, blog or on other social sites, be sure to save it to Pinterest as well.

Note: As a way to give your Pinterest content more exposure, saving a single pin to multiple boards is a good idea, but it's important that you save it to the most relevant board first – that Pin will get priority in the Pinterest feed when it is distributed. Saving pins to irrelevant boards won't help your cause and may even impede the distribution of your content on Pinterest.

What you post will depend on your business, but as statistics reveal that around 80% of all content on Pinterest is made up of re-pinned pins, aim to create original and inspiring pins to ensure that, more often than not, you are in that magic other 20%. When the pins you post includes a product, the following strategy might help: post one photo of the product on its own (e.g., with a plain white background) and another within the setting that it will be used (e.g., luxury towels in a bathroom). Some people prefer to pin simple images for inspiration, while latter strategy gives fans a way to imagine how the product can fit into their own lives. Of course, make sure to link both pins back to the same sales page of your website.

When you pin content from others, build authority within your niche by sharing stuff that is inspirational, entertaining, accurate, up-to-date, helpful, and insightful. Other Pinterest users' boards reveal a lot about their likes, interests, wishes and desires, so use what you can find to turn your profile – in addition to an advert for your brand - as a destination that serves your audience. Click on the Explore icon on the Pinterest home page to research what's hot with Pinterest users right now, then decide if it is suitable for you to integrate these trends into your content strategy. Make your account a more valuable resource by sharing pins from other boards that your fans will love.

Keep Pinterest board names short and simple
Pinterest boards are where individual, related pins are grouped together. In naming your boards, while you should be keyword-rich, keep the titles simple and descriptive so that they can be found easily in Pinterest's search - but short enough so that the names do not trail off when viewed on your profile. Each of your board names can have up to 30 or so characters (including spaces) before being cut off when viewed on your profile page - the remaining characters can be seen when the board is clicked on. In Pinterest search,

meanwhile, the cut-off point is even shorter, at around 20 characters. If your board name is more than 20 characters long, try to put the most relevant keywords at the beginning so that you give it the best chance of being discovered. Your Pinterest board name will become part of its URL, i.e. www.pinterest.com/username/your-board-name, (important for SEO), so choose wisely.

Note: Many people turn to Pinterest as a search engine (opting for it over Google, even, for certain searches), so approaching the setup of your content on the site with an SEO mindset is important - in board names, pin names and descriptions, and even the file name of your images (more on these shortly).

When creating boards, keep "niche" in mind

If you have spent time on Pinterest, you might have noticed that some of the biggest brands on the site have created *loads* of pinboards; each very specific in its content. While flooding your profile with pins might seem counter-intuitive from the "less is more" school of thought, in fact, it could pay dividends. Here's why: because people use Pinterest search a lot to find content (or come across it via a web search), creating highly targeted boards gives your pins a better chance of being found and viewed. For example, a board called "Wedding Inspiration" is very general - there are thousands all named the same and the chances of yours being found if you are just starting off as, say, a wedding accessories vendor, are slim. However, a board called "Floral Pink Wedding Dresses," although less likely to be searched for, has *much* less competition, and therefore gives it a better chance of being discovered in search results. So, when you create your Pinterest boards, think unique, specific and niche, and target the content and keywords that you think your audience will be looking for.

Select an attractive board cover

One pin from each of your Pinterest boards will be used as the board cover. This image should be eye-catching, attractive and represent the board as a whole, on your profile and in search results. In short, your board cover should appeal to users enough to make them want to click and explore its contents in full. To select a pin as your board cover, visit the board you want to change the cover of, click the pencil icon at the top, and select the 'Change Cover' button. Use the arrows to find the pin you want to use as your board cover. When selecting your board cover image, you can reposition the image to have the best part featured on the cover. Click Save to apply the change.

Rearrange your Pinterest boards by importance

Pinterest gives you the option to rearrange your boards. All you need to do from your profile page is select "drag and drop" from the drop-down menu above your boards, then hold and drag boards into their optimum positions. The idea here is to shift your most important boards onto the first couple of rows. Aside from your profile's showcase picks, think about which of your boards you want to feature most prominently - based on seasonal promotions, holidays, current trends, etc., and place them in the prime real estate area of your Pinterest profile.

Create Secret Boards to collate pins and plan marketing

Pinterest's 'Secret Boards' feature allows you to create an unlimited number of hidden boards that can be made public at any time in the future. One simple and effective use for Secret Boards is related to seasonal campaigns, e.g., Valentine's Day, Thanksgiving, Christmas, etc. Slowly build up your campaign's themed Secret Board throughout the year and when the time comes, you'll be well prepared to make it public with a wealth of content which you can continue to add to during the promotional period. To create a Secret Board, choose the option at the bottom of your profile page; or, when creating a board from the 'Add' menu, make sure to switch the Secret Board slider to 'On'.

Drive repins and web traffic with effective pin descriptions

As Pinterest is one of the world's biggest drivers of traffic to websites, crafting effective pin descriptions is essential to giving your content the best chance possible of being discovered when a user searches the site. With the roll-out of Pinterest's Guided Search in April 2014 (a tool that offers instant keyword suggestions and inspiration to help inspire users into finding exactly what they want), optimizing your pin descriptions is more important than ever. My primary advice is to write pin descriptions as a useful and searchable piece of information, including specific and distinct keywords that reflect the pin's content and your business, e.g., *"red, V-neck striped red sweater from Karen's Apparel, Denver"* is much better than just *"wool sweater"*. If the pin demands it, descriptions that mention how the subject of the pin provides value work better than straight explanations, so put yourself into the mind of a customer and write what you think they might want to know. For example, rather than saying something like *"We're now selling these diamond earrings, let us know what you think of them,"* a more effective description might read *"The way that the light bounces off these beautiful diamond earrings is mesmerizing, and they'd go well with any kind of outfit made for a night out on the town."* Some research has shown that including a call to action in your pin description also helps to encourage clicks, so you may want to experiment with these, too.

Unlike other social networks where shorter copy is king, slightly longer descriptions work better on Pinterest; just enough to spark a user's curiosity so that they will feel compelled to click through to your website for more information. Oh, and just before you publish your pin, add your site content's full URL within the description to boost its SEO. Always use the full URL, because Pinterest has a habit of marking shortened URLs (bit.ly, tinyurl, etc.) as spam. To encourage repinning (so that your pins are spread organically to a greater audience throughout the site), your description should also help people see the value of a pin and explain why they might want to repin it to one of their own boards. As for hashtags, Pinterest allows you use up a maximum of 20 (keep them broad, but relevant to your content) to help users find your content. For more specific steps on building a successful hashtag strategy on Pinterest, look to emulate the guidelines detailed in the in the Instagram chapter of this book.

Modify blog image titles for optimum pinning from readers
The title you give an image when publishing it on your blog (that's the pop-up message you see when you hover your mouse cursor over it) is the text that Pinterest lifts to use as a pin's description when that image is pinned by a blog reader. So, if you encourage blog readers to pin content from your site, make sure that the image title (and subsequent pin description) appears as you would like it to when it lands on Pinterest. I often pin from websites where this hasn't been done, and if I'm not in the mood to optimize someone else's pin for them so that it doesn't look bad on my profile, then I'll just close the window and not bother. Don't let your readers do this to you! For example, the auto-filled description generated by pinning an image of a fashionable new rocking chair from a blog might appear as "rocking-chair-new-small.jpg," when it *would,* if optimized, contain a full keyword description of the product.

Install the 'Pin It' bookmarklet and 'Pin It' buttons
The Pin It bookmarklet lets you grab an image or video from any website and pin it to one of your boards in an instant. Installing this ensures that you can quickly and easily pin top content to your boards as soon as you find it. When you visit a website and click 'Pin It' on a page where there is an image you want

to pin (displayed in your browser's bookmarks bar), the bookmarklet will display thumbnails of all 'pinnable' images on that page. Simply select the one you want to share, choose the correct board, enter a description, and hit 'Pin It'. Make sure that you install a Pinterest button on your blog, too (place it beside the Facebook "Like" and "Tweet" buttons above, below, or to the side of each blog post). This strategy ensures that your best images are made as easy for Pinterest users (at least those who don't have the "Pin It" Bookmarklet) to share as possible. Pinterest also has several choices of 'Follow' buttons, profile preview, and board preview widgets that you can display on your website to show off your Pinterest presence to potential fans. Choose the ones that appeal to you and embed them on your website where people will see them. There are simple step-by-step instructions for choosing and installing all of these widgets at the following address: https://about.pinterest.com/browser-button

On a related note (and this a strategy that will come into play once you are an established player on Pinterest), use your most popular pins as an opportunity to help drive sales *outside* of the social network, whether in real-life or on your website. Case in point is the retailer Target: it highlights various in-store items with a "popular on Pinterest" card to catch the eye of shoppers (particularly if they are Pinterest users), and it also has a section of its website - the Awesome Shop - dedicated to its most pinned content for visitors to explore. The idea is that when someone sees that a particular item is popular on Pinterest *and* that is has been given the seal of approval by their peers, they just might be encouraged to invest as well.

Set up Rich Pins for greater visibility, and Buyable Pins for products
In May 2013, Pinterest began to roll out Rich Pins, a way to make pins more useful and engaging. With Rich Pins enabled, you'll be able to feature things like the price and availability of a product, recipe details, maps, etc. on top of and underneath relevant pins. Rich Pins update this information automatically and display it below a pin in real time by lifting data from your website. To get started with Rich Pins, you'll need to prep your website with meta tags, test out the function and apply to get them on Pinterest. Getting Rich Pins to work right requires some coding and technical knowhow, so if you're unsure what terms like "oEmbed" and "semantic markup" mean, I recommend getting together with a web developer for a chat and pointing him or her to http://business.pinterest.com/rich-pins/ for more info. Once you overcome the slight technical hurdle, there are plenty of reasons to use Rich Pins

including the likelihood of increased likes, repins, web traffic, and sales - definitely worth the effort!

Note: Pinterest's own research shows that Product Pins (the type of Rich Pin related to products) get higher click-through rates than regular pins and make your brand more visible on the site. What's more, users will receive an email notification if Product Pins they've saved should drop in price, encouraging them to buy right away, particularly if they weren't quite ready to buy at the original higher price.

Overlay text on your images to grab attention and encourage interaction
Most Pinterest users scan the site's content and don't take the time to read the descriptions or comments associated with an image - that is unless the image grabs their attention first! Images overlaid with easy-to-read, bold text do that particularly well in drawing people's attention, clarifying the message of the pin, and encouraging interaction with a call to action. Use free services such as Canva and Adobe Spark to accomplish this result easily and stylishly. After all, while it's great to get repins and comments on your pins, one of your main goals is surely to drive traffic *off* Pinterest onto an external website.

Share videos and presentations; decide between in-feed or image-based pins
Pinned videos from sites including YouTube and Vimeo will play directly within Pinterest, so if videos are part of your marketing strategy, make sure your customers know about them via the site. Another effective idea is to use videos as a way to demonstrate your products in use, either in isolation or – even better – in a real life setting. You could also create a separate video board where you pin videos from Pinterest and around the web that complement yours, or invite others to pin their content there. To make sure your pinned videos have as much visual impact on the site as possible, make use of YouTube and Vimeo's custom thumbnail features. The thumbnail you choose will act as the image that represents your video pin, so make it compelling - take a look at the custom thumbnail tips in the YouTube Tips chapter for more specific advice on this. In addition, add the word "video" to the beginning of the pin's description to grab attention.

In addition to videos, Pinterest also supports the embedding of Slideshare presentations. If you use the "Share on Pinterest" option underneath a slideshow on Slideshare, the content in question will appear on Pinterest with a small "Play" button on top of the pinned image. When this is clicked, the pin opens up on its own page and users can view the whole presentation directly on the site. Similar to video content, you might want to add the words "slideshow" or "presentation" into the pin description to make clear what is being offered.

When you share a video or Slideshare presentation to Pinterest, the video thumbnail and first slide image respectively will represent the pin - and, to be truthful, it's not that big and visually impacting. To improve upon this situation (and if you'd prefer to use videos or presentations as a way to drive traffic to your website from Pinterest rather than having them play directly on the site), do this: instead of pinning the media directly from YouTube, Vimeo, or Slideshare, create a separate pinnable image that links to the video or presentation (embedded on your website) and pin that instead. The advantage of this method is that you have full control over the dimensions of the pinned image, meaning that you can format it to be taller than thinner, a composition that is often more engaging than the fixed short and wide dimensions of directly-pinned media. Custom images could simply be a much larger version of the video or slideshow's title, or - if you've got more time - a tall infographic-style image that summarizes some of the content's main points and encourages people to click through to get the information in full. To make it obvious that a pin contains interactive content behind it - and encourage users to click - add a "play" triangle symbol over your custom pin image. Yes, the downside here is that the video or presentation you link to won't play within the Pinterest feed, but chances are that the people who willingly make the extra click to view the video or presentation on your website without distractions are the kind that will be most valuable to your business (and more likely to convert) in the long run.

While I recommend pinboards made exclusively to draw attention to your video and presentations, don't be afraid to repin this content (whether you pinned it directly or as a separate image) to other relevant boards. For example, a company that sells handmade soaps could pin a video showing its manufacturing process to its dedicated video board, *plus* a board that relates to the specific product that is being made, e.g., *Winter Warmer Handmade Soaps*.

Note: If you pin a video from a page on your website on which the video is embedded (rather than a youtube.com address, for example), Pinterest will show the directly-playable YouTube video, but the link and description associated with that pin will be the URL and page name on your site, thus helping with Pinterest and web search engine optimization.

Interact, mention, and share your best content to community boards.
Pinterest allows you to mention other users in a comment by typing @username. People love knowing you like their content, so be sure to let them know. Create a seed-list of loyal people you can count on to re-pin your content, and @tag them in your pins to get them involved. In addition, consider using a service like PinGroupie (http://pingroupie.com/) to find popular community boards, and share your best content with them.

Encourage interaction and drive interest by adding guest pinners
Selectively encourage brand ambassadors and influencers to pin to your Pinterest profile on a group board (keep an eye on notifications for people who repin your content a lot, or draw them in from other social networks). Pinterest's messaging function (launched via the "+" icon at the bottom of the site) is a useful way to engage with your most loyal and trusted followers, and invite them to pin with you. Personalize the message to make the individual feel special and to let them know why they were chosen, what you want them to do and what's in it for them (money off vouchers, exclusive access to new products, etc.). The beauty of this strategy is that when an invited individual pins to your board, their activity shows up in both your followers' *and their* followers' feeds. If the guest pinner in question is popular on the site, you can just imagine the potential for increased interest in your brand. Be picky about the people you invite, restrict just one or two people to any one board so that they feel special, and give them as much creative freedom as you are happy to allow. To add a guest pinner, enter their username in the 'Add another pinner' box when creating a new board.

To supplement your Pinterest efforts further, consider using fan-made user-generated content to harness quality pins that don't require your time and effort to make. A simple way to curate your user-generated content effectively is to create a private Pinterest board that's accessible only to you and your team. Use this board to help you collect and sort through all of your user-generated content, and then repin only the best pins to your public board. Remember to give credit so that the user can share the thrill of being hosted by one of their favorite brands, with their own followers.

Share your Pins outside of Pinterest

When sharing your Pinterest post in a status update on Facebook, Twitter, in an email newsletter, etc., copy the URL of the pin and mark it as a link to click to "Pin for later," empowering your audience to bookmark content that interests them. On a similar note, try featuring some of your top pins (screenshot images of them and add a click-through link) in your email newsletter, encouraging the Pinterest fans on your list to join you on the site. One of the most effective ways I use this technique is with infographics. For example, let's assume the pinned infographic is called '10 Ways to Delight Your Blog Readers'. I will copy the image into a photo editor and crop it to show only the first of the ten ways. I'll then upload and post this shortened image to Facebook, along with a post that describes the infographic and tells fans to click through to Pinterest, at the link provided, if they want to see the other nine points.

Pinterest Board Ideas for Business

VIP board to feature customers
Ask fans of your brand to pin pictures of themselves with their favorite product of yours and to tag you in the description. You can re-pin those photos onto a VIP board on your profile. Not only is this a great way to play to the 'vanity' of your fans (they love to be featured on your boards), but it also serves to spread the word of your brand around the social network.

Products and services board, give sneak peeks
While you should never use Pinterest as a way to spam your customers with marketing pins, a couple of boards dedicated to your products and services won't harm, particularly as Pinterest is such a *huge* driver of sales and web traffic. Fashion brands on Pinterest are experts at this strategy, posting new boards to reflect the changing season's must-have looks and provide exclusive sneak peeks to its fans. A study by Vision Critical for the clothing brand J. Crew found that nearly a quarter (21%) of Pinterest users visited the store to buy an item they liked or pinned from its boards. The same survey revealed that a whopping 80% tended to buy an item within three weeks of pinning it. To boost this statistic even further, J. Crew tempts customers with pin descriptions like *"Love what you see? Our Very Personal Stylist team can help you pre order this look before it becomes available on Wednesday August 21.) Call or email..."*

Current campaigns board

Build a board specifically for posting information about your latest marketing campaigns, offers and deals, so that your customers can find them all in one place, e.g., Summer Offers, 25% Off Sale, etc. Make sure that you rearrange your boards to make this one appear near the top of your profile, so that these limited-time deals are given as much visibility as possible.

Meet-the-team board

Pinterest pins provide the perfect opportunity for your customers to get to know you and your staff better. Take individual photos of your employees and use the title and description to tell your customers who they are and what they do; add other interesting snippets of information, e.g., their hobbies, favorite movie or why they love working for you! In essence, take customers behind the scenes, to help them connect more closely with you and your brand.

Company history board

Take inspiration from Facebook's Milestones feature and use pins to document the history of your business. Customers love to indulge in the history and heritage of their favorite brands, and Pinterest provides the perfect opportunity to let them do this. Showing that your company has a history improves your credibility; showing your growth and new products can imply core growth, stability and trustworthiness. Examples of stuff you can feature as part of your history include storefront or website changes, product package revisions through the years - and even pictures of you in your younger days!

Tutorials and how-to board

In such a creative space as Pinterest, putting together tutorials and how-to videos related to your business or industry works really well. In a step-by-step process, use one pinned picture, GIF, or video per step to create an easy-to-follow chain of instructions and increase your exposure at the same time. Alternatively (and given the evidence that taller images get more re-pins), create a single tall image made up of several smaller step-by-step photos and instructions.

Reviews and recommendations board

A great number of people use Pinterest to get shopping inspiration and associate themselves with brands and retailers. Write up reviews and recommendations for products that people want and pin them to a board with a title such as 'Products We Love', whether the items inside are yours or not. Even if they aren't yours - good karma reciprocates good karma on Pinterest and you'll see a long-term positive trend if you feature and tag others in this kind of way.

Showcase your blog and website
Create a board specifically to pin blog posts and articles that you have created on your website - it helps to drive traffic to your content. Also use these boards to highlight and re-purpose old (but still great) blog posts that were posted before you joined the site.

Create and share infographics
Infographics are a hugely popular way to share information on the web and they look fantastic in Pinterest's vertical layout. Consider creating your own infographics to share with customers (don't forget to plug your business at the bottom of them). Also, repin the best infographics you find on Pinterest or around the web, as long as they are relevant and interesting to your audience. I created a Pinterest board dedicated to social media infographics and its content is among my most viewed and re-pinned.

Pinterest contest strategy
Like other social media outlets, Pinterest is a great way to hold contests to increase engagement and loyalty. The easier your contest is to enter, the simpler it is to setup and the more entries you are likely to receive. Examples include asking entrants to pin images from your business website to enter, asking fans to upload original images of their favorite products from your brand (either to their own board or one a brand new one with a name that you decide), or asking them to pin creations they have made by using one of your products (for example, a sausage company could ask participants to pin images and recipes of meals they have concocted in the kitchen).

Run an offer on Pinterest
People love offers - anything with the word 'free', 'discount' or 'giveaway' in it - and the visual nature of Pinterest is a great way to get them noticed. Either pin images from your website and add a description of the offer featured there, or upload a pin direct to the site for an 'exclusive to Pinterest followers' offer. And how about getting even fancier, with something like a 'pin it to unlock' campaign? Upload a pin detailing a special offer and tell your followers it will only run once the image has been re-pinned 'X' number of times, encouraging them to like, comment, and re-pin to unlock it!

Pinterest analytics strategy

Pinterest's built-in analytics tool (accessed via the drop-down menu on your profile page or directly at https://analytics.pinterest.com/) provides a top-down statistical overview of how often content is being pinned from your website, how many times your pins are re-pinned, how many people are seeing your pins each day, how many are clicking on them, which devices they're accessing your content on, and who these people are (based on location, gender, interests, and languages spoken). You can also glance at the most recent, most repinned, and most clicked content; click the "Export data" button to generate a spreadsheet that will give a complete breakdown of likes, comments and repins of each post. Another very useful section of Pinterest Analytics is the demographics and interests data underneath the Audience tab. Use the insights you find here to help tailor future content based on the types of people who engage with your content *and* investigate potential partnerships via boards that like to repin your posts, or brands that your audience also engages with.

Advertising on Pinterest – Promoted Pins

Advertising on Pinterest comes in three main forms – Promoted Pins (in various guises), One-tap Pins, and Search Ads. Let's take a look at each in turn, and some best practices:

Promoted Pins are a way for you to expand the organic reach of pins that you want more of your audience to see, to build brand awareness, or to drive traffic to your website. They appear in regular search results and category feeds and are marked with a "Promoted Pin" label. Pinterest users often save their favorite Pins (paid ads included) to their own boards, and so, Promoted Pins generate a lot of impressions and engagements as they get resurfaced time and again. When you pay to promote a pin, you only pay for the initial "boost." One amazing feature of a Promoted Pin is that when someone shares it on their board, the "Promoted" mark disappears, meaning that Promoted Pin essentially becomes an organic Pin. What's more, any other engagement or traffic that is generated via comments or re-pins (even after the promotion ends) is all free, so, done right, they can be a very cost-effective way of marketing your content and driving your business goals.

Promoted Pins also include the option to share videos, but while videos at standard width are the same size as all other Pins on Pinterest, paid ad videos at maximum width display at around 4x bigger and span right across Pinterest's two-column grid. For maximum impact, promoted videos should be short (between 6 and 20 seconds is a good target to aim for), include your logo and feature strong branding, ideally visible in the first few seconds to Pinterest users scrolling through the site. Cinematic Pins are similar to video Pins, but, only animate when users scroll past them in their feed.

Like ordinary pins, the most successful Promoted Pins are informative, inspirational and useful not overly promotional. They blend in! Their branding and logos compliment (not dominate) the pin; they include soft calls-to-action in an image's text overlay and in the description (e.g., "Up to 40% off," "Shop our sale," "Free shipping") - not price; and their descriptions are detailed. The copy should spotlight the most compelling aspects of the pin, and tease what a user can gain from clicking through. Multi-product images can also perform well, as they cater to different tastes, e.g., showing off several products from one range rather than just one.

One-tap Pins take users to an external website or landing page that you set up as soon as they are clicked or tapped (rather than showing a close-up of the Pin and its description as normally occurs). Keeping things uniform and seamless between the one-tap pin and your landing page (in terms of language, branding, coloring, filters, etc,) will help to increase your conversions. Your aim is to make your ad and webpage look seamless so that your prospects will trust they're viewing the same brand when they're on your product page.

Search Ads were rolled out to all business on Pinterest in the Fall of 2017. Search Ads allow you to build and serve targeted ads based on searches for potential products, which essentially give you the opportunity to put an ad in front of a customer at a moment when they've signaled intent or interest in an idea or product. Search Ads also give you the ability to auto-target relevant searches based on Pinterest's extensive "Taste Graph," which includes more than 5,000 interests.

1. To get started building any ad type, visit http://ads.pinterest.com and choose what sort of promotional campaign you want to run, based upon your goals, e.g. Build brand awareness, Get traffic to your website, or Increase installs for your app.

2. Next, name your campaign and add in a daily and lifetime spend cap to ensure that you do not blow your ad spend budget. The Campaign Placement section is where you'll choose to run your ad campaign with Promoted Pins, Search Ads, or as is the default recommended option - both. If you only want to run with one or the other, click Edit and check the box as appropriate.

3. At the top of the next page, you'll be asked to name a group of ads (several under one campaign, for example), choose the start and end dates of your campaign and provide a budget for the group of ads as a whole.

4. To reach the right people at the right time, Pinterest offers a variety of targeting options to show your Promoted Pins to specific audiences. Aside from location, gender, language and device, you can also target your ads by using interests (targets audiences based on other Pins they've saved and engaged with), keywords (targets people when they search for something specific) or audiences (creating an audience to target, like retargeting people who have visited our website) — or a combination of all three. As you choose, Pinterest will show you an estimate of the impressions that your Promoted Pin will receive on a weekly basis.

5. Choose relevant keyword terms to describe your pin and help your target audience find it. Pinterest will suggest related terms, which you can include if you wish, and the site recommends that you add at least 30 terms - a mixture of broad and specific - to increase the reach of your Promoted Pin. When deciding upon which keywords to target with Promoted Pins, use Pinterest's Search to help you determine what type of keywords people are using to find information about your service or product. In addition, Pinterest ads' robust keyword search tool can be used as a powerful generator of ideas regarding subjects to base your promotion around.

6. Choose a CPC (cost-per-click). You only pay when someone clicks through to your website. Select when you want your campaign to begin and end (or just keep it rolling). You can choose to promote an existing pin (search by name or URL), pin an image from your website, or upload a new piece of content from your computer. Hint: pins that are performing well organically (check your analytics for the data) can be great ones to promote.

7. Click Promote Your Pin to finish. Within the Pinterest ads dashboard, use the conversion tracking tools to see how many clicks, engagements, and views your Promoted Pin has received. Combine this data with Pinterest analytics to see how your Promoted Pins perform and adjust your existing or future campaigns to work on improving your results.

LinkedIn Tips: Network Like Clockwork

LinkedIn is the web's central hub for professionals and businesses to connect and market their brand, expertise, and skills to the world. Those who use LinkedIn aren't necessarily doing so for enjoyment; it's a professional site, like a networking event, so your approach to it needs to be treated as such. People won't be interested in trivial products; they want to making connections and find professional solutions. As an individual on LinkedIn, you can - among other things - use the site to establish a profile and control one of the top search results for your name online, build a broad network of professional connections whose knowledge you can tap into, and discover new business opportunities. A LinkedIn Company Page is a place for companies to provide more information about themselves, their products and services, job opportunities, and a place where they can share expert insights. Any LinkedIn user can follow a company that has set up a Company Page to receive and interact with updates, which allows you a chance to drive awareness of you and your brand. Research by LinkedIn has revealed that you only need 100-200 followers of your Company Page to reach the tipping point to start making an impact and driving engagement, so it's well worth making sure both it and your personal profile are doing the best job they can.

Note: Many of this chapter's tips are prefixed with either "Personal Profile" or "Company Pages," and some with both. This will help you tell where the advice given is best applied. Where there is no prefix, the tip is a more general hint about one of LinkedIn's many features.

LinkedIn Profile Optimization Strategy

Personal Profile and Company Page: Fill them in completely
Make sure you fill out all of the sections on your LinkedIn profiles, and that you set up both a personal LinkedIn profile for you individually, and one that is specifically for your Company Page. Either page might be the first port of call for a potential client, so you'll want to make a good first impression.

Important personal profile sections

- Your personal LinkedIn profile headline is the first piece of information a potential connection will see about you, so make it catchy and individual. Something generic like "Retail Manager" is not enough - there are millions of those on LinkedIn. Think about what differentiates you, what makes you special and what you want to be known for. Craft a headline to match. At the time of writing, my headline reads: Andrew Macarthy - Social Media Consultant, Bestselling Social Media Author, Content Curator. Another quick trick is to update your personal profile headline every couple of months, which seems to help boost views within search, and ensures your profile's keywords will be found by different people typing different search terms.

- Make sure your Intro expresses who you are *as a person*. Your company website or LinkedIn Company Page is there to tell people about your company, but your personal profile is there for LinkedIn users to learn more about you!
- The Experience section is one of the most important parts of your personal LinkedIn profile, as you can really expand upon your current and past roles and responsibilities and your achievements. It's also a really good place for you to drop in some relevant keywords which will aid your chances of appearing higher in LinkedIn's search. With a quick glance at your personal profile, visitors will know what you've done at each of your jobs, can learn more about you and determine whether you're someone they want to connect with to foster a new professional relationship. To make a prospect's job even easier, use short paragraphs or bullet-pointed lists. If you use bullets, start your sentences with verbs (past tense verbs for past positions, present tense verbs for present positions). Rather than state what you did, tell people what you accomplished or how you helped the business progress. The more concrete and quantifiable you can be here, the better. The Intro section as is also crucial, as it is your first opportunity to write an overview or statement about who you are and what you can offer your audience and a chance to show what makes you unique and desirable to prospective connections.

How to Create A Company Page
To add a Company Page, sign in to LinkedIn as a personal user and click on the "Work" link in the bar at the top of the site. From here, click the Create A Company Page' link from the drop-down menu. There are a few small milestones you have to reach and a few simple administrative technicalities to

overcome before LinkedIn will allow you to get started, but it won't take you long before you're ready to roll. You must have a company email address, e.g., yourname@yourcompany.com, in order to create a LinkedIn Company Page. You are not permitted to use an address with a domain such as Outlook or Gmail. Once your Company Page is created, you can begin to flesh it out with details about your location, size, contact details, industry, etc.

Important Company Page sections
Obviously, the 'About Us' section is very important. Write a high-level overview of your business that showcases your brand and tells people what makes you unique. It is the perfect place to start spreading your message and opening up avenues of conversation with potential partners. The 'Specialties' section of your Company Page overview is also very powerful. Here, enter relevant keywords about who you are and what you do, so that there is a greater chance that you'll be found more often in a LinkedIn search.

Create Showcase Pages for specific products or services
In November 2013, LinkedIn introduced Showcase Pages, a dynamic replacement for the old Company Page "Product and Services" tabs, which were removed from the site in April 2014. Showcase Pages aren't the same as Company Pages, and they don't have all of the same features. Think of Showcase Pages as children to the parent Company Page: a way to extend your LinkedIn presence by posting regular updates about a *specific* product, service, department, business initiative, etc., rather than your business as a whole, and a place where you can share unique and specific aspects of your brand to a more concentrated and distinct audience. For example, Microsoft has a main Company Page, but several Showcase Pages for products and services Office and Microsoft Training and Certification.

Users can follow and receive updates from Showcase Pages in the same way as any Company Page, so keep the top-notch content flowing with images, links, videos, freebies, etc. If an update appeals to both your wider fan base via your main Company Page *and* the more niche audience of a Showcase Page, don't be afraid to re-purpose it. Showcase Pages have their own unique URL for easy sharing, and also appear on the right-hand side of your Company Page. After identifying an area (or areas - you can create up to 10 Showcase Pages) of your business for which a Showcase Page would be useful, here's how you create one. After you have identified business areas that need a Showcase Page, click the Edit button on your Company Page and select 'Create a Showcase Page.'

Optimum Company Page and Showcase Page branding image sizes:
Cover image: 1536 x 768 pixels.
Company Page "Life" tab cover: 1128 x 376 pixels. Logo: 300 x 300 pixels.

Note: Download a Company and Showcase page cover photo template optimized for desktop and mobile screens (and lots of other great stuff) via the *Premium Content Bundle* chapter of this book.

Personal Profile and Company Pages: add a profile photo, logo and banner images

On your personal profile, add a recent photo to humanize it your presence. LinkedIn profile pics are 200 × 200 pixels in size. Keep it smart, though - don't post a photo on your LinkedIn profile of you in your bathing suit on the beach - a head and shoulders shot of you looking smart and presentable is best. And as with your profile information, keep your profile photo updated with your changing look - hairstyles, glasses, wardrobe, etc. This will ensure that you are recognizable at meetings, conferences and events at which you and your LinkedIn connections attend!

LinkedIn started to roll out Facebook-style cover photos for personal profiles in the summer of 2014. The recommended size for background photos is 1536 x 768 pixels. Use this space to be showcase your brand personality, help people understand who you are, what you do and how you can help them - ideas include a photo of you, your contact details (email, phone, Twitter handle, etc.) and a call to action. The default landing tab for your Company Page on LinkedIn is the Overview tab, and this is where your company logo and banner image will appear. It's very similar to how your Facebook cover image looks, but the size is different.

Note: Download Personal and Company page cover photo templates optimized for desktop and mobile screens (and lots of other great stuff) via the *Premium Content Bundle* chapter of this book.

Personal Profile: Grab a vanity URL

As with other social networks, LinkedIn offers the ability to create a custom profile URL to make directing potential clients to your profile that much easier. Here's how:

1. On your profile page, click the "Me" drop-down menu at the top of the page and choose Settings and Privacy from the drop-down menu.
2. Click on the Privacy tab and click "Change" next to the Edit your public profile heading.
3. On the right-hand side, click the pencil to add or edit your custom LinkedIn URL.

Personal Profile: Optimize your location

Entering your location on LinkedIn might not be *quite* as obvious as it first seems. For example, I have spent a lot of time in Berwyn, IL, a city that is just a stone's throw from the much bigger and better-known Chicago - so let's pretend for a moment that I live in Berwyn. If a prospect scouring LinkedIn was in charge of finding people from the Chicagoland area, listing my location as Chicago will help me appear in more search results (if filtered by location), and I will also be seen as someone "local" to others within my target market. Think about how this tactic might apply to your location and adjust your profile accordingly.

Personal Profile: showcase your Accomplishments

LinkedIn allows users to add projects, languages, publications, awards, test scores, courses, patents, certifications and volunteering carried out to your profile. As you can imagine if you put yourself in the shoes of a potential connection, this will add a lot of value to your profile, both in business terms and showing you off as a well-rounded individual. So, if you have these details to add, make sure you do so.

Personal Profile and Company Pages: Add rich visual content

Visual content like images, videos, infographics and even Slideshare presentations can be uploaded to make your personal and company LinkedIn profiles more eye-catching, while showcasing your achievements, brands that you have worked with and provided benefit to, your research, and skills at the same time. Examples of great content to feature include popular blog posts, screenshots of customer testimonials (like a tweet or product review), or a video of an impressive speech you gave at a conference. Simply click the pencil icon next to any job position, then choose to upload a file or share a link to media under the Media heading.

Personal Profile and Company Pages: insert bullet points to make your pages more readable

If you've filled out your LinkedIn profile in full, you've probably got quite a lot of text there, some of which (achievements, responsibilities, etc.) would be *so* much easier for prospects to read in a bulleted list. As it happens, you *can* insert bullet points into your LinkedIn profile sections, but it's not something LinkedIn shouts about. Here's how:

1. Scroll to the section of the profile where you want to add bullet points and click the pencil icon.
2. Copy and paste a bullet point from any other source (Google Docs, Microsoft Word, the bullet point Wikipedia page, etc.) and paste it at the beginning of a line on LinkedIn. I personally use this website: http://www.alanwood.net/demos/wingdings.html
3. Write and save your text, and you're done, and your text should be bulleted.

Personal Profile and Company Pages: Write for LinkedIn SEO

When you optimize your LinkedIn pages with relevant keywords to you, your expertise and your business, it stands a chance of ranking higher in Google and LinkedIn searches. Don't make it too obvious by writing in an unnatural style that renders it blatant to readers that you are trying to crunch in as many keywords as possible - but be aware that you'll want to include them nonetheless. Whenever you gain new skills and expertise, don't forget to add these into your profile too. LinkedIn allows you to add up to 50 skills, so fill in as many as you can.

The keywords you use should be a mix - from broad terms to those that are very specific, as you never know which search terms someone will be using to potentially find you. Where you put these keywords matters, too - research by blogging4jobs.com revealed that your name, headline, company name, job title, and skills keywords rank the highest. Another important place to use keywords on your personal LinkedIn profile is in the Experience section, both for your current and past positions. Use lots of detail, going into the same amount of depth that you would on your resume about the position you held, the responsibilities you had and the goals you achieved. Don't be afraid to brag a bit!

Personal Profile: re-order job positions by importance
LinkedIn will automatically order your job positions in chronological order, but you can override this and arrange them by importance to you (and potential connections) by clicking on the "multiple lines" icon next to any position and then dragging and dropping it into whatever order you like.

LinkedIn Marketing and Content Strategy

Personal Profile: promote your company through employee profiles
Getting all employees on board with your LinkedIn strategy is crucial to its success, as it helps to create an extended network that amplifies your company's standing and influence on the site. Ask your employees to create their own LinkedIn accounts and to list your company as their employer. If necessary, provide them with training on how to build a great LinkedIn Profile (shameless plug: check out my book, *How to Build the Ultimate LinkedIn Profile in Under an Hour*, for a step-by-step guide), and pass on the benefits that growing their own professional network can provide. Rather than being scared that employee profiles will make them a target for head hunters from rival firms, see them as reflecting extremely well on your business instead. It is likely that many of your employees already have LinkedIn accounts and, sadly, there isn't much you can do to keep them from moving on if they decide to - just focus on the positives.

Personal Profile: follow other companies
Company follows make it possible for you to keep your eye on key events happening at companies you're interested in, handy for keeping tabs on the opposition and for your own inspiration. You can follow or stop following a company from the "Follow" button on its Company Page, or by finding it in LinkedIn Search and clicking the "Follow" button right within the results.

Personal Profile: Use Advanced Search to find prospects and earn trust that leads to sales/partnerships.
LinkedIn's Advanced Search function (click on the Search box and choose the "search for people with filters" link) is a great way to find and connect with potential new prospects. You can filter by relationship, industry, location, past companies, etc., then even create a search alert to be notified when new results

become available. Even if you aren't able to Connect with or contact someone instantly because they're a 3rd degree connection (and if you don't subscribe to LinkedIn's Premium InMail service in order to bypass this restriction), you might be able to pick up enough clues from their profile to contact them outside of LinkedIn, via their website or other social account.

Note: If you hit the "Connect" button on someone's profile, a box will appear prompting you to compose a customized invite (highly recommended if your invite is out of the blue, especially if you don't know the individual). Greet them by name and add a short note that personalizes your invitation, e.g., genuine evidence that you have enjoyed a blog post they wrote or a lecture they gave which you attended. Complete your invitation by offering a compelling reason why you should connect with one another. These extra touches can help to flatter a potential connection, make a good first impression, and increase your chances of developing a relationship.

Once you have successfully connected with a prospect, send a quick thank you message and then follow-up with conversation to help the relationship blossom. Depending on the reasons you connected in the first place and your overall goals, your follow-up strategy will differ. Ideally, you don't want to go pitching your service or product right off the bat; get to know your prospect first, perhaps by picking up on a commonality between yourselves from the details on their profile. It could be as simple as setting up a reminder using the LinkedIn Contacts feature to "touch base" over the course of several weeks, or to sweeten things up by offering a free quote, PDF, or other valuable resource out of the goodness of your heart. When the relationship is sufficiently strong, you can think about moving the conversation to other social networks *and* offline as a way to get things moving towards your end goal, e.g., providing a product or service or striking up a meaningful partnership.

Personal Profile: Accept quality, relevant invites
In addition to looking to connect with others, start accepting invitations from those who want to connect with you. The more connections you have, the larger your expanded network grows, in turn creating more opportunities down the line. Unfortunately, spammers are present on LinkedIn as they are on all social networks, so be careful only to accept invites from reputable and relevant profiles.

Personal Profile: recommend and endorse others

The more you give on LinkedIn, the more you'll get back later on. Recommend and endorse others often - especially colleagues and even competitors - even if they don't ask you first. Each time you give or receive an endorsement, it will appear in the LinkedIn news feed for your network, which means more visibility for you and your brand. As you'll discover, endorsing somebody almost always results in them returning the favor, and as your endorsements grow you may even want to move that section towards the top of your profile to showcase your most valuable skills to potential contacts. Do keep in mind that you want your endorsements to be received as genuine and well deserved (more so by other users than the recipient, in a lot of cases), so don't go overboard on your first round of endorsements for an individual; spread your efforts out so that it doesn't come across as spammy or a suspicious act of over-praising.

A good rule of thumb is to review each invitation request received and make sure that the person in question has at least completed their profile and added a photo. Also ensure that the connection is purposeful and relevant to you and your brand. Do they, in your mind, offer a good reason to connect, or do they personally tell you why they want to? Do you know them already, or have they worked in the same industry as you? Finally, always reply when accepting a genuine and interesting connection request. This is an easy way to start forming relationships.

Personal Profile, Showcase, and Company Pages: drive traffic with value-added updates and an emphasis on images

Like other social media sites, focus on providing interesting and value-added updates to help others succeed in business. Research shows that the types of updates that resonate most with LinkedIn users are the sharing of expertise and industry insights, but of course you may want to talk about company developments and new products from time to time, too. The updates you share on your Company Page are displayed prominently on the main Home tab and include a nice big space for images, so don't forget to make them compelling too; for personal accounts, updates appear in a feed visible when users sign in.

Personal Profile, Showcase, and Company Pages: be visible, valuable and timely

When you've built up a thriving network of connections, you're going to want to maintain that reputation. To do this, remain consistently visible, valuable and timely in your participation in all areas of LinkedIn. Your most recent activity will appear near the top of your profile, but if you're not very active, nothing will show. As with other social networks, a rate of activity that works out at about one or two updates a day is a good target to aim for. Use the Notifications option at the top of your profile to review the most recent interactions from your network and respond in a timely manner.

Personal Profile, Company Pages, and Showcase Pages: What to post? LinkedIn users are not looking for the same kind of stuff they'll find on Facebook or Instagram, for example. Your status updates should include a professional slant. One of the most in-demand content types on LinkedIn, perhaps unsurprisingly, is industry insights. Research from the social network shows that 60% of users are interested in industry insights, over half are interested in company news, and more than one in four are interested in hearing about new products and services. As with other social networks, asking questions, including visual elements, sparking discussions, etc. are all good tactics. For longer form content posted natively to LinkedIn, (discussed below), examples of popular content includes list posts to share your favorite business books, blogs, podcasts or productivity tools; asking your network to comment with questions so you can share your expertise; and career stories, like writing about a turning point in your professional life and the lesson it taught you. Being authentic and vulnerable will resonate with your readers and drive engagement.

Whatever you publish on LinkedIn, here are some ideas to consider:

- Try putting links in the first comment instead of the status update. If you find that LinkedIn's algorithm is throttling your status updates when they include links, try putting them in the first comment below the status update instead to see if that helps. If you do this, make sure to let people know at the end of your post where they can find it.

- Reply to every comment to increase reach. When you start multiple conversations in the comments section below status update, your post will be seen in many more LinkedIn news feeds. Your replies needn't be lengthy to help reach the feeds of first, second, and third-degree networks. While it could include a follow-up question to generate more conversation, it might also simply consist of a one-word answer or emoji.

- As well as composing your own content, engaging with others' posts is important to increase your profile's visibility, especially as your comments on other people's posts show up in the news feeds of your first-degree connections. For example, when I comment on my friend Mark's status, Mark's post will appear in the feeds of some of my first-degree connections with "Andrew Macarthy commented on this" above the post. My comment appears directly under Mark's post, no matter how many other comments there are. So, the more comments you write, the more visibility you'll get on LinkedIn.

- For longer form content especially, make sure that the first sentence of your status update is eye-catching. If your first sentence doesn't grab someone's attention and make them want to tap "See More," your update will be ignored. Also, write in very short paragraphs to keep readers engaged. Most people will be consuming LinkedIn content from their phones, where massive blocks of text are a big turn-off.

Personal Profile: Publish original "thought leader" content and grow a tribe of followers

LinkedIn opened up its publishing platform to all users in February 2014. It allows you to post full blogs (known as Articles) on LinkedIn that become part of your professional profile and they are also sent out to your network as a status update. Ideally, you want to use the publishing platform as a way to share value-driven (non-salesy), expert content to both your current and potential audience. Potential topics include important trends in your industry, what advice you would give to someone hoping to enter your field of work, the biggest challenges your industry needs to solve, etc. There is no word limit, but some of the best examples so far aren't "full-on blog replacement" in length either. If you are inspired to come up with something between 400 and 600 words once a week that will build your credibility and strengthen your standing on the site, that is just what LinkedIn is looking for. A bite-sized version of a recent blog article isn't a bad idea (link to the full version at the end of your post), and – for SEO purposes - make sure to give it a compelling title that differs from the original.

To start writing, click on the "Write an article" button at the top of your LinkedIn home page and a familiar word processing layout (complete with the options to add links, videos, and images) will appear. Once you've finished writing, conclude your post with a call to action if necessary, but definitely include a quick few lines of bio with links back to your LinkedIn profile, website, or blog. When the post is shared to LinkedIn, re-post it on your Company page and other social networks for maximum exposure, then keep an eye on the metrics LinkedIn provides to help determine how well your content is resonating with your audience. As you publish more and the breadth of your statistics grows, you will be able to replicate the kind of post that does well.

LinkedIn allows users to add hashtags to ordinary feed posts, but hashtags can also be added to LinkedIn Articles, helping to surface your articles to users who may enjoy them. Editing your public profile settings to "Make my public profile visible to everyone" will enable anyone who searches for that hashtag to find your article. Then, to add a hashtag to your drafted article:

1. Open your drafted article and click the Publish button.
2. In the pop-up window, include content to introduce your article and include relevant hashtags within the "Tell your network what your article is about" field.

Note: You may find that LinkedIn gives more exposure to your status updates than to articles. If this turns out to be the case, status updates - with their 1,300 character limit (approximately 250-300 words) means that you could possibly spend much less time creating content that actually gets more reach. This might not be everyone's experience, but it's worth experimenting with.

Personal Profile: join and be active in LinkedIn Groups

Whatever your industry, consider getting involved in Groups related to your industry as a way to connect with others, discuss and learn new ideas, and - more subtly - as a way to connect with key partners and find out what your target market is interested in. With the shift in social media usage in the recent years, closed communities such as Facebook Groups as LinkedIn Groups might be the next top way to engage your audience – especially if you are a B2B company. Being actively involved in one or several LinkedIn Groups can have many benefits for businesses, including:

- Building more awareness about you within your target markets.
- Positioning your company (or you as an individual) as an industry thought leader

- Nurturing valuable industry relationships.
- A showcase for your great industry-leading content and products.
- Generation of interest and inquiries for your business.
- Converting Group members to subscribers and advocates for your brand.
- Using the ideas you find - from popular discussions, statuses with the most likes and comments, etc. - to help you work on ideas and topics to feature in your company's status updates.

As with much of social media, leaping into a LinkedIn Group only to self-promote will not go down well – and may even get you removed. Instead, use Groups as an opportunity to share posts on a topic of interest to other members, and to engage in conversations in order to highlights your expertise. When starting your own discussion (whatever it may be about) draft a compelling title to encourage views and end your message with an open-ended question or a call to action to get people to reply. The more popular your post and the more active it is, the more visibility you will receive. As a result, people will see that you have important and meaningful insights into your area of business and may then decide to follow or connect in order to build a relationship.

Groups can be searched for in the search bar at the top of LinkedIn (filter with the "Groups" tab in the results). To access and manage your group participation, select the "Work" menu at the top of your LinkedIn homepage, then click "Groups." Joining local groups with less members may be beneficial, since their members are more likely to read your posts and there's a higher chance to make relevant, local connections. Regular positive interaction, like posting and commenting thoughtful topics and responses, will raise your standing in the group, while promotional, spam, negative or inappropriate content will damage it. If a group you intend to join is already well established, you can easily view and search (via the box at the top of the page) topics within it to see what type of questions and issues are drawing the most engagement and whether these are of interest to you and your business.

Start your own LinkedIn Group
If you can't find a Group that's right for you, why not start your own? Crucially, the most successful LinkedIn Groups are focused around a topic that has a natural connection to your brand, and less on promoting your brand or company directly. Having a topic that your customers care about will not only

attract them to be part of your LinkedIn Group, but it will also help keep the conversations in the group focused and make it easier for you to manage. Here are some questions to help you decide on your group topic:

- What are your goals for the LinkedIn Group?
- What are some of the topics that your brand is related to?
- What conversations can you have that would be useful to your customers?
- What are some questions that your customers often ask you?

People should join the group because they are interested in the topic, not your company. Over time, (with you as group leader), members will create a natural connection with the topic and your brand. To create a LinkedIn Group, choose "Create A Group" from the Work > Groups menu. Fill in as much detail on the Group creation page as possible.

LinkedIn Group title, Summary, description, and rules
- The right LinkedIn Group name is critical to attracting the right members, so include a simple and specific title that instantly tells people what the Group is about. Tying your Group name to a location, e.g., *"Toronto Entrepreneurs,"* or an industry, e.g., *"Hotel Industry Professionals,"* works well.
- Add a succinct and keyword-rich Summary (which will appear in, and help your Group be found, in search results. Around 140 characters of
- your Group description will appear in search before being cut off, so make them count!).
- Add a more detailed description, which will appear on your Group's profile page. Thinking about the Group description, use specific words and phrases that will encourage people to join and differentiate you from the competition.
- Lastly, but very important - focus on creating a set of clear group rules. Your group rules will help your members understand what's expected of them (e.g. no self-promotional links, profanity, etc.), and having them stated explicitly upon joining will make it easier for you to manage and moderate conversations.

Inviting and approving LinkedIn Group members
To cut out the spam that has plagued LinkedIn Groups in the past and to ensure your Group remains a trusted place for you and your members to

congregate, you can now invite only people whom you're connected to on LinkedIn. To invite your connections, click "Manage" on your LinkedIn Group homepage and choose "Invited Users" on the left. People who aren't in your connections can Ask to join the group when they discover it in search, and LinkedIn allows Group owners to pre-approve every member who attempts to join.

In order to encourage people to find your group more easily and grow its member base, optimize and edit your group information to include keywords that prospective members are likely to search for and encourage group members to invite people to join. If you have the budget, you might also want to consider advertising your group with LinkedIn Ads. It might be tempting to think that the bigger your group is, the better it would be. However, many of the largest LinkedIn Groups have thousands of members and by this stage are often filled with links and spam. It is often smaller groups with manageable moderation that have the most meaningful discussions, and the most engaged audience. Make this a consideration as you begin to grow your group; slow and steady wins the race.

Setup message templates
One very useful feature of LinkedIn Groups is its message templates, which allow you to create custom messages that are be automatically sent to people interested in joining your LinkedIn Group. These messages are a great first point to introduce your Group and your brand to prospective members. If you don't customize them, LinkedIn will send out a default message for each of the following message actions:

- Request-to-join Message (to people who requested to join the group). To go a step further on this one, if you would like interested people to fill out an application form to join the group, you can include a form in the request-to- join message. This way, you can ensure that only people that *really* fit your criteria and are keen enough to make the effort, will get through:
- Welcome Message (to people who you have approved group membership).
- Decline Message (to people who you have group membership).
- Decline and Block Message (to people who you have declined and want to block future requests).

To setup custom message templates, click "Manage" on your LinkedIn Group page, select "Templates" on the left, then click "Create Template."

Be active in leading the LinkedIn Group
As the owner of a LinkedIn Group, it is important that you maintain an active role in discussions and position yourself as its thought leader. Do not expect the Group to lead itself. Once you've created your LinkedIn Group and invited your connections, your group is likely still feel quite barren, and new members might not post anything if there aren't already any posts in the group. As a starting measure, I would recommend creating a "Welcome" post as the group's first discussion and pinning it to the top of the group (click the three dots in the upper-right corner of the post and selecting "Feature".). Here, you can welcome new members, share what the group is about, ask them to introduce themselves, and gently remind members to adhere to the group rules.

As the ball starts rolling, tips for keeping things moving smoothly include posting a weekly discussion or question (with a LinkedIn Poll, perhaps), commenting on existing discussions, and encouraging engagement through questions and feedback requests. These actions will encourage your members to post themselves and show them know the type of discussions that are welcomed. Although starting discussions and participating in them is time-consuming, your effort will pay off once you have created a culture of starting meaningful discussions. New members will mimic the actions of existing members, so if they see only quality conversations and no self-promotional posts, they'll more likely to contribute meaningfully, too – i.e., not self-promote!

Company and Showcase Pages: monitor and tweak performance with Content Marketing Score and Trending Content
In order to gain a clear insight into the performance of your paid and organic content on LinkedIn, keep an eye on your Content Marketing Score, a feature first introduced in April 2014. It measures reach and engagement with your Company Pages, LinkedIn Groups, employee updates, Sponsored updates, and more. It then gives you a single score, ranked against your competition, and provides recommendations about how to improve your score. To drill down the information for more detailed insights, you can filter your Content Marketing Score by location, company size, industry, and more. If you want to get the best idea of how your LinkedIn marketing is helping you reach your social media goals, use your Content Marketing Score in conjunction with the

rest of the site's analytics tools. Meanwhile, Trending Content is a tool that ranks all of the issues that resonate most with specific audiences on LinkedIn by their levels of sharing and engagement. Use Trending Content as a way to help tailor the content you post to be as effective and relevant as possible.

Personal Profile: Analyze your history with the Data Export Tool
The free LinkedIn Data Export tool provides you with a .csv file complete with a detailed overview of your past LinkedIn activity. Crucially, the data it holds can be analyzed to tweak and optimize your LinkedIn profile, relationship-building strategy (on LinkedIn and away from the site), and ad-targeting - well worth a look!

How to find the Data Export tool and request an archive:
1. Go to the Settings and Privacy section of your profile.
2. In the Account tab, click on the "Getting an archive of your data" section.
3. Click the "Request Archive" button.

When your archive is, LinkedIn will send you an email with a link you can use to start the download. Some of the most useful archives to explore and exploit for your benefit include:

- Ads Targeting: information to create and target LinkedIn ads more effectively, based on data about your profile.
- Ads Click Data: see which LinkedIn ads you click on.
- Skills: review and revise a list of your Interest keywords with a quick copy and paste from the .csv into your web profile.
- Connections: a full list of your connections and their basic info to help re-target LinkedIn ads.
- Endorsements: a full list of people who have endorsed you - use it to leverage and cultivate relationships with your biggest fans. Need references too? Export your profile as a PDF via the Edit Profile drop-down menu from your personal page.
- Comments: view all past comments to see if there is anything you need to follow up or elaborate upon.
- Search Queries: A way to see which successful searches you have made on LinkedIn.

Note: If you have clients who are willing to give you access to their LinkedIn Data files, the above archives will provide invaluable data on the behavior of your customers as well.

LinkedIn Advertising Strategy

The key to remember when advertising on LinkedIn is you'll be targeting ads to a professional audience; people use the platform to network, look for jobs or new hires, and connect with industry peers. As this is the case, B2B businesses will likely have the best results on the platform. Although LinkedIn ads aren't cheap compared to something like Facebook, they can provide immense value for certain businesses if they're utilized properly. Here is a brief overview (and benefits) of each of the three main types of LinkedIn ad:

Sponsored Content: Similar to boosting a post on Facebook, this increases the visibility of status updates in your audience's feeds. These ads appear seamlessly, and are only identifiable as ads by a small "Promoted" marker attached to them. Sponsored content is ideal for promoting content like blog posts or business announcements, and for driving engagement. It's also helpful in spreading awareness of your Company Page.

Sponsored Inmail: This LinkedIn ad lets you mass-deliver private messages to the LinkedIn inboxes of your audience. As an alternative to placing an ad in the news feed, Sponsored Inmail is highly personalized; users' interest is piqued by a notification of a message. You can add a call-to-action button to the messages, allowing you to drive conversions effectively, whether you're trying to get downloads of your newest whitepaper or registrations for an upcoming event. The other great perk of Sponsored Inmail ads is that they're only delivered to users who are actually active on LinkedIn.

Text ads: Similar to ads in Facebook's right-hand side bar; these will be small and unobtrusive, off to the side of LinkedIn's feed. Only available only for desktop placement, text ads are most effective if you want to show your ad to as many people as possible. You can run text ads even if you don't have a Company Page.

Note: Your ads account is organized by campaigns. Each campaign has its own daily budget, targeting options, and ads. LinkedIn recommends that you create at least 3 ad variations, varying the ad text, calls-to-action, and images each time. You can create up to 15 different ads within a campaign, and by doing so, you'll be in the optimum position to see which ads performs best. Once a promotion is live, visit your Company and Showcase page's analytics to see how it performs.

To set up an ad, visit the LinkedIn Ads page (http://ads.linkedin.com) and click Create Ad to begin. Whichever ad type you choose, you'll be able to target it towards specific audiences based on location, job title and category, company name and category, group, and more. In order to make your ad spend as effective as possible, spend time to anchor it with an appealing headline (questions work well, e.g., "Need a Web Designer?", an eye-grabbing image (the maximum size is 50 x 50 pixels; use colors that contrast against the white background of the site) and a strong call-to-action like "Download", "Try", or "Sign Up."

YouTube Tips: Video Made the Marketing Star

Despite rising competition from Facebook and other smaller competitors, YouTube remains the world's most popular online destination for video creation and sharing, and it is absolutely fantastic as a marketing tool – a destination designed around a core goal – to give audiences content that they desire and to keep them watching for as long as possible in order to share your business and its message. Almost any audience you can think of, at any time, is looking for videos that entertain, inform, and connect them to likeminded people and groups that share their passions. YouTube makes it possible for you to meet the expectations of this audience in a variety of ways that no other online platform can. Using the power of video in conjunction with other social media outlets to show your business off to the world has countless benefits and this chapter will show you how to reap the rewards with YouTube.

Launching a long-term YouTube marketing strategy can be a daunting prospect, but years of research has identified several factors that almost every successful YouTube channel demonstrates – not a bad template to follow for yourself, I'd say:

Decide what you want to create, who you want to target, and what your goal is
Build content that addresses your audience's needs – deciding whether you want to either inspire (with emotional and relatable stories), educate (with how-to videos and other useful information), or entertain (by surprising people, making them laugh, etc.) is one strong and simple entry point at which to start the brainstorming process. Choosing how you'll engage your audience in this way will help you define your core message and tone.

The more you can specifically drill down on the people you want to reach -your target audience - the better the response to your uploaded content will be. Best practices for targeting your audience. You may already have a good idea of the people you want to reach before you launch on YouTube, but simply studying content similar to what you want to create and trying to determine which demographics are engaging with it.

And with any social strategy, ask yourself what business goals you want to achieve and how YouTube will help you to reach them. For example, is it to build awareness (so that people will be able to find and recognize your brand); to drive sales (either online or offline); or to grow loyalty (encourage people to share your brand with others after viewing a video)?

Be consistent – whatever that means to you
One of the cornerstones of a successful YouTube channel is consistency. But this can mean different things to different people, or a mixture of many factors such as:

- Consistency of upload (like sticking to a weekly schedule).
- Consistency of format (like a recurring show or that is repeated again and again, or even just the same video intros and outros).
- Consistency of tone and voice to breed trust and familiarity with an audience.

Maintaining consistency is proven to increase brand loyalty, set expectations for your audience, and compels them to subscribe to watch your future content. If consistency in uploading is one of your goals, for example, build traction with an audience and maintain your presence by publishing at least one video per week. If possible, release videos on the same day every week; viewers like structure and they will know when they can look forward to new content. If you can't be around to post a video manually, use the feature to schedule your upload for posting ahead of time - this option is available from the drop-down menu on the video upload page.

Make your video series' accessible
One-off videos are bread and butter of most YouTube creators' content, but a planned series of videos will keep viewers engaged over a number of days or weeks and ensure you of some healthy watch-time statistics. A series is also useful for chopping what might be one long video into separate, shorter, more viewable chunks. By planning ahead, you will be able to cross-reference between a series' videos when relevant and include links to related videos on YouTube cards and in the video description – all promoting people to watch more. One of the other benefits of making a series or clusters of related content is that they can potentially promote each other indirectly. When effective, your clustered videos will show up as suggested and related videos for each other in the sidebar on your own channel, and on other people's videos.

One of the key markers any good YouTube series is when every episode of can be fully appreciated by a first-time viewer. In other words, your videos shouldn't isolate new viewers who stumble upon them – make them as accessible as possible. Factor this in before you even begin filming. So, when you launch a video series, make sure to actually tell people that the videos are part of a series (visually in the title (e.g., *How to Knit A Winter Scarf: Part 1*) and audibly (e.g., *"This is part one of your guide to knitting a warm scarf for winter"*), include quick recaps at the beginning of the videos to bring new viewers up to speed, and encourage them to subscribe to come back for more with an end card message and a regular upload schedule. As well as video titles, series' do best when they include consistent video tags (good for SEO), themed video thumbnails (so that people can easily see that a group of videos are related), and when they are organized into a specific playlist (so that a viewer can click "play" just once and watch the whole series of videos in one go).

Make your videos shareable

YouTube uses the term "shareable" interchangeably with "viral" - the idea that people watch your videos and want to share them straight away. Sharing or recommending videos is powerful because people are learning about your brand from the people they trust the most - their friends and family. People share videos partly because of what the videos say about themselves. For example, sharing a funny video demonstrates their sense of humor. Smart content makes them look smart. How will your videos make people look when they share them?

The importance of subscribers

We can't go any further in discussing YouTube without touching on how central growing a loyal subscriber base who return to watch all of your videos is in achieving your business goals on YouTube:

- Subscribers tend to spend more time watching your channel than viewers who are not subscribed. YouTube's algorithm looks favorably on channels and videos with higher watch time are they are more likely to crop up in search results and recommendations.

- Once a viewer subscribes to your channel, YouTube may send them notifications to highlight certain videos. They can also opt in to be alerted when all new videos are published - encourage them to hit the notification bell located next to the "Subscribe" button.

- Subscribers form the core of your channel's community. Interacting with your audience through comments and shout-outs is an important aspect of the YouTube ecosystem. Reward and engage with fans to foster a community who loves your videos.

YouTube Channel Optimization

Choose an optimum YouTube URL; link your account to Google

Choose a YouTube username that reflects your brand for your channel URL – preferably not too long or complicated, and one that represents the name of your company or product. You will then be able to send people to this memorable address, e.g., "http://www.youtube.com/user/yourcompanyname." Your username will default as your channel title, but you may want to change this for SEO purposes, or - as YouTube will ask for all new accounts - reflect the name associated with a Google profile. Having a public identity that is consistent across Google will allow you to optimize your sharing, content distribution, content discovery, channel management, and more.

Create an engaging YouTube profile and description

Don't ignore your YouTube account's "About" section. Use it to sell your channel and its benefits to potential subscribers and include all relevant social media and web links. Fill out a keyword-rich description that will tell people all about your channel, what they will gain from it, why they should subscribe, what your upload schedule is, etc. This text will be picked up by search engines and help your channel to rank higher in search results. The first 45 or so characters of your description will be visible when your YouTube channel appears in the "Channels" sub-section of the site's search results, so pack it with keyword-rich information.

Fill out your Channel Keywords

When people search YouTube, the site does not just return individual videos for people to watch, it also suggests whole channels that a viewer might be interested in. So, in the Advanced section of your account's Channel Settings (Creator Studio > Channel > Advanced), fill in the Channel Keywords section with keywords relevant to your channel, letting YouTube and Google know what industry it should rank your channel and all its videos for. Don't go crazy here, just think about the types of search terms that your viewers will be using, add a couple of keywords and make sure you separate them with commas.

Associate your website with your YouTube channel

Visit your Channel Settings' "Advanced" menu again and you'll see an option to associate your channel with a website. Doing so will help YouTube to improve the quality of its search results and verify your channel as the official representation of your brand on the site. Enter your website URL and verify that you own it via the options listed, including an HTML tag or through Google Analytics.

Brand your YouTube channel effectively

Upload a square, high-resolution (1600 × 1600 pixel) profile photo that is recognizable at smaller sizes. This avatar will be your channel's billboard all over YouTube, including in search results and comments.

In June 2013, YouTube rolled out a new channel layout called the One Channel design. This new look enables consistent branding across all devices (desktops, mobiles, televisions, etc.), allows you to reach out to new viewers via a channel 'trailer' and shows off more of your content to existing subscribers to keep them watching for longer. The One Channel layout's main branding opportunity consists of just one main banner that features your channel's profile photo to the left and links to the channel's website and social media profiles on the right. YouTube recommends uploading an image that is 2560 × 1140 pixels in size. Inside this massive space are sections that cater to different screen sizes. For instance, the whole image will be seen on large televisions, while a central section of 1546 × 425 pixels is the 'safe' area where your logo will be visible on all devices. Whatever your design, do your best to feature your brand's personality in the channel art. Make the audience feel like they are connecting with a person or character when they arrive at your channel; this is a tactic that will encourage them to stick around.

Note: Download a YouTube channel art template optimized for desktop and mobile screens (and lots of other great stuff) via the *Premium Content Bundle* chapter of this book.

Create a trailer for your YouTube channel

On the YouTube One Channel layout, viewers to your channel's "home" page will see a different featured video, depending on whether they are already subscribed or not. What this means is that you can show a trailer that will only appear (and autoplay!) to people who are not already subscribed to your channel. This is the perfect chance for you to let viewers know what your channel is all about and tell them why they should subscribe. You'll want to keep it short and to the point, eye-catching - and include a clear call to action, inviting your audience to subscribe. My trailer is about 30 seconds long, and I used the simple tools at Animoto.com to create a snazzy video that far outperforms anything I could have created alone with my limited video editing skills.

One other thing I love about channel trailers is that a good portion of the video's description is displayed adjacent to them. Use this space to describe what you and your channel have to offer, and don't forget to include relevant hyperlinks (shortened using tools such as bit.ly so that they are not cut off, as they will be if they are too long) and a call to action too. To add or edit a channel trailer, click Edit Layout on your main channel page and choose from the "For existing subscribers" and "For new visitors" tabs. On each tab, select a previously-uploaded video to showcase from the thumbnails displayed, or enter its URL in the box provided.

YouTube Video Ideas for Business

With over 400 hours of new content uploaded to YouTube every minute, you need a strategy to ensure that viewers will want to watch yours over others'. To begin, choose a territory in which you can thrive and outperform your rivals. For example, are you going to make inspirational community-driven videos to drive awareness, short and simple how-to videos to build authority, or funny and shocking videos to get people sharing? Find the point where your business' passions overlap with your customers' concerns. At this point lies something unique you can deliver to your fans to earn their loyalty.

One of the easiest ways to judge what type of content will work for your business on YouTube is to check out the YouTube Trending page (for an idea of what's hot on the site overall), or to search for and study other popular videos within your business niche, and use them as inspiration - make yours better in every way. What are they doing that resonates with their audience? What is their tone of voice, style and length of video like, etc.? That aside, here is an additional selection of popular video idea strategies:

Interview experts at trade shows

To spread your reputation as an industry expert, interview your peers at trade events that you attend and film these interactions to create a YouTube video afterwards (make sure to get permission from the subject and event organizer first, though). It's a great form of marketing, particularly if the interviewee is popular and well respected, and links to your video after you've posted it online. You could even get someone to interview you - you're an expert in your field, right? Easy, powerful video content for you right there!

Record product demos and reviews

Rather than *telling* people what your product or service can do, why not *show* them instead? Product demo videos are a great way to demonstrate your wares to customers. Alternatively, record videos of product reviews - not necessarily of your own products, but those your customers will be interested in. For popular examples as proof of how this strategy works, search YouTube for stuff like reviews of iPads, vacuum cleaners, gym equipment or any type of consumer goods.

Show viewers around; upload presentations and talks

Take your audience on a tour of your offices and city to help them feel connected with you and your brand; give them a sneak peek behind the scenes. Upload recordings of presentations you've given, to demonstrate your authority within your business niche and to show off your public speaking skills.

Ask your audience to review and promote your products

Ask your audience to use your product in their videos (like product placement in movies), or to provide reviews, and cross-promote each other. You can then feature these customer-created videos on other social networking sites to increase your exposure and play to the vanity of your customers, who will love to see themselves featured on your pages.

Ask and answer questions for your audience

One of the best ways to get and keep your audience engaged on YouTube is to ask questions for them to answer or ask them to submit questions for you to reply to. For the former, ask viewers to submit a comment or record and link to a video response. For the latter ask fans to leave a comment featuring a question for a chance to see it answered in your next video or, even better, to video record themselves asking the question, which they then email to you so that you can feature it in your next upload. Imagine how surprised and delighted a customer will feel if you show off their feedback in a video, rather than just respond to it via a reply in the comments.

Announcements and community service

Do you have key dates or occasions in your business' life? Mark them with a video and thank your customers for their support, e.g., your 1000th customer or 100th video. Highlight the causes your organization cares about and the philanthropy you carry out in the local community - make videos that show you care.

News and views - be timely and topical

Are you in a dynamically moving industry? Show your expertise by making videos to announce and discuss breaking news and information. React to trending topics in your niche with relevant content when it makes sense for your audience. Being part of what's going viral, rising search trends or breaking news can be critical for certain content. News and politics, sports, commentary, and opinion content can thrive on topicality.

Collaborate with your peers

Look into collaborating with other, relevant, YouTube channel owners in order to share audiences, introduce each other to new subscribers and publish complementary content. In the videos you create together, get your pal to ask their fans to check your channel out (or a specific video that's available on your channel), and link to it in the video description and End Screen. You'll also want your collaborator's viewers to find your channel through searches for them, so ask them to feature your name and face prominently in the thumbnail of the video, and include it in the title, tags, and description. For another little SEO boost, at the bottom of the video's Info and Settings page, you can add another creator's channel as a credit. This connects your channel to theirs in the YouTube algorithm and can boost the number of times your channel is recommended off the back of their videos. Lastly, feature brands that you like and support in the About section of your YouTube channel (and ask them to do the same). Under the Featured Channels menu, choose "Add channels", then search for your buddies via their YouTube username or channel URL.

Convert podcasts into YouTube videos

Does your company have a podcast? Turn them into videos and upload them to YouTube to expand your reach. YouTube won't let you upload the audio alone, so create one or several graphics to complement the topic of the video.

YouTube Marketing and Content Strategy

With regards to structuring your content to *educate, entertain* and *connect* for the greatest impact, YouTube proposes three complimentary types of content in the following framework: *help, hub* and *hero*.

• *Help content* refers to the type of things that your target audience is actively searching for regarding your brand or industry – the most common questions they will be visiting YouTube to find the answers to. Ask yourself what types of video can serve as your everyday, bread and butter content? Examples include product tutorials, how-to content, customer service, etc. Once you've answered the query, include an invitation to subscribe, like "Hit subscribe and turn on notifications so you don't miss our videos - there's a new one like this each week."

• *Hub content* refers to videos that are published less frequently, and it's the kind of content that gives your audience a fresh perspective on your customers' passion and pain points; perhaps focusing on one particular topic at a time. Episodic videos or a series works best as hub content.

• *Hero content* is that which you want to find to a large and broad audience; marquee events that are designed to whose hope should be to give a notable boost to your audience growth. Hero content could mean a live-streamed event, a viral video, cross-promotion with an influential figure, or even a made-for-YouTube ad. It may also revolve around a holiday like Christmas or a cultural event like the Oscars. To make the biggest impact as possible, plan ahead and promote the event with ancillary videos in the run-up to it to build anticipation, and let people know about it via your email newsletter, other social channels, etc. Ask for your audience's participation in the event in any way they can be made useful; turn them into advocates who will promote ahead of the event happening.

We'll look at some more specific examples of these types of content later on, but first here are a selection of other considerations for all of your videos:

Focus on quality, edit well, and grab FREE YouTube Music

Whatever content you create for YouTube, a basic standard of quality is essential. At a minimum you should ensure that the video quality is high definition (at least 720p), that the audio is clear and balanced, that the lighting is good, and (if fitting), you use varying camera angles to add variety and dynamism to the finished product. Viewers rarely expect YouTube content to have Hollywood production values, but watching a person talking down into the tinny microphone of their low-res webcam isn't going to give anybody a good first impression, or reflect well on your brand. If you're serious about videos as a social media tool, consider investing in a decent camera and video editing software, such as Adobe Premier. Include only necessary footage in your videos - don't be afraid to cut - and add transitions, overlays and graphics to help convey your story.

Want free music and sound effects for your videos? Check out the YouTube Audio Library. It features thousands of royalty-free instrumental tracks (arranged by mood, genre, instrument and duration) and sound effects that you can use for free, forever, for any creative purpose (not just in your YouTube videos). Access it via a link on your Video Manager page, or at https://www.youtube.com/audiolibrary/. Another extremely popular source of royalty free music for YouTube videos is Incompetech (http://incompetech.com/music/royalty-free/), with tons of great tracks available for download and use as long as credit is given.

Find your company's cheerleader and use screen capturing

Who is the cheeriest person in your office? Consider them to host your YouTube videos, as they'll appeal to your audience. Everyone shy about being on camera? If you don't have anyone who wants to be the face of your business, consider something like Google Search Stories (http://www.youtube.com/user/SearchStories) to show off your best online properties or if, like me, you do a lot of web demonstrations, use screen capturing software such as Camtasia (expensive but great quality and editing options) or Screenr (completely free, but without editing features). *Ideally*, you want to have a person in front of the camera, or a mix of screen capture and someone onscreen, as this approach will resonate with your audience best.

Find the correct tone of voice

Your tone of voice in a video is very important. Remember, it's a conversation you're having, so avoid the cheesy radio announcer voice and speak naturally.

When expressing yourself on video, be real. Robotic speech or blatantly reading from a script will not appeal to viewers. Talk directly to your fans as if you're in a room with them; it couldn't get much more personal than that.

Hook viewers with a teaser or intrigue

With low viewer attention spans and YouTube making it so easy for them to click away to someone else's content, it is crucial to use the opening seconds of your video to hook viewers in and keep them watching *your* recordings until the end. This portion of your video only needs to be a few seconds long, but its effectiveness can pay dividends towards watch time and viewer engagement. Examples include:

- Showing off the finished result in a "how to" video and telling your audience that this is what they'll have learned to create by the end of your clip.
- Offering a mysterious line or quip like, *"What is the link between a potato and unbelievable sales conversion? Keep watching to find out..."*
- Stories are another way to pique viewers' interest, as we are all hardwired to enjoy them. When you begin your video with a story, people will naturally want to stick around to see how it unfolds. In addition, personal stories endear the presenter viewers and can often provide a helpful segue into more complicated ideas.

No matter you hook viewers, make sure your opening gambit relates directly to the title of your video and that you get into it quickly. After all, that's why the viewer clicked in the first instance.

What is the best video length for YouTube?

The question *"How long should my YouTube videos be?"* is a complicated one, and the answer depends on a myriad of factors, including the subject of your videos and your target audience. In short, the "right" length for a YouTube video is exactly as long as it keeps people watching. Ultimately, the right length for a video is just long enough to get all of the information across without unnecessarily padding. You don't make a video longer just for the sake of making it longer, as that's a sure-fire way to put people off. Although creating long videos might seem counterintuitive, given the famously short attention spans of online viewers, longer videos – especially on YouTube - equate to more watch time, which will lead to a boost for your content in the algorithm.

Some basic rules to keep people watching include keeping content relevant to your audience *and* especially in relation to your video's title and custom thumbnail (more on both of these coming up), knowing what message you want to communicate and sticking to it, and editing out all unnecessary waffling or distraction. If you saw two videos offering exactly the same information - one 3 minutes long and the other 20 minutes long, which would you click on? Similarly, if you started watching a short video and the information promised was not being delivered quickly, you would be very likely to give up on it.

Feature calls to action within your videos, build an interactive End Screen

Depending on where during the video would be most effective, include calls to action (CTAs) to direct your viewers - do you want them to visit your website, call you for a quote, watch another video, reply to a question in the comments, subscribe for more great content, or click the link in the description? Tell them! CTAs can be implemented in several ways, including direct from the video host, or as interactive on-screen cards.

YouTube also offers a *mobile-friendly* End Screen tool that lets you engage viewers right as your video finishes and encourages them to watch more. In the last 5-20 seconds of your videos, you can choose to show overlays that prompt viewers to watch your other videos, subscribe to your channel, visit collaborators' channels, and more. YouTube offers several templates to make setup quick and easy. Research has shown that the Best for Viewer End Screen works really well, letting Google select the best video based on the viewer's past viewing habits. But if the video is part of a series, make sure you point viewers to the next video in that series or to a playlist so they can keep watching. In addition, a Subscribe End Screen will add an on-screen link featuring your profile photo for people to tap or click to subscribe to your channel – there's really no reason *not* to include it in your videos. As a general rule, the more CTAs you provide, the less likely people are to choose any of them, so it's a good idea to include no more than three links to your End Screen. To set one up, navigate to the End Screen & Annotations option within Video Manager and build one from scratch or use one of several templates.

Note: End Screen Cards must be inserted on a per-video basis, but once you have a favorite or one that performs well (monitor the success of your End

Screens and refine your strategy based on the data via Creator Studio > Analytics > End Screen), you can quickly import it into every new video you publish. Click Import From Video option and select the video from which you want to import End Screens.

Experiment with YouTube Cards – the evolution of annotations
 Launched in the spring of 2015, YouTube cards provide a new way to add a layer of interactivity to your videos. Cards can be used to direct viewers to other videos, merchandise, websites, playlists, and more, and unlike annotations, they also work on mobile devices. The six types of card currently available are: Merchandise, Fundraising, Video, Playlist, Associated Website and Fan Funding. To create a card, click on the "Cards" tab in your Video Editor.

How YouTube cards work
When a card is applied to a video, a teaser for it will appear for a few seconds at a time you designate. If clicked, the full card will appear for use. Here, a viewer will - depending on the card type - see a link, customizable image (cropped to a square), title (50 characters max), and call-to-action (25 characters max). At any other stage of the video, viewers will notice an icon appear if they hover their mouse over the player (desktop) or when the player controls are visible (mobile). At any point, they can click on the icon to view all cards that are applied to the video.

Making the most of YouTube cards
- Cards should be inserted in a contextual manner as a way to help you reach your business goals through video, while also providing an enriched experience for the viewer. Up to five cards can be used in any one video.
- Don't physically point to a card in your video as it may appear differently depending on the viewer's device.
- Cards work most effectively when they are not placed too close together, so try spacing them throughout your videos at key points.
- Analyze the performance of cards - and use the date to improve their function - within YouTube Analytics.

Create Associated website annotations
Associated website cards enable you to add a clickable link to a non-YouTube URL within the video player itself. They work great for branding purposes, and

as an easy way to direct people either audibly or visually to click through to your website. Here's how to set one up:

1. Verify ownership of your YouTube account by telephone at http://www.youtube.com/verify

2. Add your website as an associated website and verify ownership of it via Google Webmaster Tools - visit https://www.google.com/webmasters/tools to do this. You'll need back end access to your site to add some code, so contact your web developer if you need help here.

3. Back on your YouTube Video Manager page, visit the "Advanced" section of the Channel Settings menu. Here, add your website URL to the box next to "Associated website." When confirmed, a green "Success" circle will appear.

4. You're done! When adding an annotation to your videos, choose the Associated Website type from the drop-down menu and add your full website URL into the box provided.

Add a branding watermark to your videos

A branding watermark allows you to embed a channel logo to appear across all of your videos. When clicked, it allows non-subscribed viewers to quickly and easily subscribe. To access and set it up, click on the Channel settings within Creator Studio and choose the Branding option. An effective strategy I have employed is to create a branding watermark that is also a call to action. Mine is an image that reads 'FREE Social Media Tutorials' and sits in the corner of all my videos. Whichever image you choose, best practice denotes that it has a transparent background and uses just one color, so as not to be distracting to viewers – especially those watching on mobile devices.

YouTube Video Optimization Strategy

After Google, YouTube is the world's second-largest search engine. In fact, as Google owns YouTube, the search feature on both platforms is engineered to do one thing: provide the best answer to an inquiry. Videos based upon highly-searched topics will surface in search results, and some search terms remain popular for years. Videos that address these search queries will have a longer shelf life on YouTube. To have your videos rank well in YouTube search results, your aim should be to reverse-engineer your content to be as close as possible to the best answer for a particular search term. Before you even hit record, know what the title, tags, and content of the video are going to be. When someone searches for your video on YouTube, the site uses a variety of factors to judge where it will appear in the list of results, including the number of views, how long people typically watch it, its tally of likes and comments, how many subscribers your channel has, how often the video has been embedded, and more.

Note: Through your research, you also want to know what content your video will be competing with, so perform a few searches to see what's already out there and think about how you can improve on it - so that your video will eventually perform better.

To maximize the chances of your video being found, it is imperative that your videos' metadata is optimized. Here are some tips to do just that:

YouTube video title SEO
When coming up with a title for your videos, think about what your audience is likely to search for and reflect that in the words that you use. For ideas, look for keywords (either individual words or phrases) in Google Keyword Planner, or go to the YouTube search bar, start typing, and see how it finishes your sentence. Those predictions are what real people search for in order of importance. Your video title should be keyword rich and *match* the content that your video contains. Only the first ~45 characters of your video title are displayed in the YouTube search results on mobile devices, so make sure you front-end load the title with your primary keyword phrase(s). Here are some quick pointers to help get even more from your video headings:

- Use deliberate capitalization of words to highlight your content, e.g., 'The Top 10 Reasons Facebook Marketing Works' instead of 'The top 10 reason Facebook marketing works'.
- Add colon after your initial keywords and rephrase your title. For example, your video on saving money "Save Money Easily: The Simple Money Saving Plan." This will help capture those people who are searching for videos by using two similar (but different) phrases.
- Make your titles catchy in a way that will encourage users to click. For example, in a video that teaches people how to tie a bow tie - and do it in 30 seconds or less - which of the following would be more appealing: "How to Instructions and Advice About How to Tie A Bow Tie" or "Tie A Bow Tie in 30 Seconds or Less."

- Include keywords at the start of your video title and branding near the end, e.g., "How to Fix A Cracked iPhone X Screen | The iPhone 10 Wizard Tutorials".

Write effective video descriptions

The first few sentences of your video description will appear in YouTube search results, and the same few lines of it will appear below your content on the video's individual page followed by a "See More" link that must be clicked in order to read the rest. Therefore, good practice is to use the beginning of your video description to accurately describe what your video is all about in one or two sentences, as this is the most valuable snippet for SEO purposes. For people who click to view your description in full, consider adding the following information to all of your video descriptions:

- A description of your channel and a link to your channel page.
- A call to action asking viewers to subscribe and a link to click.
- Links to more episodes or related videos and playlists.
- Links to your website and social media profiles and a call to action to follow you.
- Information about your channel's video upload schedule, e.g., "New videos uploaded every Friday."
- Links to useful time-codes for long videos using the X:XX format, e.g., "Talk of squirrels starts at 3:44."

Lengthier and more detailed video descriptions that include multiple relevant keyword variations have a better chance of ranking high for relevant web searches, because contextual keywords are the heart and soul of Google and YouTube search queries. A detailed description can help you rank for many possible related searches, and may even boost your chances of snagging attention for keywords or phrases you didn't use.

Note: Often, the links listed above are placed at the beginning of descriptions for maximum visibility. When adding links in your video description, type out the entire URL to your website, including the "http://" prefix, so that YouTube will automatically hyperlink it. Otherwise, people won't be able to click through to your site.

Tags are descriptive keywords that help people find your videos, so the more relevant your tags, the more discoverable your video will be. The following list will help you write tags as effectively as possible:

- Come up with a set of standard tags that can be applied to any video you upload, e.g., sports, film, food, videogames, etc. - Set video info defaults for these to automatically appear via Channel Settings > Upload defaults.
- There is no perfect number of tags, but they should always be topically accurate and concise, and you should use enough to thoroughly describe your video's content.
- To help you come up with tags, think about the different keywords that viewers will search find your video; if your video was split into sections or themes, how would you describe them in a single word or phrase?
- Install a browser extension like VidIQ or TubeBuddy for Chrome to reveal the tags used by other popular videos in your niche (visit any YouTube video and they'll appear), and see if you can spot any inspiration for your own. These tools will also give you an idea of how your keywords are ranking once a video is published - and educate you on improving your approach in future. If the extension's data for keyword ranking seems all over the place initially, don't fret. YouTube is constantly testing your video in the opening hours, letting it spend a few seconds or minutes in a certain market or with a certain number of users to see how it performs.
- To boost your video's search ranking, use quotation marks to isolate important keyword phrases with multiple words, e.g., "how to make a paper airplane", as well as typing the phrase without the punctuation.
- Use keywords and phrases from the video title in your tags.
- Actively update and optimize archived videos with relevant tags when new search trends emerge.

Note: In July 2018, YouTube began to allow uploaders to add hashtags to descriptions and video titles to make it easier for viewers to find channels and content. When clicked, YouTube's hashtags will show a results page with other videos tagged with the same hashtag. Up to three clickable hashtags can be included in a video title, but if there are no hashtags in the title, the first three hashtags in the description will display above the video title. So, as well as considering strong keywords for your YouTube video titles and descriptions, adding one or two relevant hashtags (such as a location or brand-specific hashtag) in the title, as well as a smattering of a few more in the description, would be a wise move. Try not saturate your description section with hashtags. YouTube will ignore all hashtags on a video if it has more than 15 hashtags.

Select the right video category and add a location
Make sure that you submit your YouTube video to the right category - choose the one that your viewers are most likely to look under to find your content. If there is no exact match (and there often isn't), choose the category that most closely fits your upload. Videos submitted in irrelevant categories may not get relevant traffic, so this step is important. If your video could fit into two categories, select the one where you think it might have least competition to increase the chances of it being found or even featured. Meanwhile, adding your location to your YouTube videos will make them geographically searchable, which can help you get more relevant views. To add a location to an existing video, go to Video Manager and click Edit next to the video you want to edit. Below the video, click Advanced Settings and enter your location under Video Location.

Caption all your videos; add the transcript to the description
YouTube's AI is now smart enough to actually listen to the content in the video to confirm that the substance of the video matches the tags, so words and phrases that match with (and are related to) the title and description, can provide you with an extra SEO boost. YouTube will automatically add closed-captions to your video with its best guess. You can edit and improve automatically-generated captions in the Edit Video interface using the Translator Toolkit. In addition, paste your transcript in the video description, too, as it's a good way to add relevant, keyword-rich information to your content, which will benefit you SEO-wise. In addition, it will give people an easy way to refer back to different sections of the video, which is particularly useful if what you are discussing is an in-depth or complicated subject. To create fully new captions for a video, type out the text of all the audio, upload it via the "Subtitles and CC" tab, and it will automatically sync to your content.

Create a custom video thumbnail (or choose the best default option)
Thumbnails act as mini marketing posters for your content and are important in attracting viewers to your videos wherever they are seen - either on YouTube, in Google search results or embedded on websites. Thumbnails,

more than any other element, can make or break your videos' success on YouTube. The reason? Suggested videos. Suggested videos provide the biggest source of traffic on the site. As someone is watching a video, your video thumbnail – assuming it appears in the Suggested videos section - needs to stand out and entice the viewer to click it next.

Assuming your account is in good standing, you may have the option to upload a thumbnail once your video has uploaded. If the feature isn't enabled (mine took a good few months to appear) be patient as you can always go back and add them later. In the meantime, you can choose the best option from a default selection of three thumbnail images that YouTube offers you after your content is uploaded. Here are a few more tips for creating a compelling thumbnail:

- Make sure the thumbnail accurately represents the video content. No one will stick around to watch, or trust your other content, if the thumbnail is deliberately misleading.
- Attempt to tell a story with your video thumbnails to encourage people to click on them. For example, construct an image that sets up or teases a particular situation; make the viewer wonder what happens next, or what happened to cause what they see. If the thumbnail works with the video title to amplify the story you're trying to tell, that's even better.
- YouTube recommends a custom thumbnail be sized to 1280 x 720 pixels, and you can create them in an image editor like Photoshop or GIMP, or easily online at sites like Canva or Adobe Spark. However, nobody ever sees a thumbnail at that size on YouTube or anywhere else. While you should still upload the image at that size, its actual design should be constructed with smaller sizes in mind. Is your thumbnail still going to be as impactful when seen in search results or on a mobile device, for example? To check how your thumbnail will look in practice, zoom out wide during the design process so you can get an idea.
- Give your thumbnails a consistent look and branding, so that fans can recognize your videos at a glance in the subscription feeds.
- Some of the other general guidelines YouTube recommends for thumbnails are making sure they are clear, in-focus, hi-resolution (640 × 360 pixels min, 16:9 aspect ratio); bright, with high-contrast; well-

framed with good composition; and a foreground that stands out from the background.

Note: The first 24 hours after a video is published are critical to its initial (and potentially long-term) success. If it attracts views and watch time right away (and to a lesser degree in the subsequent 7 days), YouTube will notice and use the measure of that activity to determine where to rank the video more favorably. To maximize the chances of your video being found upon its release (and for weeks and months to come), you want to encourage as much traffic as possible in the first 24 hours, whether it's from people on your email list, via posts on social media, or even using some paid traffic to get a little bit of a boost on that first day.

Increasing Views on Your YouTube Videos

Create playlists and sections to group and feature great content
Playlists will lure people in to experiencing the breadth of the content you offer and encourage multiple video views in one session.

Playlist best practices
• From the controls on your main Channel page, build playlists to feature your "Best of..." and most viewed content and to ensure people view a series of videos in the order that they were intended.
• If a playlist requires context, upload a short and snappy intro video and place it at the beginning of the list.
• Use Playlist Notes to write conversational asides about individual videos.
• Use call-to-actions, end-cards and links to direct viewers to playlists.
• Feature playlists on your channel page by creating a new Section. Sections are used to organize videos, playlists on your channel. Sections can sub-divide your content by genre, theme, show or any other criteria. Effective organization will help your audience to find the content they are looking for.

Post a bulletin to your subscribers
A bulletin is a text update you send from your Channel page to all of your subscribers. You can tell your subscribers about a video you're working on, remind them of an awesome video you posted recently or include a link to a video you recommend, with a comment about it. When you post a bulletin, it will appear on your subscribers' recent activity feed (on their homepages) and

on your Channel page in your recent activity feed. Here's how to post a bulletin:

1. Sign into your YouTube account and visit the URL http://www.youtube.com/user/[yourchannelname]/feed
2. Type out your message in the "Share your thoughts" box.

Blog about your videos
Every time you post a new video, compose a blog post regarding the video and share it with your fans and followers and social media. Conversely, if you write a blog post that is particularly visual and would work well as a video, then why not screen grab it while you talk through it and turn the blog post into content for your YouTube channel? I often use this strategy for step-by-step guides, and as a bonus the blog text sitting right in front of me is a helpful reminder of what I want to say!

Embed a YouTube Subscribe widget on your blog or website
A YouTube Subscribe widget is a little box that you can embed in the sidebar of your website to encourage people to subscribe to your channel, or click through to check it out. It displays your YouTube channel icon, subscriber count, the number of videos you have published and, of course, an all-important Subscribe button. What I like about it most is that it acts as a permanent advertisement for your video content. I combine my widget with an embedded playlist that displays my most recently-published video to compound its effectiveness. For a look at a YouTube Subscribe widget, further instructions, and the code needed to embed one on your own website, visit the following link: http://bit.ly/youtubesubscribewidget

Leverage other social media to increase reach
- Post your video to Facebook (making sure to choose the best thumbnail).
- Tweet about it on Twitter with a couple of relevant hashtags (also include the prefix "Video:" before the video title, as although a shortened YouTube URL will show, it may not always be immediately obvious to your followers that you're sharing visual content - something they are more likely to engage with.
- Pin your video to Pinterest and make sure that the video's title and a short description is posted along with it, as well as a couple of

relevant hashtags. All of these details will improve the chances of your content being found by others in their Pinterest search.

- Consider submitting your video to other major video sharing sites such as Dailymotion and Vimeo. These sites might not have the massive popularity of YouTube, but it could be that your most lucrative customers only ever browse those video websites.

Manage comments effectively, keep engagement ticking over in between uploads

Be sure to keep a tab on the comments being left on your video via the Community option, found in the Video Manager portion of your account. Let commenters on your videos know that you appreciate what they have to say, and respond as often as you can. They'll appreciate the time you take to do so, and YouTube will see it as an engagement boost which could help your video rank better. Every time you answer a comment on YouTube, your reply counts, too. So, if you have 30 comments and reply to all of them, your video now has 60 comments. If you can reply to every comment, you'll double the engagement on a video. If everything else is equal but you get 60 comments and your competitor has 30, your video will outrank theirs.

In addition, consider the Community tab on your YouTube channel, which gives you a simple way to engage with your viewers and express yourself beyond video. You can discuss topics through text, launch live video, share images, animated GIFs and more, giving you a more casual way to engage with your fans more often in between uploads, and in real time. Viewers will be able to see your posts in the Subscriptions feed on mobile and they can also opt into receiving notifications when you post.

Paid Advertising on YouTube

YouTube is one of only a handful of websites with over 1 billion monthly active users. With such a large and diverse audience, it makes sense to consider experimenting with paid advertising on the site. Its current model allows you to achieve video clicks for just a few pennies based on keyword and audience targeting, with the potential for very satisfactory cost per acquisition. YouTube ads are fairly cheap; a budget of as little as $10.00 per day should allow you to experiment and collect some valuable data. The following advice relates to the most user-friendly ad setup process for YouTube, accessible via http://www.youtube.com/yt/advertise/index.html. If you would prefer a slightly more advanced approach (including more in-depth setup, scheduling, and targeting options), head straight to the main AdWords dashboard at http://adwords.google.com and choose to launch a new video campaign.

Most effective YouTube video ad type
There are several types of YouTube ad available, including traditional banner ads positioned around the site, and others that overlay the videos. My preference, however, is to use TrueView in-stream video ads - skippable ads that are inserted before, during or after a video on the site (these are the default option in the basic setup method). Not only are they the most engaging ad type with the option to drive clicks to your YouTube channel or website, but you won't be charged if your video is skipped or if a viewer does not watch at least 30 seconds of your ad. This also ensures that viewers pay more attention to your ad because they've actively chosen to watch it.

TruView video ad basics: length and content strategy
- Try to keep your video ads relatively short – between 30 and 60 seconds long is a good target - long enough to formulate a compelling visual story, but not too long that viewers will get bored and skip past it.
- Show viewers what your channel is all about. Feature clips of your content and produce the ad in the same style as the content on your channel.
- Use a call to action. Tell viewers exactly what you want them to do after watching your
- ad: to subscribe, comment, check out a playlist, watch your newest video etc.
- Give users time to take action. The last ten seconds or so of your video ad should be reserved to give users time to click or tap, based on your call-to-action. Guide them even further by creating a static call to action in an end-card.
- Give your video ad a compelling title. Ad titles are visible to viewers, so don't call it an ad. Use this space to double-down on your call to action in a prominent position.
- Upload a compelling thumbnail. Use a clear and creative thumbnail to entice users to click and watch your video ad.

Setting a budget and target audience

As mentioned above, you don't have to spend a fortune to begin to see if YouTube advertising might work for you. The site will recommend a daily budget, including a maximum cost-per-view (the highest price you're willing to pay for someone to view your video ad; it starts at just a penny, but obviously the more you bid, the more likely your ad is to be played to someone), but you can enter any amount you like. As with any ad campaign, it's only going to be a success if the right people see it. Under the target audience option, identify where you want your ads to be shown - based on, age, location, interests, gender, and web activity. As you play around with your budget and targeting options, keep an eye on the box that estimates how many views the amount is likely to give your video.

Note: One tactic favored by a lot of TrueView YouTube advertisers is to begin a paid campaign with a " blast" that aims to reach a broad target audience in the first three to five days after a new video is published. As you don't pay if a user chooses to skip your TrueView video ad, there's little financial risk in this strategy. This approach allows you to promote your content to a wide potential audience and helps the video to surface in ordinary searches, which will give a boost to organic views - kickstarting the virtuous chain of events described above. Afterwards, switch to a more targeted approach. Use remarketing to reach users who have already visited your channel and continue to generate new views at an optimized cost.

Tracking the progress of YouTube ads

When your YouTube ads are live, you can track their performance via your AdWords account. To get a detailed overview of your ad performance metrics in AdWords, connect your AdWords and YouTube accounts, and in AdWords for video, enable the "audience" columns to see the number of views and subscribers generated as a result of them. More success metrics are also available in AdWords including conversion, reach, frequency and website clicks. For a quick overview, meanwhile, navigate to the "Traffic Sources" report in YouTube Analytics to see how much of your channel's viewership is being generated from your ads. As with all paid advertising on social media, don't be afraid to experiment with different approaches - cull what doesn't work and concentrate your time and money on what does.

Instagram Tips: Snap-happy Marketing Strategy

Instagram has taken the world by storm since launching in October 2010. Hundreds of millions of people use Instagram as a way to transform everyday photos and videos with filters and frames, into memory-laden content, which can then be shared with the world. Chances are that snapshots and recordings of your brand are already on Instagram, and all of this content acts as authentic peer-to-peer endorsements of you - essentially free advertising. With a sound strategy of your own, you can only help to compound this effect, increasing brand loyalty and driving sales as a result. Some have even dubbed Instagram "The World's Most Powerful Selling Tool," such is the level of passion its users show. They're young, they're engaged, and many of them are ready to buy.

Understand the "Culture of Instagram"

The top-performing brands on Instagram all have one thing in common: they understand what makes the app unique compared to other social networks and use this knowledge to their advantage. While the definition of "Instagram culture" will inevitably change over time, at its core are users who are *proud* of the content the images they post (video can be a different matter, more on this with Stories later) - you won't see hundreds of impulsive selfies and blurry photos from some the most successful accounts, for instance. As such, there is a definite lean towards quality over quantity, which sees creators taking their time to carefully compose and construct photos and videos, cropping and editing until they are *just* right so that when something does eventually get posted to their Instagram feed, it is poured over by impressed followers, complemented with lots of likes and comments, and attracts new fans (*"Wow, these guys post great stuff and get a lot of love; I'm sticking around for more!"*) in the process. One of Instagram's central mantras is to encourage people to "find beauty everywhere." For businesses, this means showing how your company sees the world, sharing imagery that pushes people's ideas of you deeper than the common perception, and offering a view into the lifestyle that your product or service makes possible both through your own eyes and those of customers who use them.

In short, whereas visual imagery for sites like Facebook and Twitter might sometimes be more ad-hoc in nature or Pinterest simpler, mood board-y or salesy, your preference on Instagram should be more creative, arty, and *special*, with even more of an emphasis on visual storytelling, turning ordinary situations into artistic moments and capturing the essence of your brand throughout. Immerse yourself in the culture of Instagram by reflecting this more imaginative style of photos or videos in your own feed (clearly expressing a defined personality and voice and mirroring the attitude and preferences of the app's majority audience) and you'll be in a significantly more powerful position from the get go.

What are the elements of a top-quality Instagram image?

As you now know, posting any old photo onto Instagram just won't cut it with the app's savvy audience; you have to be much more inventive and selective. One of the best ways to discover what kinds of photos Instagram really wants brands to post in order to keep fans happy is to look at its recommendations for Instagram ads:

- No heavy use of image filters as a way to mask the "reality" of a shot, and no text overlays are allowed.
- Brands cannot feature their logo in Instagram ads other than as a natural, non-obvious part of the scene.
- Images used as ads must be "true to your brand", i.e., not shocking or cheesy, and no use of gimmicks.
- Photos used for ads should capture "moments", not products. In other words, ads must not just be a shot of your product, but something more creative and inspiring.
- Ads should use ideas and take cues from the existing Instagram community, especially from popular hashtags.

As you read through the rest of the advice in the chapter, keep these ideas in the back of your mind as you think about how you want to shape your own Instagram strategy. As with a lot of social media theory, they won't apply to every situation all of the time, but as a good basis for your activity? Pretty good stuff. By the way, there's plenty more information and strategy for Instagram ads at the end of this chapter.

Understand the Instagram algorithm to use it to your advantage

In March 2016, and in response to data showing that people miss on average 70 percent of the posts in their feeds, Instagram overhauled its algorithm from showing all posts from people users follow in chronological order to one that prioritizes what is shown first based on *"the likelihood people will be interested in the*

content, their relationship with the person or business posting and the timeliness of the post."
In short, if you want your Instagram posts to be seen by more people, they need to consistently connect with your audience. The more fans like and comment on your posts, the more likely Instagram's algorithm is to favor subsequent content - pushing it to the top of news feeds, and limiting the need for paid promotion to get it seen. The biggest challenge, then, is developing an Instagram strategy that generates engagement. As you start testing ideas, listen to your audience and pay attention to the comments on each post. When someone takes the time to comment or send you a message, they are telling you they enjoy what you are posting, so continue along that path. In addition, making personal touches, especially at the start of your Instagram journey, can help you gain meaningful
growth. For example, taking the extra few seconds to like and reply to comments shows people that their engagement matters to your brand. As a result, next time you post content, they are more likely to engage with your account again. Take the time to build a strong relationship with your followers because their engagement will cause more people to be exposed to your activity, and this can lead to a snowball effect in terms of growth.

Instagram Profile and Content Optimization

Optimize your Instagram bio; add a profile photo that fits a circle
One of the easiest ways to connect with would-be Instagram followers is to optimize your bio. Use the whole 150 characters allowed to encourage followers: give them a reason to follow you, tell them what makes you unique, remind people that they'll be among the first to know about special offers and promotions, first to get a sneak peek at new product lines, and have the first chance to enter Instagram competitions to win stuff! Don't forget to add the URL to your company's website in your bio section too – the only place on Instagram where a URL is directly clickable.

Note: If you have an additional Instagram profile or hashtag to promote, adding its @username or hashtag to your bio text will make the handle or hashtag clickable on your profile. It's worth remembering that including a hashtag in your Instagram bio does not make your profile searchable within that hashtag, so just stick to using your own branded hashtag rather than something you think might attract new views through search.

Equally as important for your bio is to add a photo of yourself if you're the figurehead of your company (ideally of your smiley face) or, instead, your company logo, as this will represent you all across the service. Instagram uses a circular profile photo, which suits faces better than it does company logos. If your logo is square and messily cropped when you upload it to your Instagram profile, use my *square-logo-into-circle-fit* template as an easy fix. Grab it via *Premium Content Bundle* chapter of this book.

Keep the tone of your bio light and fun, include relevant keywords (for SEO), and Emojis if the mood fits. Instagram also has the option to include additional contact information buttons to Business profiles. Call, Email, and Directions. Switch your personal account to a Business one (you'll also get access to real-time analytics), and add them in.

Instagram action buttons
In addition to Call, Text, Directions, and Email buttons, depending on your business type and goals, through external app integration, you may also be able to choose from action buttons like Book, Buy Tickets, Start Order, and Reserve. The action button that appears on your account will tie directly into the app you select for the button integration. For example, if you use and select OpenTable, you'll automatically get the Reserve action button. To add an action button to your Instagram account, you need to have an existing account set up with the third-party with which you plan to integrate. To add an action button to your Instagram account:

1. Select Edit Profile, scroll down and select Contact Options. From the Contact Options screen, tap the Add an Action Button option.
2. Select the third-party app you want to integrate with, e.g., Acuity Scheduling, Atom Tickets, Booksy, ChowNow, EatStreet, Eventbrite, Fandango, Grubhub, MyTime, OpenTable, Reserve, Restorando, Resy, SevenRooms, StyleSeat, Tock, Vagaro, and Yelp.
3. Enter the URL for the account or page you use on the third-party app to which you want people from Instagram to be directed via the action button. Tap Submit.

To maximize your results with the action button, use a call-to-action in post captions and Stories to let customers know they can book or reserve directly from your Instagram profile. You could also include a short CTA in your bio description to encourage customers to click, or offer an Instagram-exclusive coupon code.

Instagram Name tag
A Name Tag is a special image (like a QR code) that anyone can scan to instantly visit your Instagram profile and follow you. Your Name Tag allows you to promote your Instagram account in a lot of different ways - on your website, email signature, store window, on product packaging, etc. To create your own custom Instagram QR code, tap on the Name Tag icon on top of your screen. From this Name Tag screen you can create your custom Name Tag, save your custom Name Tag to your Camera Roll or send it to someone and scan someone else's Name Tag to go to their Instagram profile. The default Name Tag design is a rainbow-colored gradient background, but tap the background to change it if you wish. Alternatively, you can customize your Name Tag with Emojis or a selfie and stickers.

Instagram web profiles
In late 2012, Instagram rolled out official web profiles for users. Login to your account; your web profile URL will be www.instagram.com/yourinstagramusername. When an Instagram image link is posted to Twitter, Facebook, and other sites, a user will be directed to your web profile when it is clicked. Web-based profiles mean that these people can comment and/or like the image direct on the web - no mobile app is required. Marketers can use this knowledge as an opportunity to promote more interaction among fans.

The Importance of Hashtags on Instagram

Starting from zero – 3 steps to gain traction and grow your following
As a way to underline all of the ideas and information already laid out in this chapter and a preface to lots more to come, what follows is a no-fuss strategy that outlines how any brand can grow a new Instagram account from scratch. Building an organic follower base on Instagram is, in theory, simple: just get people to see your content and have them hit the "Follow" button on your profile. This happens in one of three ways:

1. A user sees someone they follow share your content, then taps through to your profile.

2. A user sees your content while browsing various hashtags in Instagram search and then tap through to your profile.
3. A user gets a notification that you followed or liked them, and then taps through to your profile.

Note: And of course, there's paid advertising, which, as mentioned above, I go into more detail about later in this chapter. Paid ads can obviously help to amplify growth, but the ideas described in this tip are all focused on helping you to grow a strong foundation of genuine, loyal Instagram followers from scratch.

Outcome no.1 is obviously the most desirable, as it means your Instagram content is admired enough for it to be shared to others, and seen by all of their followers. However, if you've just launched an Instagram profile and haven't got any followers to promote your content for you, this is a non-starter. Instead, let's focus on the other two suggestions – hashtag strategy and user notifications - to see how they can work for you.

Instagram's system of hashtags is central to any brand's growth strategy on the platform (more than any other social network) and it is, to some degree, very democratic. For example, every photo of someone's brunch tagged in its caption with #fridaybrunch will appear in that hashtag's search results, ready for someone to view it. However, if this brunch-sharer happened to be your brand and someone who found it in search liked the photo enough to tap through to your profile, they might hesitate to hit "Follow" when they see that your follower count is pitifully low. Why follow your brand when they can follow a similar account with hundreds of thousands of followers, more content, and perhaps slightly snazzier production values?

So then, posting great content isn't enough on its own. You need to put some work in to get your profile in front of people and schmooze just a bit to create a bond to start growing a following. Here's the three-step process you need to follow:

1. Develop your content. Think up a niche or subject for content that you will be able to continue produce fairly easily and at a steady rate - aim to post at least one photo per day, at least in the early stages of your growth strategy. Make sure the images are high quality, speak to people's emotions (inspires, makes them laugh, motivates, etc.), that

the overall aesthetic is cohesive - similar branding, filters, colors, etc., and most importantly, that your Instagram profile's grid represents your brand as a whole.

2. Develop a list of hashtags to start driving organic traffic. There's a lot more about how exactly to come up with a set of powerful hashtags in the next tip, but in essence they should be relevant to your content and chosen to target keywords that will help your brand to grow. Pay close attention to how different groups of hashtags affect the reception of your content. Start with a couple (rather than the maximum of 30), change them around, and use the resulting follower growth (or lack thereof) to discover hashtags that work best for bringing in genuine fans.

3. Network with others. This is the biggie, and the step where most brands fall short. Putting in the legwork through cold outreach is central to growing an Instagram account from scratch. If people within your community don't know you exist, they can't follow you. Be genuine about it. Perform a hashtag search and visit the profile of someone in your niche who you think might follow you. If their content confirms your initial gut feeling, like a few of their posts, leave nice comments, and follow them. With any luck, the theory of basic reciprocity (I've done something nice for you, now you want to do something nice for me) will mean that they follow you back.

And remember, this strategy won't necessarily produce results overnight – patience is the key. Repeat the aforementioned steps for a couple of months as a no-fuss way to kickstart growth on an Instagram account you're building from scratch.

Choosing the right hashtags to boost engagement and get discovered

There's a good reason why many popular Instagram profiles use oodles of hashtags (up to the 30-hashtag limit) in their posts. Through its search and explore options, Instagram gives major weight to hashtags as a way for people to discover things like. People use hashtags to search for content on Instagram, so using the right hashtags can help put your content in front of people searching for keywords and phrases associated with your business. Which hashtags should you use? Use a good mix of broad hashtags related to your business and industry as a whole (and the post in question): those that return over 1m results, as well as some more "niche" options - between 1,000 and 10,000 search results returned- as well as some in between - between 20,000 and 100,000 search results. Find inspiration from auto-completed hashtag suggestions in Instagram search, in the "Related" hashtag suggestions displayed when you click on a search result, and in the captions of popular Instagram accounts within your industry.

There are two main reasons for selecting a mixture of broad and niche hashtags to include in your posts (as well as some "in between"): to hopefully get your brand to appear regularly within the Top Posts and Recent Posts sections of the Instagram search results page. 9 "Top Posts" display at the top of every completed search and are "stickied" there for at least several hours - these will garner you plenty of attention. Meanwhile, Recent Posts refresh near the top of search results in real-time - for a tiny duration, but seen by more people when a mega-popular hashtag is searched (e.g. #fashion) - and for a longer amount of time, but seen by less people when a less-popular hashtag is searched (e.g. #greywoolcardican). For a full explanation of this strategy, as well as a more scientific breakdown for selecting and tracking appropriate hashtags, see the blog post I have written at this link: http://bit.ly/instagramhashtagstrategy.

Should you max out the hashtag limit? A study by Trackmaven, found that using between 5 and 11 hashtags maximized Instagram interactions, but what works for one business might not work for yours – you'll need to play around to find a sweet spot. One simple idea is to spy at how many hashtags influencers in your industry and your competitors use in their posts and to fall into the same kind of ballpark, or to track the engagement of your posts when you experiment with using different amounts of hashtags.

Note: If you use the same group of "base" hashtags often, save the list in your phone's Notes or utilize the text shortcut option in iOS or Android Settings to pre-populate the list in an instant. In addition, to keep your posts looking neat and tidy, hide a long list of hashtags in the first comment of your post (simply comment right after posting) - Instagram will still pick them up as if within the post's main caption.

Discover and engage by following hashtags
At the beginning of 2018, Instagram allowed users to start following hashtags, meaning content from people who are using the hashtags you follow will pop

up in your home feed. It presents an amazing opportunity to engage organically with other accounts – like current and potential customers – and as well as a way for you to discover more people, it's also a way they can discover you. And if you are thoughtful with your comments, they might even reciprocate and check out your account. To follow a hashtag, go to the Explore page, type a hashtag and then tap on the "Follow" button.

Taking Great Instagram Photos

The types of images and photos that resonate with Instagram users reflect many of the themes we discussed in "The Best Types of Content to Post on Social Media" chapter of this book (featuring customers, promoting products, going behind the scenes, etc.). Here, you'll find advice about shooting and optimizing images especially for Instagram's dominant user base, but it can also be applied to images across all of social media.

Only post your best photos, find inspiration from other users
As mentioned earlier, best brands on Instagram are extremely picky about the images they post on their Take your time in creating a collection of photos that you are really proud of - your very best efforts - as it is this that will catch the eye of users both when viewed as individual pieces of content and when your grid is browsed as a whole. Many of the biggest brands on Instagram post just once per day, sometimes even less. Here are some basic photography tips and guidelines that will help to lift the quality of your work on Instagram:

See the world in squares (but don't fret about it too much)
Traditionally, photos on Instagram have been squares - like an old Polaroid snapshot – and this remains the most popular type of composition on the social network. So even before the shutter closes on your widescreen camera view, try to imagine how your composition might appear as a square once the sides are cropped. However, if there's a critical element of your content that a square will frustratingly crop out, you'll be relieved to know that Instagram, in August 2015, added the ability to publish photos and videos in portrait and landscape mode. When uploading content, just tap the format icon to choose the orientation.

The rule of thirds
Just as with other forms of photography, the 'rule of thirds' is deeply rooted in many of the great Instagram shots. Imagine your viewfinder is split into thirds,

both horizontally and vertically (or turn on the iPhone Camera grid view via Options); now balance your composition between these areas.

Get symmetrical

Symmetrical shots look great with Instagram. You'll finish with a perfect square crop of your image. When taking your photo, the key is to center yourself perfectly and make sure all your lines are absolutely straight.

Play with angles and lines

Instagram is all about encouraging its users to see the world in a new way. We're all so used to viewing the world from head height, so experiment with high and low angles, from behind, or at the side, to add interest and intrigue to your snapshots. In addition, think about incorporating lines into your photos - natural elements like a line or trees or a road stretching into the distance - to draw people's eyes into the image, or toward whatever it is you want them to focus on.

Zoom in on details

To make the most of the relatively small real estate of mobile devices (where most people will be viewing your Instagram content), make a habit of focusing in on particular details of products or service in order to draw customers in, rather than making blander long or mid-range shots. For example, a clothing store might highlight the quality dye and material in a garment, while a decorating service could go a bit more abstract and use the close-up shot of a pot of paint and a brush to represent a job well done.

Find inspiration

If you are lacking inspiration, use Instagram's Explore tab (the compass points icon) to see the latest emerging trends on Instagram, and consider implementing them in your own work.

Brand your images with consistent filters and image editing

Instagram's popularity blew up, in part, due to the ease with which users can transform ordinary photos with its vintage filters. While these overlays remain central to the app's appeal, over the years its image editing tools - in response to competition - have expanded to include a variety of additional options for photo-tweaking, including straightening, lux, brightness, contrast, tilt shift, sharpening, and more. Instagram allows you to set the strength of each adjustment with a simple slider. Overall, I'd suggest applying them in a way that is subtle (to align with Instagram's preferred approach for brands, i.e., natural), and decide on a filter that you will use consistently; one that helps the image to reflect your brand culture and personality (e.g., fun, playful, serious, professional, etc.) *and* makes your style immediately identifiable within the feed of fans. What's more, this consistent style will be a big, eyeball-pleasing hit to those who tap through to view more content within. As well as focusing on each individual piece of content, think about cohesiveness that will be created when they all sit together within your full grid of images. Ask yourself, does your content look like it belongs as part of a whole, or was it thrown together in any old style? In order to create a distinctive branded account on Instagram, learn what your fans like about you and consistently create content around that theme. By the way, Instagram allows you to manage (and easily access) your favorite filters by selecting the gear icon at the end of the filter list -handy!

Consider not taking your photos in Instagram

If you shoot a photo within Instagram, you are instantly locked into using its filters and editing tools. As expansive as these options have become, it is often a better option to shoot a photo with your mobile's native camera app (or any other digital camera). Doing this will provide you with a 'clean' image that can be imported into whichever photo editing app you like (VSCO Cam or Afterlight, for instance - tools that may provide more unique and diverse filter and image editing options). When you're done, you can then import the photo into Instagram for final tweaking and publishing. This approach is how the pros get such great photos - ones that look so different from anything that Instagram alone can produce. Of course, if Instagram already provides you with the look and feel that you want your photos to have, then that is totally fine as well!

Stories: An Instagram game-changer

When I mentioned earlier that not all Instagram content requires the same meticulous care as the photos in your main profile feed, Stories is what I meant. In one of its biggest ever updates, Instagram rolled out Stories in the summer of 2016. The feature allows users to add a continuous string of photos or videos to their profile, that get automatically deleted after 24 hours. Unlike Instagram's highly-curated main profile, Stories gives individuals and brands a fast, immersive and fun ways to share photos, videos and text. People use Stories to share and discover content they're interested in, and businesses can harness the power of Stories to connect with customers when they're already engaged with the content you produce; a way for you to promote products, build brand awareness and drive sales in a way that fits seamlessly into their customers' browsing experience.

With this in mind, think about Instagram Stories as a way to supplement your main Instagram content with bonus info for loyal followers and to hook in new eyes to your brand and your main feed with additional posts. For example, after publishing something special in your main feed, go into more depth about the shot or video in a story - show how the shot was setup, etc., talk a bit about it in a casual video, etc. Alternatively, use Stories to remind viewers about your most recent blog post; find 3-5 key points that will grab your followers' attention and turn them into images. Don't forget to tell viewers how to read more (either with a short bit.ly link, or by prompting them to click the link in your bio).

Whatever your Stories entail, make sure to keep your social media goals in mind. For example, having a call to action in your Instagram Stories that is not too pushy - build a message that gently says "this is what I want you to do and why." After all, if you're going to take the time to craft a story, you want to have a reason for doing it that's going to benefit your business.

Note: Here's a quick tip to maximize the watch time of Instagram Stories. Images play for approximately 7 seconds on Instagram Stories. However, videos can play for up to 15 seconds. If you want to keep your text or image on the screen longer, craft your image and convert it into a video.

Stories features to maximize your Instagram strategy
Since 2016, Instagram has rolled out a swathe of new features to Stories. Here's a quick summary and strategy for each:

Stickers and drawing tools: Stickers are fun and colorful overlays that can be added to your Instagram Stories - time, temperature, polls, etc. For example, the interactive questions sticker lets your followers submit questions for you to answer. It's a fun way to start conversations with your fans and customers, and can be a great way to open your brand up to them, while also learning more about what you can do to improve your products and services. Add a question sticker to your Story by selecting it from the sticker tray after taking a photo or video; type out your prompt, position the sticker as you like, and share it to your story. When people see the sticker, they can tap it to reply — and they can reply as many times as they want, right from the sticker.

Crucially - hashtag and location stickers can also be added. To add a sticker, snap a photo or record a video, then tap the smiling-face icon to bring up the stickers library. Drag the sticker around to place it and use pinch-to-zoom controls to rotate it and/or change its size. Here's the best bit: Instagram users can search for a location or hashtag, and if included - see story posts by you that include that location sticker, hashtag sticker, or hashtag in the caption. Location Stories from nearby places (but not Hashtag Stories) will also appear featured in the Explore tab. Only content tagged with a location sticker, hashtag sticker, or underlined hashtag will appear in the associated Stories.

Boomerang, Rewind, and Superzoom modes: A format picker underneath Stories' record button lets you select these playful settings. Boomerang allows you to stitch together a burst of several photos into a short video that plays forward and backward; make videos that play in reverse with Rewind, (create visual tricks like drop an object and watch it fly up into your hand; capture water in motion and share a rewind of the flow floating back up, etc.); while Superzoom adds dramatic and suspenseful sound effects while automatically zooming in on a single subject in three stages (the resulting video lasts 3 seconds but can be extended up to 15 seconds by holding down the shutter button longer).

Mentions and sharing posts: Mentioning people in Stories works the same as in ordinary Instagram captions and comments. When you add text to your story, type "@" followed by a username. The person's username will appear underlined in your story and, when someone taps the mention, they'll see a pop-up that takes them to that profile. Mentions are a great way to give a shout-out to customers (like contest winners or people you regram), influencers you're working with, or others.

You can also share your posts or anyone else's in Instagram Stories. The post will then be clickable in your Instagram Story, and people will be redirected to it instantly -perfect for sharing a post from your feed in an Instagram Story or if you want to feature someone else. To do it, go to the post you want to share, tap on the paper plane icon below the post, and select "Add post to Story". To help the post stand out, you can: tap on the post to change the style of card;

pinch the post to change its size; or use the Pen tool to change the background color.

"Swipe up" links: Only available to verified Instagram accounts at present, this could be huge for businesses if rolled out to everyone. When a user swipes up during a story, they'll see a designated landing page or a specific site page. In many cases, the "Swipe Up" prompt will be accompanied by text like "Learn More" or "Shop." When you create a story, tap the link symbol at the top of the post to add swipe up links.

Stories Highlights and Archives: Rolled out in November 2017 to offer a way for Instagram users to showcase story content that would otherwise disappear after 24 hours, Stories Highlights allows you to group together Stories you've shared into highlights and feature them at the top of your profile. In addition, to prevent your stories from disappearing forever when they expire, all Instagram Stories can now be automatically saved to your Stories Archive when its 24 hours is up. To turn your Archive on, visit your Instagram Settings, select 'Story Settings' and turn on the 'Save to archive' option.

Combining the Highlights and Archives features allow your brand can re-surface the most popular parts of previous Stories, showcasing it to your audience as a "new" post that sits in prime position on your profile. Some ideas for business-related Instagram Story Highlights include producing a welcome message for viewers, promoting a sale, showcasing customer reviews or testimonials, or highlighting a selection of posts that utilize your brand's own hashtag. If you want to get clever, you can combine stories and highlights to drive web traffic – that's if you have the "Swipe Up" tap-to-view-a-link feature, reserved for accounts with over 10,000 followers.

How to Create an Instagram Story Highlight
1. Tap the profile icon in the bottom-right corner of the screen, then tap the + button to begin creating a new Story Highlight.
2. Scroll through your archive of past Stories posts and select each post
3. you want to add to the Highlight. When you're done, tap "Next."
4. Type a name for your Highlight, to appear under it on your profile.
5. Tap "Edit Cover" to change the Highlight's cover image.
6. Tap "Add" to save the Highlight to your profile.

Note: Want to make custom-branded Highlight covers for your Instagram profile? The Canva mobile app makes it easy. In the app, choose the Your Story template, get designing, and save the image ready to upload. To setup a Highlights cover without sharing it in your Instagram Story:

1. Press and hold your finger on a Highlight.
2. Select "Edit Highlight"
3. Select "Edit cover"
4. Press on the "image" icon at the beginning of the list.
5. If you have a lot of photos and in a Highlight, you might have to scroll all the way to the left. Then you will see the "image" icon.
6. Choose a cover from your camera roll.

Live video: Going live on Instagram is easy — just swipe right from the feed to open the camera, select "Live" and tap the "Start Live Video" button to start sharing. When you go live, followers may be alerted with a push notification, encouraging them to click and view it. If you're lucky, your video may be chosen to appear in the "Top Live" section of Instagram's Explore section, which could put you in front of a much bigger potential audience. You can also save your broadcast after it's over, to edit and repurpose it on Instagram or other social sites later on. If you're keen to experiment with it – to answer Q&As, run contests, give people a behind-the-scenes look at your business, etc., let as many fans beforehand know when you're going to go live! Here are a few best practices (for more tips on succeeding with live video, check out the *Explained: The Best Types of Content to Post on Social Media* and the *Facebook Tips* chapters of this book, where I've also included more general advice):

- Use a combination of Instagram Stories posts and ordinary Instagram posts to promote your upcoming live videos - a way to boost live views and replay views.
- You can also let viewers join live video streams within the app via the Go Live With option. Once the other person is added to the live stream, the screen splits into two with the host on the top and the guest below.
- Pin a comment at the beginning of your broadcast to tell people what
- you'll be talking about. To pin a comment, type in a comment of your own, post it, then tap on the comment and choose Pin Comment. The pinned comment will retain a banner that helps it to stand out

against all other comments and it remains at the top of the screen for viewers to see.

- Upon ending the live video stream, a recap screen appears. You'll see how many viewers watched the video and have the option to let your video be viewed again on replay for the next 24 hours. Tapping Share will upload the replay to your stories.

- Straight after a live broadcast, publish a new post to your regular Instagram feed, letting your audience know the replay video is available. Outline the topic and key takeaways in the video so that they get a taste of what you're offering.

- Encourage replay viewers to send you a DM in response to the video to ask clarifying questions, and use it as a way to foster relationships.

- Live video stats are available when watching your replay. You'll see the number of viewers and who those viewers are while reviewing your own video replay (no one else can view this data). When in your own video replay, you'll see the number of views in the bottom-left corner. To get more detailed information, tap on that number of viewers or swipe up on the screen to open a screen with a list of viewers. As the video replay will disappear after 24 hours, if you want to collect this data, make sure to do so before the video is removed for good.

Insights: Instagram Stories also includes useful insights to allow you to track their performance. You'll see the number of impressions, number of replies your stories received (tallied when a user clicks "message" while watching a story), and the number of exits made before your story was complete. You can view story information from the past hour, seven days, and fourteen days.

Instagram Content Optimization Strategy

Experiment with multiple image posts in Instagram

In February 2017, Instagram introduced the ability to upload between 2-10 photos (or videos, or a combination of both photo and video) to feature together in one single post via a swipe-able gallery, with one shared caption for the lot. In the app, you'll see an icon allowing you to select multiple photos and videos. Once uploaded, you can tap and hold to change the order, apply a filter to everything at once or edit them one by one. For brands, this provides yet another way to create interesting and engaging content. Some examples include:

- *Showing a step-by-step process:* like a recipe or product demonstration, one step per photo or video.
- *Asking a multiple choice question:* Feature the question in the first image (such as asking for input on a new business logo), offer several choices numbered 1, 2, 3, etc. in the next few images, and ask fans to comment to vote for their favorite.
- *Expand a panoramic shot:* If Instagram's traditional square format is going to constrict a really great widescreen image, why not split it into multiple sections and then upload them together? The joined-up result delivers a really nice, smooth effect where users can swipe from left to right, taking in the full detail.
- *Showcase multiple products:* launching a new product range or just want to showcase a single product from multiple angles? This feature is perfect for that.
- *Tell the story of an event:* If you look at Instagram Stories as a way to curate a dynamic tale about your day as it unfolds, multiple image posts allow you to present a more considered overview for your feed. Pick the best photos or videos to sum up the events over a day and present them to your audience in one succinct post.

Make the most of the photo caption

The photo caption that accompanies every image on Instagram exists as a small but crucial part of your marketing strategy - never leave it blank. Use it as a way to anchor the content of the image and to reflect your brand's personality and tone of voice. Examples of uses for the photo caption include adding a description of the product you are featuring, asking a question or starting a discussion and adding a call to action or including a URL that you want fans to visit. URLs written within Instagram descriptions cannot be clicked on, so make sure that they are short and memorable, using a service like bit.ly to facilitate this if necessary. Related to this point, another popular strategy to drive click-throughs from Instagram captions to a destination of your choice is simply to include a phrase like "click the link in our bio." Your bio is always just one tap away and since the "Website" URL there *is* active, it will save people the time and effort of opening up a separate browser and typing in a URL, if that is their preference. Interestingly, Instagram captions do not have a character limit. Some brands, like National Geographic, use this to make each caption read like a mini magazine article. It's a tactic that, combined with high quality images, keeps viewers immersed in their content for longer, seeing them as more than throwaway snapshots. Need to edit a caption for typos or additional detail? Tap the "..." icon next to your photo and choose "Edit."

Got a physical location? Geotag your Instagram posts

Tagging your Instagram posts with your business' physical location - geotagging - can provide a multitude of benefits - detailed below. First, you'll need to create a Location for it - via Facebook. Simply go to create a new post on the Facebook mobile app, click "Check In" and enter your brand's name. From here, tap the "Add" button and set up information about your brand and once submitted, you can search Instagram to see your result. Use the same named location as much as possible to build content around the location so others will be encouraged to share as well.

Stickers in Stories: Instagram Stories allows users to use digital stickers on photos or videos that are based on a geotag. By selecting the "Location" sticker, you can set it to the geolocations already around you. Remember, you have to create a location first in Facebook if your geotag doesn't show up on Instagram.

Hashtag Locations: Utilizing the right hashtags on Instagram can give your content more visibility, but you can also use hashtag locations like #london or #miami to give your content the chance of being suggested to people who are near you. Hashtag locations can also be used in Instagram Stories, making it easy to tag locations through a hashtag sticker.

Find local influencers: Imagine you want to get the word out about an upcoming event you're hosting, and you want to find local people who might be the right fit to help you promote it. In the Instagram search bar, ensure the Places tab is selected and type in your location. Browse through the results to see which users would be a good match for your brand, then DM them to see if they're interested in working together.

Comment on location posts: If you have physical store location, it is wise to keep on top of the local location geotags as much as possible; you areas have a plethora of content your brand can use to further engage users.

Encourage sharing content to your location or hashtag

Promote your geotag location and encourage users to share content to it. You can even run contests to get users to engage more with your location. Set out the rules and make sure entrants tag your specific location correctly.

"Regram" other users' photos

There is no better promotion for your business to new customers than to show photos of existing customers enjoying what you offer. Ask for photos to be submitted to you by happy customers, or - even better - proactively track them down using specific hashtags. When you find an image you would like to use, utilize apps like Regram for iOS or PhotoRepost for Android to share these images on your own feed, and don't forget to tag the person who originally took the image so that they are notified. For example, pen manufacturer Sharpie regularly features sketches drawn by its customers, and Starbucks "piggybacks" on the popularity of Instagram users with large follow bases, reposting images (with permission, of course) that feature their products.

Schedule posts to maximize the impact of campaigns and promotions

Scheduling Instagram posts will come in handy if you have a lot of stellar content that you want to post consistently, but can really come into its own as a way to pace and maximize the impact of campaigns or promotions, e.g., posting themed photos at exactly the same time every day, or releasing contest details at a set time (having trained customers to come back to view both). Third party tools like Buffer, Hootsuite and Latergramme (at http://latergram.me and as an iOS app) will allow you to queue content (including caption and hashtags) for posting on a day and time of your choosing.

Instagram contest strategy

Instagram contests are hugely popular and can provide a quick, cheap, and powerful way to encourage fans to engage with your brand and spread the word about you across Instagram and beyond. Here is a series of simple steps to help ensure your Instagram contest is a success:

Choose a prize: Choose a prize that is unique to your business, e.g., a product or gift card so that you will attract entrants who are genuinely interested in your business, not just in winning an iPad or $500 cash, for example. Also, try to make the size of the prize proportionate to the effort it will take to win it, which leads us to...

190

Decide on an entry method: Some of the simplest contest entry methods on Instagram include asking fans to like a photo, follow your account, or re-post an image (with an app like Regram or simply screen-grabbing your published photo). You can also decide to advertise a contest held elsewhere, like on your Facebook Page or your website, via your Instagram account, and drive people to those destinations via a memorable shortened URL in your image's caption or a clickable link in your Instagram bio. Alternatively, some of the most common entry methods ask users to post a photo or a video on Instagram in order to be entered; often tied to a particular theme, e.g., food, colors, seasons, their favorite product from your offering.

Build your contest: When you launch the contest with a post on Instagram, featuring an attention-grabbing title with a short call-to-action will help maximize entries, e.g., *"Enter to Win a $100 Gift Card from Sean's Salon!"* A photo of the prize is a great way to entice people to enter to win it. If you're giving away a gift card, for example, include an image with the gift card value in text and a product that people can buy with it. Write the entry method and prizing info in the description - a paragraph with info about the prize, how to enter and any rules or restrictions for your contest, linked to with a short URL or a clickable link in your bio.

Monitor progress: To help gauge the success of your Instagram contest:
- Use hashtags to easily track how many photos are being shared on Instagram that have your contest hashtag (ask fans to use one in the caption for the photos or videos they post as a requirement for entry, but make sure beforehand that your chosen hashtag is unique and hasn't been used by someone else before).
- Set up Google Alerts to monitor mentions of your contest across the web.
- Use Wishpond or Woobox Instagram contest web apps for real-time campaign reports, which allow you to track views, entries, and conversion rates.

Promote your contest: In addition to organic marketing of your competition, send an email to your mailing list (these are the people most likely to enter), promote your contest on social networks, and add a banner to the home page of your website. You may also choose to stream contest entries to your website or a custom tab on your Facebook Page based on a specific @mention or hashtag, to help spread the word - the latter can be achieved via a service like Woobox.

Follow-up actions: After your contest is over, follow these steps to wrap everything up neatly:

- Showcase winning photos on your Instagram account and other social channels.
- Share a video showing you choosing the winning photo to create excitement.
- Post teasers for future contests on Instagram to keep your followers hooked, keep momentum going, and prime followers for future contests on your Instagram account.
- Run regular contests on Instagram (weekly or monthly) to get fans into the habit of looking forward to them and entering.

Embed your Instagram photos and videos

When you view an Instagram photo or video on your desktop web browser, you'll see a share button on the right-hand side (just under the comments button). Click this button and you'll get an embed code that you can copy and paste into your website, blog or article. Handily, the embedded image features an Instagram logo which, when clicked, will take viewers to your Instagram profile where they can discover more of your content.

Track and analyze your Instagram activity

While Instagram doesn't have a native analytics tool, there are plenty of third party options out there, both free and paid. Two of my favorites are Iconosquare (http://www.iconosquare.com) - a free analytics service that provides a variety of metrics for your Instagram account, including your Top 5 most-liked and followed photos, how often you use filters and which are your favorites, and your most engaged followers, as well as management tools like the ability to follow or unfollow users, like and comment on posts, and use Emoji in comments - and Collect.to (http://www.collect.to) – a platform with both free and paid options that provides you with analytics and data to help you run Instagram campaigns and contests. A paid account provides you with enhanced filtering options for date, hashtags, locations, etc. Whichever you choose, sign in with your Instagram details and use the stats to monitor which of your Instagram activities best resonate with your audience and use this as a basis for future content. Don't forget, too, that you can use a service like bit.ly (http://www.bitly.com) to shorten links and track their visits. Links aren't clickable within Instagram photo captions, but they *are* in your Instagram Bio, which you can direct people to via a message underneath a photo or video that you post.

Video Content Strategy for Instagram

In June 2013, video recording was rolled out to Instagram. The feature allows users to film clips of up to 60 seconds to share with the app's huge community and across other social media. The following selection of tips will help you make the most out of shooting video for Instagram.

Plan your shoot, record outside of Instagram
As editing on the fly is so limited within the Instagram video app, it is wise to plan your video in advance, as well as the shots that you will use. Without being forced to record within Instagram, you are free to use your phone's own camera and/or other apps to create potentially more compelling content before sharing it to a wider audience via your Instagram profile. Some good options include combining your phone's native camera with video editing and filter-adding apps like iMovie, Vintagio, and 8mm Vintage Camera (iOS) and Magisto or Videocam Illusion (Android).

Jerky camera work? Turn on "Cinema" mode
One of the features Instagram is most proud of is *Cinema*. With the tap of a finger, Cinema aims to remove as much wobble from your video as possible, making it seem as smooth and professional as if it was filmed by a Hollywood camera operator with a Steadicam. At the same step that you choose a filter for your video, you will notice an icon of a shaky camera. Simply tap this icon to turn Cinema mode on.

Choose a compelling cover frame
After you have recorded a video and added a filter, Instagram will ask you to add a cover frame. This will act as a thumbnail for your video in the feeds of your followers and in search results, so use the slider to choose the most compelling still shot available from those provided. The more appealing the image is, the better chance it will catch someone's eye enough for them to want to check it out!

Instagram video enhancement
Instagram video's editing and enhancement options are basic at best, but a whole variety of apps exist to add a touch of style and distinctiveness to your

mobile video efforts - if your video creation exists outside of the Instagram app, that is. Some of my favorites include iMovie (of course), Videohance (iOS), and Vidtrim (Android). The Flipagram app can also be used to stitch multiple photos together in order to create a story-driven slideshow video.

Experiment with Instagram's Hyperlapse app

In August 2014, Instagram launched Hyperlapse, an app that allows you to create cinematic, stabilized time-lapse videos on their mobile device - even you move around while shooting. Simply tap to record (for up to 45 minutes), choose a video speed (up to 12x faster), and share your creation instantly to Instagram and Facebook. It's worth noting that that 3 minutes of recording sped up at 12x will generate 15 seconds of video, the current limit for videos on Instagram, so plan around this figure or you'll have to trim your footage if you plan on sharing your creation with your Insta-followers. Whether you choose to share right away or not, all recordings are saved to your Camera Roll for, if necessary, further editing and disseminating elsewhere. Coordinate your use of Hyperlapse with other Instagram marketing strategies (e.g., capturing the atmosphere or story of an event, demoing a product, using filters to create an on-brand vibe) to produce captivating and engaging content.

Note: As Hyperlapse outputs video at high speed, try to keep your mobile device stable while you record so that changes of direction aren't too jerky - there's only so much that its automatic stabilization can do. Talking of stabilization, the app will crop the edges of your video while achieving this effect, so try to keep your scene/subject in the middle of the frame.

For more tips about the types of video content that resonate with Instagram users, check out the *"Explained: The Best Types of Content to Post on Social Media"* chapter of this book.

Shopping on Instagram: Seamless Selling to Customers

In March 2018, Instagram rolled out its much-anticipated Shopping feature to a much larger set of brands, including to businesses in the UK, Australia, and Spain. Shopping on Instagram allows your followers to browse and buy your products seamlessly through the app. Simply add tags to items featured in your posts (just like you would tag a person or profile); shoppers can tap on a tagged post within the Instagram feed (or through the Shop button on a business profile) to browse and buy.

Note: If you don't have the ability to set up Shopping on Instagram as detailed below, keep a close eye out for when it appears, as the potential benefits are significant.

To get your business approved and setup for Shopping on Instagram, you need to:

1. Ensure your Instagram account includes a business profile, or convert an existing personal account to a business type.
2. Connect and manage your Instagram business profile to a Facebook catalog of products. This can be created and managed through a new or existing Shop section on your Facebook Page (add one via Page Settings > Add A Tab > Shop) or via third-party websites like Shopify or BigCommerce.

One you've done this, your account will be reviewed and hopefully approved, normally within a few days. Once approved, to enable product tagging on Instagram, tap the Get Started alert at the top of your profile. If you don't see the alert, go to Settings > Shopping > to add a product catalog.

To tag products in your posts:
1. Select a photo and add a caption, effects and filters.
2. Tap Tag Products from the Share screen.
3. Tap the products in the photo you want to tag.
4. Enter the names of the products you want to tag, then select them as they appear in the search box.

6 Ways to optimize the Shopping experience on Instagram
1. Create at least 9 shopping posts to activate the Shop tab, which will then appear at the top of your profile. Tapping it will allow customers to browse and shop through every post that contains tagged products.
2. You can tag up to a maximum of 5 products per single-image post or 20 products per multi-image post.
3. Double check that each tag touches the correct product, so shoppers know which product each tag refers to.
4. You can tag products in already-published posts on Instagram, so don't forget to return to older posts to capitalize on any potential customers who might come across them.

5. Create an Instagram Story to let your fans know that they can now shop your posts.

6. Use Instagram Insights to understand your customers better, and utilize a catalog containing the most relevant products, currency and language for your them.

IGTV: Another Channel For Businesses on Instagram

Launched in the summer of 2018, IGTV is a standalone app that integrates with Instagram. IGTV lets users upload videos of between 15 seconds and 10 minutes to so-called Channels. Crucially, Instagram wants IGTV to be populated with new and unique content, not just rehashed Instagram posts. Many commentators see IGTV as Instagram's first real foray into competing with YouTube. If your brand finds that Instagram is its natural home, then creating new content for IGTV might be a good way to extend your reach and influence.

You can't record video directly within the IGTV app, you must upload external video files onto your channel. By requiring videos to be 15 seconds or longer, you can't simply repurpose your Stories videos to IGTV. And by requiring you to upload from an external source, Instagram is presuming you've created separate video content for your IGTV channel. Once you upload a video, it's available to view by all of your existing Instagram followers. Your current followers automatically follow your channel and can only unfollow it by unfollowing your Instagram account. IGTV also recommends multiple videos to each user on the app, increasing your chances of having your content distributed to new followers who have an interest in content similar to yours.

How to setup your IGTV Channel
Your IGTV channel can be setup on either on mobile or desktop. The process is similar on each, but here I'll summarize the mobile method in two steps.

1. Download the separate IGTV app (while it's a separate app, you and your fans can access IGTV directly via an icon at the top of the Instagram app as well). After installation, open the IGTV app and connect your Instagram account.

2. Tap on your profile photo, select the Create Channel option, and follow the prompts to set up your channel. Once connected, your Instagram account info will populate into your channel and you'll be asked to upload a video. After you've created your first IGTV video, you'll notice the IGTV icon in the highlights row of your mobile profile. Tapping on this icon will take any user to your IGTV channel and your list of videos.

IGTV tips and best practices

- Videos can be in vertical or portrait mode, and the ideal size ratio is 9:16, but a ratio as close to square as 4:5 is also supported.
- Give your video a descriptive title that will encourage viewers to watch. Do note that IGTV video titles get cropped off the thumbnail at around 20-25 characters, so try keep the title relatively short or else include the most descriptive information at the beginning.
- Add a unique cover photo. The default cover frame is not likely to be the best to attract the attention of viewers, so add your own. To edit your cover photo, select Edit Cover. From the pop-up screen, upload a separate image for the cover photo or choose any frame from the video.
- Instagram Live videos saved to your device (even if shorter than 10 minutes) don't appear in the gallery of videos to upload. A workaround for this is to save the live video to another folder on your device (for example, save it to your Google Photos folder).
- After selecting the video to upload to your channel, edit the title, description, and cover image.
- Use hashtags in video descriptions. Like in the main Instagram app, hashtags a are crucial for helping to gain exposure for your content. When you can include a list of hashtags in your IGTV video description, your video will appear in search results for those hashtags.
- Add clickable links in video descriptions. Any URL typed into an IGTV video description will become a clickable link, which you can use to drive traffic to any website. As is popular on YouTube, make sure to include important URLs near the top of IGTV descriptions and encourage viewers to click or tap on them in accordance with your brand message and goals.
- Share IGTV videos to Stories as a way to promote your channel. Open your Stories as normal, then upload a video, photo, or screenshot of

your IGTV video cover. Tap the link icon, select the IGTV video you want to share, and now - assuming your Instagram "swipe up" function has been granted - viewers will be able to swipe up to see it.

- Analyze your performance. Instagram has provided video insights for all IGTV uploads directly within the app. To view your insights, tap on the three-dot button on any video on your channel and select Insights. Use the information in your Insights - such as engagement and retention rate - to help inspire and optimize future content.

Instagram Direct: Private and Group Messaging

In December 2013, a new function – Instagram Direct – was rolled out to the app. Instagram Direct is a private and group messaging function that allows users to send photo or video messages to select people – either to a single individual or to groups of up to 15 people at a time. Whereas in the past, any content posted on Instagram was sent to the feeds of everyone who followed you *and* was publicly viewable via your mobile or web profile, Instagram Direct messages do not appear publicly. When you send a message directly (after you take a photo or shoot a video and are finished editing, select "Followers" to share the content with everyone or "Direct" to selectively choose who it goes to), you'll be able to find out who's seen your photo or video, who's liked it and also watch the recipients commenting in real time via the "folder" icon that sits at the top of the Instagram home screen. Photos and videos that you receive directly from people you follow will appear immediately in your inbox, but if someone you're not following sends you a photo or video directly, it will be held in your requests list until you decide that you want to view it. If you choose to view it, further private messages from that user will no longer need approval.

Instagram Direct is primarily aimed at casual users of Instagram to share messages privately between one another, but brands and businesses can also take advantage of this added functionality. Here are just a few ideas on how:

Welcome new followers
Record and share a 15-second welcome video, genuinely thanking someone for following you and telling you what you want them to do next - check out more of your posts, click the link in your bio, keep following for great new content, etc. When people can see you and hear your voice, they'll instantly feel more intimately connected to you and your brand. Depending on the rate your

profile is growing, this strategy can be time consuming – especially if each video is individually tailored to the follower (mentioning their name or username, for example), but could also pay dividends in the long run.

Target your most engaged fans by location and demographics
As you can message up to 15 people privately via Instagram Direct, you can use this as an opportunity to segment and target your audience based on location and demographics. To track down your most engaged fans, browse through your photo stream for the people who most comment and favorite your content, or often tag their friends as a way to spread awareness of your brand. Once you've identified your most active fans, you can formulate different group messages to send to various segments of your audience. Use these as a way to share news on new products, announce giveaways and contests, conduct Q&A sessions, drive traffic to your website, and more. Of course, since these messages will be largely unsolicited, you should be *very sure, and extra careful,* that sending them will not upset people who are most likely to be your biggest brand ambassadors.

Conduct customer service
Previously, any customer service issues that arose via Instagram were often forced to be dealt with within the comments section underneath a photo or video. Now, public disputes can be ushered into the more private setting of Instagram Direct. This prevents your comments from being clogged up by unsightly feedback and prevents your brand image from being damaged. To make the transition, reply to a complainant in the comments telling them that you will send/have sent a direct message to them to help solve their issue, and then go from there. Photos, videos, and text can be used as a way to help solve problems - choose whichever means of communication works best for you. To further enhance your customer service via Instagram Direct, advertise in your bio that people can contact you privately and actively monitor negative mentions of your brand via your notifications and Instagram search to jump on and deal with problems before they get the chance to stew and escalate. You can - similar to Twitter - also explore Instagram for hashtags associated with your product and services, then see if you can offer helpful advice to anyone talking about your area of expertise, as a way to break the ice. Again, this tactic works best if you are quite sure that your "out of the blue" message will not upset the individual in question.

Offer coupon codes / exclusive deals

While occasionally sending coupon codes out to all of your Instagram followers is a sound tactic in itself, messaging them to an exclusive group of followers can be even more effective. Make sure that each coupon code you create is unique so that you can track its success easily and also limit the quantity and set deadlines for their use to encourage their redemption and discourage abuse. Tactics include:

- Send a direct message including a coupon code to new or milestone followers (e.g., 50th, 100th, 1000th).
- Send a coupon code as an apology for a customer service issue.
- Send a coupon randomly to surprise and delight a follower; encourage the recipient to share it with their friends both on Instagram and elsewhere.

Give ultra-exclusive sneak peeks

In a very savvy move - and one you can emulate - Kardashian Kollection offered 15 of its followers an exclusive behind the scenes photo from its latest fashion collection. To enter, Instagram followers were asked to screen grab the image which told them of the entry instructions and re-post it with the hashtag #KKDIRECT. The promotion received over 4,000 likes and 650 comments in under 24 hours… and the really clever part? By requesting followers to re-post the entry instructions, they put their fans to work in helping to drive more participants. After the promotion, screen grabs of the private messages being sent to the chosen 15 were posted publicly for transparency.

Run Instagram contests

Private messaging on Instagram gives you the chance to run more types of competitions via the app and enables promotions that can be held "ad-hoc" with smaller prizes. Example strategies include:

- Hold a contest where the first person to reply privately with the answer to a question, or post a certain photo, or tweet with a certain hashtag wins a prize, e.g., *"The first 10 people to send us a photo of themselves wearing a Shawn's Sweater while standing in a bucket will win a $10 gift voucher towards their next purchase!"* or *"The next 5 people to post a video eating at Bob's Burgers with the hashtag #lovebobs will get a very special Direct message from*
- *us…"*

- Hold a "friend referral" contest where the winner is the first person to get 5 friends to follow you and mention the username of their referrer in the direct message.
- Host a scavenger hunt, where a clue is sent out to an exclusive set of followers and the next one is only delivered once you receive the correct answer to the first. The winner is the user who reaches the end of the hunt - in the real world or virtually (finding clues hidden on your website, for example) first.

Video chatting in Instagram Direct

In the summer of 2018, private video chat in Instagram Direct was rolled out, either as a conversation with one person or a group of up to four people of whom you've already shared direct messages with within the app. Video chat gives you the experience of real time video in a private space and helps you feel close and connected to fans, customers, and prospects. To start a video chat, swipe into your Direct inbox and open any message thread. Tap camera icon in the right corner, and the video chat will ring your friends' phones so they don't miss it. You could use video chat in Instagram Direct to:

- Provide customer service. Schedule calls with customers to answer their questions or resolve issues with a real person on-camera.
- Close a sale. If a potential customer has questions about your product or service, or is on the fence about purchasing, a quick live call could be the nudge they need to decide to buy.
- Show product demos. Whether offering a first look to prospects or helping a customer with a newly purchased product, a live demo can show them how to use your product.

Advertising on Instagram

Instagram's history with advertising stretches back to 2013, when it tentatively began to test sponsored content with a select number of big brands, including Ben & Jerry's, Michael Kors and Mercedes. Over two years of research and experimentation later, in September 2015, the app's advertising opportunities were opened up to *all businesses.*

Instagram ads can be used to build brand awareness, drive consideration and action like website traffic and conversions, to help buyers discover your products, and optimize your campaigns for your desired business objectives like driving website leads, app installs sales. Ads for Instagram are built via the Facebook Ads tool (Instagram was bought by Facebook in April 2012), so you will need to have a Facebook account to set them up. In this section we'll cover some of the essential information you need to craft successful Instagram ads.

Setting up Instagram ads
To link a Facebook Page to an Instagram account, visit your Page and click Settings. In Settings, click on Instagram Ads and follow the instructions to add an account for Advertising. You can also create a new Instagram account here if you need to. If you use Facebook Business Manager, you can assign an ad account to an Instagram account by clicking Business Settings > Instagram Accounts > Click Assign Ad accounts. To authorize one or more of your ad accounts to use the Instagram Account, check the box next to each ad account and click Save Changes.

Instagram ad basics
- Instagram ads (which can be a photo or video) appear among the ordinary stream of content within the app, identifiable as they are marked "Sponsored." Ads can be created in a square or landscape format.
- All ads will feature a linked call to action button such as "Learn More", "Shop Now", or "Install App".
- The recommended image size for an Instagram ad in the square or landscape format is 1080 x 1080 pixels. The aspect ratio for an Instagram ad in the square format is 1:1. If you use the landscape format, your image or video should have an aspect ratio of 1.9:1.
- Video ads should be no more than 30 seconds long or 30MB in size.
- The caption you use for your Instagram ad will appear below the content and can include up to 300 characters. As a best practice, avoid using URLs in your Instagram ad's text. URLs will not be clickable from your ad's text field.
- Instagram ads should adhere to the same guidelines as Facebook ads, including the 20% text rule.

Instagram ads best practices
As you should now be well aware, Instagram is a place people go to discover and become inspired by the images they see. The best practices for ads reflect much of what you have learned about content marketing on Instagram so far – make ads seamless to the experience, not disruptive. As a business, it is

recommended that you focus your Instagram ad campaigns around 3 key objectives: on brand, concept driven and well crafted.

On brand

Like organic Instagram content, your ads should be creative, showing your brand's personality. Find unique ways to incorporate your brand's logo, icon or a color, but stay consistent with your style between organic and paid content to drive familiarity.

Concept driven

When planning your Instagram ad, know what you want to make your audience think and feel, and what your core message is. With that, you'll find it easier to apply some of the following ideas:

- Tell a story: Take a series of images that tell a story about your brand and share them over a period of time.
- Experiment with visual styles: Use different filters and color schemes to create a visual mood with your images. You could even use a series of different filters to show a change in mood.
- Develop a theme: Create a series of unique images that all share a common theme, e.g., different events from a single day or an object in a variety of settings.

Well-crafted

With a bit of practice, anyone can create compelling images for Instagram – ads or not. Here are some ad-specific tips.

- Strong Focal Point: Avoid making your images too complex or busy. Instead, focus on one or two places where you want to draw people's eyes. As a best practice, one focal point should include a brand logo or another brand element that's recognizable to your audience.
- Framing & Balance: Straighten out images to make them look cleaner and consider symmetry, the rule-of-thirds, and other composition basics as you're photographing or shooting.
- Lighting & Detail: Be sure to use clear and high-resolution images. Pixelated images and those with bad lighting or other flaws may not perform well.
- Caption and hashtags: Don't forget a compelling tagline and, crucial
- for Instagram, a selection of on-brand and relevant hashtags.

- Ad guidelines: To avoid your Instagram ads being flagged and rejected, follow the Facebook Advertising Policies, including the 20% text rule. You can check to make sure your image doesn't have 20% or more of its pixels dedicated to text, by using the grid tool to check your photos.

Instagram Stories Ads

Instagram Stories Ads let brands insert a short, full-screen ad - either a static image displayed for up to five seconds, a carousel ad with up to three images, or a video of up to 15 seconds long - between stories that users watch within the app. Stories ads can be utilized just like other Instagram or Facebook ads, to drive brand awareness, announce sales or special events, start a conversation via direct message, or re-target existing or lapsed customers – all viewers have to do is swipe up when they see the call-to-action. However, as Stories ads don't appear in the normal Instagram feed and pop up instantly between story posts, they're a super direct and intimate way to put your brand in front of potential customers. Like ordinary stories, Stories ads disappear forever after 24 hours.

The creation process for Instagram Stories ads is carried out via the Facebook Ads tool, just like any other Facebook or Instagram ad, *but* to make the biggest impact, you'll need to optimize Stories Ads for viewers. Here are a number of tips to help drive more action through Instagram Stories ads:

Grab attention straight away

Just like an ordinary Instagram story, if a user taps on an Instagram Stories ad, it will be skipped instantly - and there's no "back" button to save the situation. That said, the initial second or two of your ad needs to be attention-grabbing so that viewers stop to view it. Use a combination of visuals, copy, and font to stop viewers in their tracks. But whatever you do, keep the message clear and simple to prevent viewers getting confused and tapping away.

Show your brand name (but avoid these placements)

People tap through Instagram stories quickly, so ensure that your brand name and product is clearly visible. That way, even if they don't swipe up to take action, they might remember who you are to visit later on. Avoid placing any text in the top-left of the ad or at the bottom in the middle. These areas are where people's handles and your chosen call-to-action message appear respectively.

Don't make your ads look like an ad

Instagram users are hypersensitive to ads and can easily tell the difference between a typical post by a friend versus one made by a slick brand marketing team. One of the keys to success with Instagram Stories Ads is to advertise while not looking like an ad, by mirror the expectations of Instagram users as they watch Stories. For example, a large proportion of organic Instagram Stories feature videos of real people in real life situations, so video could, depending on your audience and product, be the best option overall, rather than graphics and text alone, which sometimes run the risk of looking like traditional ads. In addition to the basic format of your ad, experiment with other creative techniques to make them more "authentic," with the use of elements like emojis, handwriting, stickers, and built-in Instagram tools like Boomerang, Hyperlapse and Superzoom.

Optimize the call-to-action

Your Stories ads need to include a clear call to action that encourages people to swipe up to perform an action. To make swiping up more appealing, use interactive elements like arrows, stickers, and action-orientated copy to let viewers know what you want them to do. In addition, use the last few seconds of your ad to focus solely on the CTA. This two or three seconds lets the user know that the ad is over and it gives them time to swipe up before the story disappears.

Re-purpose existing content for Stories ads

The full-screen dimensions for Stories Ads is different from anything on Facebook; the recommended resolution is 1080 x 1920 pixels. If you want to experiment tentatively with Stories ads without building whole new visuals from scratch, start off by re-purposing existing content created for your social media marketing campaigns. To make the task easier - specifically for content not already designed and formatted for Stories - Facebook's Ad Manager provides full-screen support for all ads to be used in Instagram Stories. When you upload an image or video within Ads Manager, it will be transformed into the full-screen format of Stories, allowing you to run Stories ads more quickly and efficiently.

Use fast clips with audio

For ads with more than one scene or clip, edits to make the video fast-paced make for better ads. Facebook found that top-performing Stories ads, on average, included brief clips with quick scenes. On top of that, Instagram's research shows that 60% of stories are viewed with sound on, so make sure that the content you share sounds just as good as it looks.

Google+ Tips:
Plus One Your Marketing Strategy

When Google+ first launched in 2011, many assumed – probably correctly – that Google's social network was aiming to be the search giant's answer to Facebook. While its user base grew to well over 500 million by 2014, Google+ never really blew up in the way that Google might've hoped, and the site began to reshape and refocus to compensate. By late 2015, instead of a kind-of Facebook clone, Google+ was fully redesigned and re-developed to put Communities (a place for people to gather to discuss any topic they are passionate about) and Collections (a way to group posts by topic, providing an easy way for people to organize everything that they're into) front and center. In essence, Google+ is now a stripped back version of what it was, a place for people to gather to share and discuss their interests.

Despite the major changes to Google+ in 2015, Google's dominance of search on the web means that the site can be beneficial as a place for businesses to maintain a presence. There is no easier way to increase visibility of your content on Google search than to encourage comments, shares, and +1s (the social network's equivalent of Facebook "likes") on your Google+ account. The major caveat to this? You will have to commit to building a Google+ community against competing social networks, especially Facebook and Pinterest, neither of which have undergone such a dramatic transition, and all which have a much more active use base (an average of 20 minutes per day on Facebook vs just seven minutes per month on Google+, according to DMR). However, if you and your audience are prepared to put in the time and effort, then the opportunity remains.

Google+ Profile Optimization

A solid Google+ marketing strategy begins with a profile that knocks the socks off customers and prospects. Here's how to make that happen. Use the following tips to build, brand, improve search engine ranking and form relationships using Google+.

Get a Google+ brand page, not a profile page

As with Facebook, make sure you create a Google+ brand page for your business rather than another personal profile. Google My Business is the way for businesses, products, brands, artists, and organizations to manage their online presence with Google. When you add your business using Google My Business, you'll automatically create a Google+ page. Customers who follow your business page can show appreciation and give feedback with posts and comments and they'll also be able to use the +1 button to endorse products and services on Google Search, Maps, or on ads. To start, visit https://business.google.com/manage and follow the short setup steps. Google My Business pages are indexed in Google search results, and display reviews, additional details and photos of a business beside it. As a result, a well-produced page that includes all of your most important business information has a good chance of getting high engagement with users.

Upload a compelling cover image, grab my template

Use your Google+ cover image to express your brand image, tell people where you are, showcase new products, advertise upcoming events, or for whatever you like, really. As of November 2013, the recommended size is 1080 pixels × 608 pixels, and the smallest image size you are allowed to upload is 480 pixels × 270 pixels. By uploading the larger size, you ensure that your cover will be seen in its best light on mobiles and desktops.

Note: Download a Google+ cover photo template optimized for desktop and mobile screens (and lots of other great stuff) via the *Premium Content Bundle* chapter of this book.

Add a circular profile photo or a transparent logo

The Google+ profile image switched from a square to a circle in March 2013. Its minimum size is 250 × 250 pixels, and this will be scaled down to 104 × 104 pixels when re-sized. If you have a square company logo, you might find it tricky to get it to fit fully *inside* Google+'s profile photo circle on your page, even with the cropping and sizing tools that present themselves when you upload. The trick here is to upload your profile image as a .png file with a transparent background. Upon upload, drag the cropping edges right to the corners so that the while image will show on your business page. If your image still doesn't look right at this stage, click on it from your profile and choose More -> Auto Enhance -> off from the menu at the top.

Add a compelling tagline

In your 'About' section, Google+ allows you to add a 140-character tagline to appear underneath your profile's business name. The tagline acts like an elevator pitch to visitors, will appear as the description when somebody shares your page, and as the first sentence when your Google+ page is found in Google search. Keep it short, snappy, descriptive and keyword-rich, or as a message to explain who you are and what you and your business is all about. Check out a few examples from these well-known names for inspiration: Yahoo! News - *"The official Google+ page for Yahoo! News. All stories are hand-picked by the Y! News team."*, Volkswagen: *"Take a look around, kick the tires, and ask questions to get to know our community."*, and ESPN: *"We +1 Sports"*

Add a +1 button and Google+ badges to your website

If you write a blog, be sure to add a +1 button widget to your posts, so that your fans can share your content on Google+ easily. Just search for "Google+ button" or grab the embed code from the following link: https://developers.google.com/+/web/+1button/ Meanwhile, the Google+ badge is the equivalent to the Facebook "Like" box in that it lets readers follow you on Google+ without leaving your site. In addition, however, it also has benefits within search results. When you embed the Google+ badge for pages on your site, an active Follow widget will show up next to your website's listing in Google search results. To install the Google+ Badge, simply search online for "Google+ Badge" or visit https://developers.google.com/+/web/badge/.

Google+ Marketing and Content Strategy

Google+ might not have as much mainstream appeal as its competitors, but some of its features - especially discussion and conferencing tools - make it an extremely powerful destination for relationship building if the site is where your audience or prospects like to hang out. Let's take a look at some ways to maximize the impact of your approach...

Share top content, boost your SEO

Your Google+ audience may differ from those on Facebook and Twitter, so get to know them by asking questions, polling, sharing great and relevant content, and interacting. Posting great content on Google+ does more than reach out to your fans and other users — it also "markets" to search engines. Any time you post content to Google+, Google immediately indexes it, giving you faster exposure to new viewers. When you share a link to an article on your Google+ page (whether it is your own content or someone else's) write the first sentence of the post mindfully with relevant keywords and phrases. The first sentence of a post makes up part of the title tag in search results and can affect its ranking. If you notice that your post isn't getting much attention, try editing the text you used to see if that improves things. The longer a piece of content exists, the longer it's in the index of Google, so as people continue to search and interact with it, it will continue to show up near the top of search results. What's more, your content is more likely to appear in your contacts' online searches, thanks to Google's personalized results.

Note: In May 2015, Google+ introduced Collections, a way to group your posts by topic - very similar to Pinterest boards. Collections can be shared publicly in your timeline, or privately. Create yours via the "Collections" tab on your page or profile, and use them as an easy way to curate and share images, links, videos – maybe as a "catalogue" of your products, a hub for breaking industry news, your newest offers, etc.

Embed Google+ Posts on your website
Like Twitter and Facebook, Google+ allows you to lift posts you publish and embed them onto your website or blog, which can help to give your content an extra lease on life and boost its engagement. When someone encounters the Google+ embedded post on your site, they can +1, comment, or follow you, all without leaving your site.

How to embed a Google+ post
1. On Google+, move your cursor over the right corner of a post to reveal a down arrow. Click the arrow to expand the post options and select "Embed post."
2. A text box containing HTML/Javascript code will appear. Copy and paste the code in the location of your article where you'd like to display the post.

Use Mentions and hashtags
As with Twitter and Facebook, @mentions and hashtags are important on Google+, both in tagging other users in your posts and grouping related content. To hyperlink someone's name in your posts, type "+" or "@" and then his or her name. Unlike other social networks, Google+ uses hashtags to help people *explore* tagged content rather than simply curate it. This is typified by Google+ search, which returns related hashtags and trending topics when

you submit a query. As such, adding hashtags to your Google+ statuses will help people with *related* interests find it - even if you're not connected to them - and you can also see what related hashtags appear on key searches for *your* industry, then incorporate the ideas you find into future content.

Google+ contest strategy

Although Google+'s contest terms are strict (they begin with the rather damning sentence *"You may not run contests, sweepstakes, or other such promotion directly on Google+ or in a manner that requires use of G+ features or functionality."*, there are still several ways to leverage the platform to engage your community through giveaways without violating its promotions policy. These include:

- Asking fans to suggest ideas to improve your business, anchored with a specific hashtag to post along with submissions (the one you like the best get early access to your next product before everyone else). Classify entries as "applications" so not to break the promotions policy.
- Asking fans to show you how they use your product or service in their everyday lives and showcasing the best examples on your page. In this case, recognition and a feature on your page is the "prize."
- Google+ does allow you to *"display a link on Google+ to a separate site where your Promotion is hosted,"* so use this as an opportunity to promote a contest on your Google+ page (but one that is not hosted directly on the site). Read up on Google+'s full contest rules here: http://www.google.com/+/policy/contestspolicy.html

Hunt for prospects and brand ambassadors on Google+

As with Twitter, you can use Boolean search techniques on Google+ to find people who are talking about your brand, services, or products using the search bar at the top of the site. To begin, enter keywords, as well as hashtags that are related to your brand or niche, then filter your search by content type (posts, photos, most recent mentions, etc.) to find mentions with the most potential. Utilize searches as a means to discover potential customers (e.g., people with problems you can solve or desires you can meet) or existing brand ambassadors (people saying nice things about you) and target them to build strong, long-lasting relationships that will convert into further sharing of your content, leading them to influence the emergence of new customers and conversions further on down the line.

Hashtags are particularly useful for prospect hunting on Google+ as they allow you to deepen your investigation to find and interact with new communities and potential brand ambassadors. When you search using hashtags, the results will return Collections, Communities, People, and Pages that have mentioned or are related to the topic.

Use Google+ Communities to engage and gather feedback

The Google+ Communities tab gives people – your customers included - a place to gather with one another and discuss almost anything, including your products and brand offering. When you create your own Community, it has the potential to become an invaluable resource as it allows you to get feedback and engage with your customers in a personal and meaningful way. What's more, all of the content posted within a Community page (whether Public or Private to invited members) is indexed by Google search. Compared to posts on your Google+ page, Google+ Community updates should be longer and more conversational, with more detail on a specific topic or a fuller explanation of the content you are sharing - something like you might see on a web message board, for example, complete with a question to finish in order to encourage feedback. To create a Community, simply select the Community tab in the sidebar of Google+, then click 'Create A Community' from the "Yours Tab". Don't forget to tell your fans and customers that it exists and encourage them to get involved.

In addition to setting up your own Community, search for Communities within your business sector or niche and actively participate in them to make connections, share expertise, and set yourself up as an authority figure. Once you are an established member of a Google+ Community, you begin to share content you have created regularly, to encourage more views and engagement with it. Carrying out this kind of self-promotion is *okay* when you are new to a Community, but you don't want to do it too often and risk coming over as spammy and unprofessional, which could eventually get you blocked from the Community altogether.

Test, measure and apply

As with all social media, the key to finding what strategy works best for your business on Google+ is to try experimenting with different types of posts and Hangouts and seeing what your followers engage most. Measure your performance via Google Analytics, as this is key to gaining more meaningful insights into your followers' behavior towards your activity. To focus specifically on the progress of custom campaigns and referral traffic, use Goals in Google Analytics in conjunction with giving links custom URLs via the Google URL Builder, found at https://ga-dev-tools.appspot.com/campaign-url-builder/

Snapchat Tips: Self-Destructing Social Media

Snapchat, launched in September 2011, is a photo and video-sharing app centered on one simple premise: all messages shared between friends via Snapchat will self-destruct, never to be seen again. In most cases, photo and video messages - Snaps - will disappear between one and ten seconds after being opened by a recipient (the time limit is specified by the sender), and if the Snap is not opened, it will automatically delete itself after 30 days. The only exceptions to this rule are a "one-time or infinity-repeat option for any single snap, Snapchat Stories, and the potentially game-changing Memories (more on these features below). Before sharing content with fellow contacts, Snapchat users have the option to add filters and annotate photos and video with colorful text and markers.

While media shared via Snapchat only exists for a matter of seconds, if you switch your thinking to view the time limit as an *opportunity* rather than a limitation, there are plenty of ways that it can be used for effective marketing. Think about it this way: when a customer is notified of a Snapchat message from you, first they're excited about what mystery it holds and second they know that as soon as they open it, they need to pay close attention as it will soon disappear forever. And if they don't keep checking the app daily, they'll miss messages, creating sense of urgency to keep up with fleeting information. Often it's addictive! By today's standards, 10 seconds of someone's *undivided attention* like this - especially on a medium as personal as mobile - is gold dust. One of the biggest emotional triggers for brands on social media is creating the feeling of FOMO (fear of missing out), and the format of Snapchat's content delivers this in spades. Like all social media, the best Snapchat content is framed in a way that mirrors the style of the majority of its users who take advantage of the platform. Where Snapchat is concerned, this involves humor, sharing secrets, having fun, holding small conversations, and capturing "shareworthy" moments: the promise of one-of-a-kind, real-time content is your customer's incentive to follow you, even if they already do on other channels.

Unlike other social networks, Snapchat isn't about portraying perfection or driving people to directly buy your product. It's a fun, genuine way to promote the personality of your brand and share your story in an off-the-cuff, genuine way. Let's look at some ways that you can make the most of Snapchat for your business...

Take advantage of Snapchat Stories

The Snapchat Stories mode allows you to join multiple snaps together to create a rolling 24-hour reel of content for *all* of your followers to enjoy again and again. When any snap is added to your story ages over 24 hours, it disappears and must be replaced with new photos or videos if you want the story to remain active. If no new content is added to your story, it will disappear once the newest piece of content expires, and a whole new story will need to be created. To add content to a story, just choose the '+' icon after taking a photo or recording a video with the app.

While the previous Snapchat content strategies in this chapter allow you to specifically target individuals, stories are more of a "catch all" approach that give followers a better opportunity to view collections of snaps multiple times. They also act as a central hub to which you can direct fans when you want them to engage with your Snapchat efforts over a prolonged period of time and enjoy a more substantial narrative of events. For example, the Washington Wizards basketball team uses stories to document its game days, making snaps that show the players arriving, a glimpse of the locker room, half-time fun, and the result at the end of the game. Similarly, the fashion brand Jack Wills employs stories to allow its fans to tag along all day at photo shoots for its newest ranges of clothes, while the online food-ordering service GrubHub uses stories to give its fans extra time to catch its latest promotion blasts and coupon codes. What's more, with the story replies option, anyone can reply to a specific photo or video within a story by swiping up from the bottom of the display and opening a new chat window. This means you can receive instant feedback (and reply to fans!) and it is an invaluable way to gauge how a live campaign is going.

Note: A sure-fire way to boost the view rates on all of your stories is to think about the three pillars of storytelling: each one needs a logical beginning, middle, and end, where each pillar of the story gives your fans a reason to view until the end. Invite viewers on a journey and keep them asking *"What's next?"* Brands with successful view rates tend to keep their snaps brief and their stories anywhere between 1 and 2 minutes long. Any longer than that may negatively impact view rates. One common mistake amongst businesses who are new to Snapchat is creating mixed-message stories that don't connect with their audience. For example, they will create a story by combining random snaps without context or overarching story. If you *do* plan to take a bunch of one-off snaps, use a longer frequency between each snap to minimize any confusion.

Use Memories to develop new, repackage, and re-purpose content
In the past, only photos and videos shot within Snapchat could be posted as snaps or as part of a story. The Memories feature, introduced in July 2016, changed this by allowing users to upload content from their device's Camera Roll and save and share old snaps from inside the app for later use. So, now it is possible to create content in any app or software to be uploaded to Snapchat, opening up a whole new world of opportunity. Snapped a photo or shot a video made for Facebook, Twitter, or elsewhere? Now you can re-purpose it for Snapchat with very little effort. For example, a long YouTube video can be chopped into 10-second clips to be repackaged as a serialized Snapchat story. Or if you want to export a top-performing snap to share on another platform, that is just as easy to do.

Access Memories from Snapchat's home screen by tapping on icon of two mobile phones at the bottom of the app's opening screen. Here, you'll be able to import content from your Camera Roll to use within Snapchat. Alternatively, to save a completed snap to Memories for future use, tap the arrow pointing downwards at the bottom of the screen. This icon used to save snaps to your phone, but now tapping on this icon will save your snap directly to Memories. Saved snaps can be shared to other social networks to promote your Snapchat content, like attaching it to a tweet or Facebook post, creating an album of Snapchat photos to tell the story of a day, or stitching video clips together to create a vlog for uploading to YouTube. Memory snaps are differentiated against ordinary snaps because they appear with a white border and a timestamp. Like stories, multiple memories can be stitched together.

Snapchat Content Ideas

Ask simple questions
As the ability to type long text replies is limited by time and space on Snapchat, the best kind of questions to ask are those that are easy to digest and demand a visual response, either by photo or video. For example, a shoe brand might ask their fans something as simple as "Show us your shoes!" or "Snap us a photo when you're in our store!" The quicker and easier you make it for fans to respond, the better.

Show sneak previews

Snapchat media's brevity makes it a great platform for showing a sneaky peak behind the curtain of your business, whether it's news of a new product launch, an upcoming offer, or something else exclusive only to your friends on the app. If need be, tease out the content over the course of several snaps to keep it digestible and to encourage people to look out for more. MTV UK used this marketing method several times to preview photo stills and video clips from the new season of its reality television show, *Geordie Shore*. The content was memorable and impactful, reminding people to watch the program and visit its website.

Offer coupons and special offers

Use Snapchat as a way to send out time-limited coupons or special offers to your customers. As the promotion will be seen so briefly, make sure that your message is extra clear and succinct, e.g., "10% off today only with promo code SNAP" *and* consider sending out a "heads-up" snap to alert people to the day and time that a promotion will be landing in their inbox. The 16 Handles ice cream chain put an interesting spin on this strategy. First, they asked customers to send them a photo via Snapchat of them eating the chain's ice cream. 16 Handles would then reply with a coupon code for money off their next purchase. The customer had to keep the self-destructing message unopened until they placed their order at the register, then quickly show the cashier the coupon to receive a discount.

Hold a Snapchat contest

As you know, a contest can be a highly effective way to boost engagement and awareness of your brand on social media. It is no different on Snapchat. Here are several methods you can use:

- *Scavenger hunt:* Share photo or video clues to a secret destination, either in the real world or online, and allow your followers to compete to be the first to find it.
- *Word or picture quiz:* Send out word or picture clues over a set period of time, building up to a way that followers can win a prize, e.g., visiting a special page on your site to enter a keyword revealed over the course of a week, or by sending back a specific snap.
- *First snap wins:* Send out a photo or video asking followers to snap back something specific or tweet you a screen grab from a snap, and the first one to do it wins a prize.

Have fun, be funny

Snapchat's majority audience is teenagers and young adults and the app is dominated by fun and humorous pieces of content. If your brand image allows, don't be afraid to have a little fun - pull faces, doodle on top of your snaps, use Emoji and stickers to tell a story, or surprise your audience with something that might raise an eyebrow or two! Handing over your Snapchat account to partners, customers, and different employees can also a great way to vary your content and make it feel more authentic. Branded content on Snapchat is like nothing else out there, so if you can capture the imagination of fans in this way, they are more likely to keep opening the snaps you send... which means the odd promotional one, too.

Note: Make it a goal to create snaps and stories that are engaging from start to finish and screenshot-worthy (a trackable metric in Snapchat – more on this shortly). As covered in previous chapters, examples might include useful checklists, inspirational quotes, and discount codes.

Use Paperclip to drive traffic to your website

In a landmark rollout that is an immense help to brands – and will help you tie many of the suggestions above to your brand's social media goals - Snapchat introduced Paperclip in July 2017. The feature allows you to attach a website URL to a snap. When a user swipes up on the snap, the link you've entered will open within Snapchat's internal browser, allowing you to push fans and customers to your content instantly and directly within Snapchat (a feature previously limited to paid ads). The tool can be accessed by tapping on the paperclip icon within Snapchat's toolkit, directly after taking a snap photo or video.

How to track customers on Snapchat and measure ROI

Unlike some of its rivals, Snapchat does not yet feature an in-depth set of tools for businesses to manage and track detailed analytics on the app – some out-of-the-box thinking is needed until a time when official means of carrying it out is possible. Here are several metrics you can utilize go help you determine how successful you're growing and engaging your Snapchat following:

Total Opens: This is the total number of views across all of your Snapchat stories. To track your opens and views, you can use a third-party tool like Snaplytics.io.

Average Open Rate: This is the percentage of total estimated followers who have engaged with any given Snapchat story - comparable to engagement rates on Facebook. This metric is closely tied to the number of opens.

Screenshots taken: Screenshots is the total number of screenshots taken by users for all of the snaps within a story. This metric tells you how many times people have saved your snap to their devices. Screenshots are a great indicator that people found your post valuable or entertaining (whether you asked them to or not).

Completion Rate: Completion rate is the percentage of followers who viewed an entire story from beginning to end; a way to measure the loyalty of your audience. Do they watch your stories in their entirety or swipe away before finishing?

Follower growth: Follower growth by source is the key metric to determine where your Snapchat followers are coming from. From there, you can adjust your strategy.

To view the number of opens and screenshots of individual snaps and stories, and from this data, figure out the other metrics listed above, tap the three little dots that appear to the right of where you click on your story in the app.

How to grow your Snapchat following – Snapcodes and friend referrals
Other than the obvious "market your Snapchat presence and username everywhere", one of the simplest ways to encourage the growth of your audience on Snapchat is to ask existing followers to encourage their friends to add you on the app. Following is made easy courtesy of your profile's Snapcode, which when photographed by a customer using the app's built-in camera, will add you automatically – grab an editable, printable version at https://accounts.snapchat.com/accounts/snapcodes). When asking existing fans to refer their friends, make sure you get them to snap you the name of the friend who will be adding you, and when they do, send both users a little reward as a thanks (discount code, unique content, etc.)

Custom URL Snapcodes

In addition to "follow our profile" Snapcodes, in early 2017, Snapchat added a feature that allows users to turn *any* link into a Snapcode that can be used to open web pages within Snapchat. To create a Snapcode:

1. Open Snapchat Settings, select Snapcodes, and then "Create Snapcode.
2. Paste the URL of the chosen web page and add an image that will appear within the Snapcode (Snapchat will automatically pull images from the web page as possible options).
3. The completed Snapcode will be saved to your camera roll and can be inserted anywhere you like: embedded on a website, posted to Facebook, Instagram or Twitter, on flyers, menus, etc.

As a way for brands to track Snapcode usage, Snapchat provides in-app analytics (total number of scans over the past three months, as well as the percentage of people who opened the link after scanning it) for Snapcodes that have been scanned at least 100 times. If you're not reaching that number consistently, converting your link on bit.ly is an alternative method to track Snapcode progress.

Combine Snapchat with other social channels

Given Snapchat's fluid and destructive form of messaging, it often helps to combine the app with other social networks as a way to switch up or more easily preserve the momentum of your strategy. For example, you could launch a contest using a Snapchat story, but ask fans to submit their entries to you via Instagram or Twitter, using an @mention and a specific hashtag. Not only would this help you tell how effective your Snapchat marketing is, but also provide some extra exposure on other social networks.

Quick and effective Snapchat content creation tips

To make the most of visuals on Snapchat, do this first: Navigate straight to Settings (cog icon), tap "Manage" under the Additional Services option and turn on Filters, and Special Text.

- The Loop tool for videos lets you decide if your Snap plays once or loops until the viewer is ready to tap to the next Snap – very handy if you're going to be stringing together multiple, short video clips.
- To add background music to video snaps, begin playing a track on your mobile (either one saved to your device or streamed in an app like Spotify), then open Snapchat and begin recording – the portion

of the track that plays during the recording will be dubbed into the video automatically.

- Snapchat provides hundreds of cute and vibrant emoji and stickers to decorate your snaps. To access the emojis and stickers, take your snap then tap the folded paper icon on the top of your screen. Tap to choose a sticker, drag it around, pinch and twist to resize and rotate. You can add as many as you like! To "pin" an emoji or sticker to a moving object in your video snaps, tap and hold it above an object to stick it in place.

Advertising on Snapchat

Snapchat advertising is an exciting advertising channel for marketers, especially if your target audience is in the 13-34 age bracket, who make up the vast majority of its users. With Snapchat's data, you can target users based on their demographics and their online *and* offline interests and behaviors. You can also use your own data to reach your customers and similar users on Snapchat. There are two main types of advertising available to all marketers on Snapchat. Let's take a look:

On-Demand Geofilters
Snapchat geofilters are user-made filters that appear when a Snapchatter fires up the app in a designated location, like a city, a park, or near a restaurant; typically, they do not have a time limit. On-demand Geofilters – specifically targeted at business users – allow you to create and host a geofilter in a specific location for a chosen amount of time, ranging from a few hours up to 30 days. This feature opens up huge marketing opportunities for small and medium-sized businesses. Imagine a restaurant using an overlaid on-demand geofilter to advertise a new dish, or a theater promoting their newest production. The cost? As little as $5.00, depending on the length you want the geofilter to appear, and how big the area you want it to generate within is. To begin the geofilter-creation process, visit http://geofilters.snapchat.com/purchase or within the Snapchat app, on the settings screen, tap On-Demand Geofilters. If this is your first time creating an on-demand geofilter, Snapchat will walk you through a series of questions and templates as you create your design. Otherwise, if you have existing geofilters and want to create a new one, tap the Create icon to get started.

Snap Ads

Snap Ads are full-screen vertical video ads that begin with an up to 10-second video, and then offer the option to add an interactive element when the user swipes up: watch a longer video, read an article, install an app, or visit a website. Snap Ads appear in between friends' stories an curated content like Snapchat's own or publishers' stories. Snap Ads are created in the Snapchat Ad manager, and if you are already familiar with the Facebook Ads Manager, the Snapchat Ad Manager is similar. You can set up and login to your business account on Snapchat at https://ads.snapchat.com/. Like Facebook, you will be creating choosing a goal for your ad (drive traffic, grow awareness, video views, etc.), selecting a schedule and choosing a budget (it is recommended that you set the bid amount to how much each goal action (e.g. video view) is worth to you. If you are not getting the results you expect, you could try increasing your bid.

Here are some targeting best practices from Snapchat:
- Keep your audience size less than 20 million people for the same creative.
- Create an ad set for each unique group of people you're trying to reach.
- Test Lookalike Audience for prospecting and finding new customers.
- Try using multiple ads per ad set so you can see how different creatives perform with the same audience.

There are several ad types available on Snapchat, including:

Top Snap: A Top Snap is the three to 10-second video ad that users will see. Top Snaps won't feature a swipe up call-to-action because there won't be any video or link attachment.

Long-form video: This ad type acts as a trailer for a longer video that can be up to 10 minutes long.

Web view: This objective allows you to drive traffic to your website as a means to encourage purchase of a product, to read an article, etc.

App install: This ad type drives traffic to your app page in the Google Play or Apple App Store for users to download your app.

As mentioned, all Snap Ads are required to be in a vertical format. If you are not confident about making vertical video ads, no problem: hit "Create" and you'll launch Snap Publisher, Snapchat's online video editing app. You can either create a video from scratch or edit one of the pre-designed templates. As for the content of your Snap Ad, it's up to you! If you're stuck for ideas, a simple selfie video is a good first option, because they look like stories from friends and make the ad experience familiar to other users. Snapchat's own research shows that *"Ads which feature UGC [user generated content] look and feel, Snapchat inspired features, and speaking to camera are significantly stronger at driving view-through."* Whatever your creative, here is a selection of best practices to help ensure your ad is effective:

- Establish brand moment before the two-second mark to maximize your ad's awareness, but avoid opening on a solid frame with a logo or product shot only; start with immediate action and a compelling element, like a product reveal or brand iconography
    - opening with moving footage provides a moment to hook viewers. Ensure that your ad is descriptive about what the user gets once they swipe up.
- Ads should seek to mirror the bite-sized and linear storytelling of Snaps. Although the maximum length of video permitted is 10 seconds, Snapchat actually recommends trying to keep your ad's duration closer to below 6 seconds. Its research reveals that between 3 and 5 seconds is the sweet spot for Snap Ad length to drive action, and that an offer message (if available) should be delivered within second two or three.
- Use voiceover call to actions to encourage users to swipe up, and choose the most appropriate of the available call to action buttons to display, e.g. Install Now or Download for app installs.
- If promoting an app, feature a person using it, and screenshots of it, along with key metrics to demonstrate the value of downloading it.
- Test all types of Snap ads from video, to stills, to gifs or cinemographs (one per ad set)
- Align creative with targeting where possible- Higher relevancy leads to higher swipe and conversion rates!
- Interestingly, Snapchat has found that incremental exposures to an ad increase lift in resonance metrics (i.e. the more times a person sees an ad, the more they are likely to remember it), despite having a negative impact on view duration. So, it recommends that you focus on driving resonance metrics rather than view duration. This is why

capturing your audience in the first few seconds, and persuading them to swipe up if called for, is so important.

The final step of Snap Ad creation is to tell Snapchat the website, app page, or video that you want users to see when they swipe up. Once your Snap ad is launched, you can visit the Snapchat Ad Manager at any time to monitor its performance, edit the schedule or budget, or download a report about your results.

Blogging Tips: Captivate With the Written Word

Although maintaining a blog doesn't constitute social networking in the most modern sense, blogging as a practice can so often act as the cornerstone of a great social media marketing strategy that I really wanted to include it in this book. As a central and stable hub for sharing detailed and valuable information with your audience (and having them share it with others), a blog is not only a fantastic way to build authority within your business niche, but also a place to re-purpose social media content, amplify your brand's voice, personality, and core values, *and* ultimately sell your offering to a legion of engaged customers. What's more, if all of your social media profiles were to disappear tomorrow, your website and blog will be one strong asset that you can say you own. And if you're encouraging people to sign up to your email newsletter here, too, you've still got perhaps the most direct method of contact to them, still available.

When people share your content, Google listens - the more your blog posts are shared, the better your site will rank in search engines and the more traffic will find its way to you. Of course, there are a *ton* more factors that go into making a blog successful, such as website SEO, plugins, copywriting skills, and more - way more than I can cover here. Instead, this chapter will explore some of the ways that you can prepare your blog for the *social* world and reveal some of the best types of content to create in order to captivate your audience.

Starting out and what to write about

Before you even start a blog, it's useful to figure out, in a wider sense, what your readers want from you. What key issues and information can you write about to engage your audience? The more relevant your content, the more successful it will be. To find out what your readers want, you could study the performance of existing blog posts or ask your readers directly through survey sites like Straw Poll (http://www.strawpoll.me), or in a post on Facebook. With that down, you can start to find specific topics for blog posts. It can be tough to keep coming up with fresh new content, but here are five simple and effective strategies to help aid the process:

- *Keywords:* Research keyword opportunities with sites like BuzzSumo (http://www.buzzsumo.com) and Answer the Public (http://answerthepublic.com/) and then come up with ideas around the results you get.

- *Inspiration:* Keep an eye out for popular discussions in your industry and think about what ideas could be could discussion or learning points around each topic.
- *News:* Look out for breaking news stories within your industry. Pick apart the essential information for your audience and explain what it means for them.
- *Past experience:* Come up with ideas based on posts that have performed well.
- *Intuition:* Occasionally, you'll come up with a blog post idea based on the intuition you only get from running a blog for a long time and getting to know your readers well.

When you've nearly settled on an idea, it is useful to refer to a set of criteria relevant to your blog and business goals: questions like "Is this relevant topic to my audience? Does this help them solve a challenge they face? Has this topic been written before and if so, can we add more value? Is there interest in this topic (keyword research will help with this one)? Writing only blog posts that meet these criteria can help to keep the quality of your content consistently high.

Integrate social sharing into your blog; include a call to action

No blog worth its salt will forgo the installation of good, clear social sharing widgets to allow users to easily share its content to the biggest social networks including Facebook, Twitter, and Pinterest. Even the best bloggers in the world don't have their work found without a little help from their readers, so you need to empower people to *easily* share your blog posts with their social connections. Visit any popular blog and you'll see an array of social sharing options above or below (or above *and* below) each post, often coupled with a call to action to encourage people to hit "Like", "Tweet" or "Share." There are plenty of ways to install and customize the way your blog's social sharing buttons display (some of which we've already covered earlier in the book), but one of the easiest and most popular options is through AddThis (http://www.addthis.com), which is a plugin that will place the buttons on your page in just a few clicks. In addition to the established social media sharing options, provide a 'Subscribe via RSS' button in a prominent place on your page, so that people can have your posts pushed to them in their Google Reader or RSS feed as soon as soon they are published.

Ways to encourage social sharing and encourage engagement also extend to the blog content itself, whether it's through pre-populated tweets containing valuable snippets of the article's information - ClicktoTweet (http://clicktotweet.com/ will facilitate that), or teasing the article but not revealing *all* of it until they share your link (the WordPress plugin Social Locker does this). As the latter requires people to act before they have even read your content, I would use it with great caution - reserved for premium content you believe people will desperately want to see.

Produce top content, make some of it evergreen

First and foremost, always aim to produce inspiring and educational content on a regular basis that is *shareable*. At the core of many great blogs is a set of evergreen posts (articles that will never go out of date, or are updated periodically to make sure that they won't). Evergreen blog posts can act as the backbone of your brand and its expertise online, position you as an authority figure with your finger on the pulse, and help to drive interest in your company. The types of evergreen posts that do best include articles that are written to help beginners (the people most likely to be searching online for assistance), e.g., *"The Complete Beginner's Guide to Choosing Your First Electric Car,"* and ones that answer FAQs, e.g., *"Is Paragliding Safe? Here's Everything You Need to Know."* As I mentioned above, be sure to revisit these posts from time to time to keep them up to date and *the* definitive online resource for whatever the topic might be. To promote evergreen content and give site visitors a clear point of reference, think about creating something like a "Start Here" page, a menu link to training guides, or a "Top posts" widget in the sidebar of your site.

Write effective headlines: be clear and concise

Learn to write keyword-rich headlines that will make people want to read the rest of your article, especially if all they have to go on is the blog post title they see in a list of search results or within a tweet. Don't try to be too clever or cryptic with your headlines; be as clear and direct about what the post will offer someone who might come across it, e.g., *"Hot or Cold? The Experts Tell All"* is pretty ambiguous next to something like *"Hot or Cold Water? Expert Opinion on How to Shower."* Some tried and tested ideas for powerful headlines include asking questions, e.g., *"How Do I Craft Amazing Blog Post Headlines?"*, teasing content to attract click-throughs, e.g., *"When one man's son was on the brink of flunking college, three words changed his whole life around..."*, or making references that tie your content into readers' interests or scenarios they often encounter, e.g., *"This is how America's #1 Mom Potty Trained Her Kids in 24 Hours."* Think about which keywords your customers will be using to find the content that you provide; replicate them in your blog post titles. For example, a customer is much more likely to search for *"how to bake chocolate cake recipe"* rather than *"Omnomnom, check out our great chocolate cake recipe"*. So your heading might read, *"Recipe: How to Bake A Delicious Chocolate Cake."*

Popular blog post frameworks for highly-readable posts

Sometimes you'll have the best idea for the subject of a blog post, but trouble finding a way to structure it in a way that is concise, clear, and easily read by your audience. Here is a variety of common ways to give a framework to your blog post ideas:

Versus posts

The power of the Internet has given consumers more choice than ever when it comes to buying products and services, or deciding between one idea or another, so much so that the decision is often overwhelming. A great way to solve this dilemma, and put together a great blog post, is the X vs. Y article. For example, a company that specializes in beds and mattresses might write a blog post explaining the pros and cons of sprung mattresses as opposed to memory foam. Similarly, *"What is the best X?"* types of posts work in a like fashion. These types of posts help consumers make a sound decision, make you stand out as a trustworthy authority figure, and are easy to put together.

Problem-solving posts

One of the main reasons that people search online is to find solutions to their problems, whether seeking to learn how to sew a button back on to their shirt, how to house train their dog, or how a guy makes himself irresistible to the opposite sex. Focusing on the solution to problems, especially for businesses, is a great way to come up with new ideas for blog posts and attract web traffic. Think about the problems that your customers want to solve - and then use your expertise to tell them how you (or your business) can help. To use dogs as an example, a pet store owner might blog about the best way to stop your dog from barking, or how to teach it to sit or fetch. Think about how you can become an invaluable resource for your customers *and* for those searching for solutions to their problems on the Internet.

List posts

'List posts' are extremely popular in almost any industry, as they can be read quickly and are great for sharing, e.g., *10 Top Marketing Tips For Your Blog*. There are three common types of list post: Brief list posts are long, bulleted snippets of information that users can use as a platform to search for more detailed information elsewhere (sometimes useful, but not always the best way to keep readers engaged on your site!); detailed list posts provide more complex, valuable information - like these tips, and hybrid posts lie somewhere in the middle.

Break news, offer opinion, and ask questions

Writing blog posts about breaking news within your industry sector is not only one of the best ways to come up with new and original content, but it also positions you as an authority figure in the eyes of readers. However, rather than simply regurgitating a press release or something you found on a big news site, frame your story in a way that makes it relevant to your audience, positions you as an authority, and encourages people to interact: offer an opinion, and ask readers to share their own as a way to drive engagement. One of the easiest ways to illicit a response is to close your blog posts with a simple request, e.g., *"What do you guys think? Tell us in the comments"*. You'll be surprised how much interaction this garners, especially if the question you ask is simple and quick to answer.

Spin hot or detailed topics into multiple posts

One of the biggest challenges that many bloggers face is creating fresh content, week in, week out. One of the techniques you can use to combat this is called "spinning". In a nutshell, it involves taking one important topic that you know your audience will lap up and writing about it from a variety of different standpoints. Let's take an article about painting a garden fence, for example. Several different blog posts about that one topic might be: *'A Beginner's Guide to Painting A Garden Fence'*; *'5 of the Biggest Garden Fence Painting Mistakes'*; *'Video: How to Paint A Garden Fence in 5 Easy Steps'*, or *'How [Brand X] is Revolutionizing Garden Fence Painting'*. Get the idea? Drilling down on individual topics like this (as opposed to being more general) may be beneficial in terms of attracting people hunting for more specific information or advice.

Guest posting

Offer to write guest posts on other influential bloggers' blogs, and provide a link back to your own blog at the bottom of the post in return, as part of the agreement. This is particularly useful if you manage to post on a blog that is much more popular than yours! As well as guest posting on other blogs yourself, be open-minded about other experts posting on yours to help build a strong network of friends within your industry.

Celebrate milestones

As traffic to your blog grows, celebrate this in specific blog posts, thanking readers for their continued support. Use these posts to highlight your most popular content so far, to encourage new readers to go back and revisit, increasing page views and time on your site.

Note: In an online world packed with strong opinions, research-backed blog posts are often more persuasive (and therefore popular) than those that are solely story based. For this reason, quoting authoritative resources, citing statistics and studies, or even showcasing your *own* data, can be an effective way to back up your arguments, emanate credibility, and create stellar blog content that stands out from the competition. For example, which blog post title would you be most likely to click on from the following: *"How to Run Faster and More Efficiently"* or *"How to Run 20% Faster and More Efficiently in 4 Weeks"*? Where the circumstances call for it, the data-backed title will always win out.

Use awesome images in your blog posts

As I discussed in the *Facebook Tips* chapter of this book, social networks like Facebook (and Google+) will pull in a photo from your blog to display when someone shares your blog link. If the photo is poor (or there isn't one at all), then there is little chance of your plain link catching the eyes of people browsing through their news feeds. One blog post image is good, but several are even better. Multiple images within a blog post help to break up long blocks of text, make your articles more memorable, and can be used to enhance a written fact or opinion. Check out the *"Explained: The Best Types of Content to Post on Social Media"* chapter for advice on where to find, and how to use, great images.

Note: Adding alternative text (alt-text) to images is not just important for search engine optimization (they can't see pictures, but do grab the text and include it in image searches), but it also acts as the description of images pinned to Pinterest. Alt-text is what pops up when you hover your cursor over an image and it can be edited in the image upload process on most blogging platforms, including <u>WordPress</u> and <u>Blogger</u>.

Encourage email subscriptions

The harsh truth is that when someone has visited your blog once, there is a good chance that they will not return for a second visit. To combat this, you need to position yourself to target these people in future at a location where it is hard to ignore you - their email inbox. By gathering email addresses, you have a ready pool of willing contacts with whom you can share new blog posts and updates and slowly help to convert them into more passionate brand ambassadors. In addition to placing a box for people to sign up to your newsletter in a prominent position on your home page, *also* add a sign-up box to the bottom of a handful of your most popular blog posts from the past (use Analytics to find out which these are). Be sure to let visitors know what they are signing up for before they hit 'Submit' so that your emails are not considered spam, and consider including a discount code or free gift (like a PDF guide) as a way to sweeten the deal.

The blog post length and how often to post

There is always plenty of debate about the optimum length of a blog post, particularly when you are dealing with an audience who is short of time, who can easily look elsewhere, and are forever skimming quickly through content. I would suggest forgetting about the word count, at least to a degree. Instead, focus on creating interesting, well-formatted content that web and mobile readers will love, whether it takes 100 words or 1,000 (do note, however, that long form content generally has less competition). Don't let worries about the length of your post dictate its overall quality.

How often you should publish new blog articles is different for every business: it's a balancing act between how much time and resources you can invest into researching, writing, editing, and promotion whilst maintaining the upmost care and quality in your output. If you have the scope to pump out multiple world-beating articles a week, fantastic! But even if you can only manage one or two articles a month, as long as you are consistent and they are finding an audience, you'll be on a much steadier path to traffic growth than if you publish a lot of sub-par content for the sake of populating your blog.

Use descriptive URLs for SEO

For improved SEO, ensure every blog post URL is descriptive rather than just functional, e.g., www.yoursite.com/10-top-blogging-tips-for-business.htm

instead of www.yoursite.com/post345.htm. On most blogging platforms, the URL is normally generated from the words used in the blog post's title. If you are able to edit the URL to make it even more optimized for SEO, and you think it can be improved over what has been automatically generated, go ahead and do it.

The 'deep linking' and 'linking to other sites' trick

Whenever you refer to a previous blog post while writing, be sure to add a hyperlink to it, so that readers can go back and check it out. On that note, you want readers to stay on your page as long as possible, so if you link outside of your website for any reason, be sure to set the link to open in a new window.

Share and re-purpose your blog post for maximum exposure

The most savvy marketers repurpose their blog posts into content optimized for maximum effect on each social media platform – both through the text caption and image you use. It might not make a *huge* difference in driving traffic to your blog, but it does mean that your content will stand out against competitors who are not tailoring theirs to each platform. As such, when it comes to thinking about your industry in future, hopefully customers will remember your brand first. Here are some examples of ways content can be repurposed:

- Create Instagram stories with the key points of the blog post and invite followers to check out the full post.
- Create short videos using the content in the blog posts to share on Twitter and Facebook, and a longer form video on YouTube.
- Use a tool like Lumen5 to convert your blog post into an animated video with captions.
- Lift key data from your blog post and turn it into an infographic.

Get shares from industry influencers

Not all shares are created equal. If you want to encourage your awesome blog content to be a runaway hit, think about how much easier this would be if you could get influential people within your field to share your link with their hundreds or thousands of loyal fans. The best way to go about this is to work backwards. Spend time building a relationship with the influencer(s) first (commenting on their own blog, tweeting them to ask a question about their work or for a quote to use in your work, etc.) and at the same time analyze the type of content they are already sharing, so that you can reflect this in your own posts. This strategy works because people love to share things they've been involved in, even if they weren't directly responsible for putting it together.

Re-share evergreen content

As mentioned near the beginning of this book, automation on social media can, in the right circumstances, be very beneficial to you - a time saver, and a chance to give the content you slaved over as much exposure as possible. One case where this is certainly true is the automated scheduling and posting of evergreen blog content across multiple social networks, which can help to extend its useful life over and over again. For example, you could tweet a link to the same blog article two or three times in the same week, then keep the same frequency for the next few months using alternative post titles to see which performs best. Some ways that you might want to restyle a social media post featuring the same blog article - as an alternative to [post title] + [link], include: posing a question as a lead into the post, quoting a striking sentence or statistic from the article, or showing off just a little, e.g., "Our most popular read from last month..." My tool of choice is Buffer (http://www.bufferapp.com), which allows you to bulk-upload and organize content to be posted to Facebook, Twitter, Google+ and LinkedIn at a date and time of your choosing.

Relaunch old blog content

Depending on your industry, the information in any blog post (especially popular evergreen ones) can become outdated. Instead of just writing new blog posts to, it is often quicker and more effective to update existing blog posts that have outdated information and even more potential for traffic through search:

- Seek out underperforming content - posts that rank low on the first page or onto the second page of Google, posts where organic traffic has fallen, posts that didn't meet your expectations traffic-wise, and posts whose content is *okay* but could be improved.
- Improve and update that content: for example, update the copy, refresh the images and update screenshots.
- Republish your post: Update the "Published" date to today's date (the day of the relaunch). That will bring the blog post to the top of your blog.

Monitor progress with Google Analytics

Use Google Analytics to monitor the volume and quality of search terms which are driving visitors to your site, and use the information you find to tailor the direction of new content - expand on the most popular topics and tweak or ditch those that aren't working quite as well. Above all, keep in mind *why* your blog exists – for example, to build your brand, increase reach, and drive sales – and aim for consistant forward momentum. Alongside traffic, keep a close eye on the number customers referred by the blog, Metrics like this will give you a sense, in hard numbers, of how the blog provides real business value.

General Strategy and FAQs for Super Social Media Marketing

Social media marketing is an ever-growing, ever-changing sector, but there are a number of core elements that will help you ensure a steady foundation to your social media ventures.

5 Easy Ways to Promote Your Social Profiles and Gain Followers

Add your social profiles to your email signature

Think about how many emails you send per day. Now imagine each email you send is a chance for someone new to find out about your social media profiles. Stick your social media URLs in your email signature along with a 'Like Us' call to action, and a reason why people should visit and 'like' your Page, e.g., *"Like us on Facebook for exclusive vouchers and discount codes!"*

Blog about your social profiles; give reasons to follow

If you have a company blog, why not create a post specifically to promote your social media presence? Give your readers five compelling reasons why they should 'Like' your fan pages in a blog post - e.g., exclusive offers, news to their feeds, sneak peeks at upcoming products. Don't beg them to like you; just give reasons why they'll benefit and watch the like box numbers trickle upwards.

Promote your social media profiles in the real world

Anywhere you can display your social media URLs is free advertising for you. Just think how many people would see a car bumper sticker with your Facebook address on, or a sign in the office or store window asking visitors to follow you on Twitter. In addition, combine offline and online by letting the people you meet in real life know about your social profiles by printing those URLS on your business cards, letterheads, etc.

Ask different sets of followers to like your other profiles

If a person follows you on one social network, chances are good that they will want to follow you on another too. For example, give some compelling reasons to your Twitter followers as to why they should join your Facebook community, much as in the example for your blog post promotion mentioned above. A tweet might read, *"Great discussion about our newest garden tool offering happening right now - get involved!* http://www.facebook.com/yourfacebookpage.*"* In addition, don't be afraid to directly promote your social profiles once in a while. Unlike the approach above, here you simply point people to your page with a message along the lines of *"Enjoying our tweets? Why not join us on Facebook too? Click here:* http://www.facebook.com/yourfacebookpage*"*. Create and save three or four different variations of this message, so that you don't repeat the same tweet over and over.

Ask your email list to like your social profiles

Got an email marketing list? Consider sending a dedicated email asking your subscribers to follow or like you on social networks - again with compelling reasons as to why they most definitely should. Whenever you send out future messages to them include links to your social profiles underneath the main message.

Social Media Marketing FAQs and Miscellaneous Advice

Should I keep my social media posts short?

While many studies will advise you to keep text in your social media posts to a minimum in order to cater to low attention spans and mobile users, my advice is different. The reason? Studies like these will have covered a spectrum that includes text-heavy posts with low engagement that are often the result of poor writing practices, and short posts like memes that only generate lots of cheap, low quality engagement. My advice is to put the *quality* of your written content first and see how a mixture of lengths affects your engagement rates, rather than worrying about sticking strictly to a set character limit.

When is the best time to post on social media?

Depending on which study you read, the "best" time to post on social media to maximize organic reach and engagement will differ wildly. Some will offer general guidance: advising you to post at the time of day when most people are likely to be checking social media, i.e., first thing in the morning and in the evenings. Others will recommend that you use hard evidence - tools like Facebook Insights and its "When Your Fans Are Online" data, and Google Analytics' activity - to determine what time of day your posts receive the most engagement, and stick to posting around those hours. Alternatively, there's the "late night infomercial effect" school of thought. This states that you should post content in the twilight hours, at a time when there will be much less competition in peoples' news feeds, when an international audience (if you have one) is most likely to spot your updates, and to boost the chance that your posts might - as a result of being published at night - be the first thing fans see when they wake up in the morning. As goes the advice on similar issues, there is no "one size fits all" answer, so the key to finding out when *your* best time to post on social media comes down to experimentation. Use all of the suggestions above to run a few tests, then tweak your strategy until you find the single method (or a combination) that works best for you. As always, re-evaluate your approach from time to time to ensure your posts are performing as well as they can be.

Don't post for 'empty' engagement

One of the biggest traps that many businesses fall into is that of posting certain kinds of posts as bait to encourage likes and comments. The most obvious examples of this are *'Fill in the Blank'* and *'Click LIKE if you think X is X..."* sort of posts on Facebook. While these are great for occasional use, they do not give you a very accurate overview of fans and customers who are really engaged with your content and how successful your efforts really are. Anybody can post an image of a cute kitten to get likes, but what real impact does it have on your fans' opinion of your brand?

Search the web for social mentions of your brand

While I've touched on the different ways that you can use individual social networks to discover and track mentions of your brand, one popular (and free!) "catch all" solution to see real-time activity, understand your content's reach, and get a top-down idea of your brand reputation, is SocialMention (http://www.socialmention.com).

Type in and search for your brand name and keywords related to your company and experiment with the different filters found in the drop-down menu. For each mention found, the site provides a set of overall metrics particular to it, including the sources where it is found and whether people are interacting in a positive or negative fashion. Hover over each metric with your cursor for a short definition of each.

Free and Premium Social Media Video Tutorials: 250+ Videos and 10+ Hours of Content

Bite-sized YouTube video tutorials

To support the content within this book, I record and post regular social media videos onto YouTube. No filler, just free, clear and simple information that will help you with your social media marketing. The majority of the videos are screen recordings, with my voice guiding you step-by-step, and each major set of tutorials is grouped together into playlists for easy viewing. There are over 250 videos so far and that number is growing all the time, so why not head over to check them out? And don't forget to subscribe to the channel, so that you're the first to see future tutorials!

Subscribe to My YouTube Channel:

http://www.youtube.com/500socialmediatips

Comprehensive premium video courses

I also offer premium video courses on the website Udemy - an interactive hub for people who have something to teach and people who want to learn. These courses are considerably longer and more detailed offerings than my YouTube uploads - fully comprehensive guides to help you master different social networks and other related topics from start to finish. You get lifetime access to all updates once you enroll, and can even interact with me right there on the site with any questions you may have. Sign up to my newsletter and you'll receive a deep discount as a thanks, too - details on how to do this in the next chapter.

Enroll on my Udemy Courses: https://www.udemy.com/u/andrewmacarthy

FREE E-Book Version Updates

The very nature of social media means that the tips and tricks in this book will need to be updated and amended often. To prevent you from being provided with out-of-date information, *500 Social Media Marketing Tips* is updated regularly. To see a summary of all the changes made to the book over time, please visit: http://bit.ly/500smmtupdateslog

E-book version updates

An updated version of *500 Social Media Marketing Tips* is uploaded to the Amazon Kindle store at the beginning of every month, complete with all of the changes made in the four weeks prior. **These updates are available for free.** Unfortunately, Amazon's processes mean that you may not be notified when a new update has been made available, but when available, they can be downloaded via the Manage My Devices > Kindle section of your Amazon web account.

The Kindle version of *500 Social Media Marketing Tips* is available at http://bit.ly/500kindle

Paperback version updates

Updating the paperback version of *500 Social Media Marketing Tips* is a little more challenging than its electronic cousin, so barring the requirement of a lot of important amendments, updates normally occur on **quarterly basis** - once for every season - spring, summer, fall, and winter. These updates will include all of the same tips from the e-book version of the book available at the time of printing. To check that you are buying the latest version, please look for indications of the version in the book's product description, on the front cover, and on the copyright page.

The paperback version of *500 Social Media Marketing Tips* is available at http://bit.ly/500paperback

Download My Essential Social Media Marketing Premium Content Bundle

What is the Premium Content Bundle?

My Premium Content Bundle is a selection of incredibly useful social media marketing resources - instantly downloadable - to help you reach and surpass your social media marketing goals. It includes of the following:

- **18 Social Media Profile Branding Templates:** Expertly designed templates for Facebook, Twitter, YouTube, LinkedIn, and more.
- **Ideal Social Media Image Size List:** an at-a-glance view of the optimum image sizes to use for posts, profile design, and ads.
- **Social Media Strategy Plan Questionnaire:** 24 questions to help you plan and shape a social media marketing strategy.
- **2 Social Media Content Calendars:** plot your social media posts in advance for a more stress-free, optimized content strategy.
- **Social Media Strategy Progress Tracker:** Track and chart the growth of your social profiles – followers, referral traffic, and more.
- **50% off my premium Udemy video courses:** Half-price access to my top-rated Udemy video courses, *How to Use Instagram for Business* and *How to Use Snapchat for Business*.
- **10% off my Social Media Marketing Services:** an instant discount on all of my consultancy and design services. Nice!

...and more!

How much is the Premium Content Bundle?

The Premium Content Bundle costs **$7.00**. There are two payment options:

1. Purchase access for a one-off $7.00 to grab all the goodies within a 7-day time frame, OR
2. Purchase a subscription for $7.00 per month to show your ongoing support for me and my work (free Kindle book updates, blog posts, video tutorials, etc.) and to have *unlimited* access to all of the latest/updated Premium Bundle Content wherever and whenever you like.

Where do I purchase the Premium Content Bundle?

For more information about the Premium Content Bundle goodies and to purchase yours, visit www.andrewmacarthy.com/premium

Hire Me: Social Media Design, Analysis and Management

Since writing *500 Social Media Marketing Tips*, I have been contacted by many businesses who want help with their social media strategy - either from the beginning of their venture, or just for reassurance that they are on the right path. I am pleased to say that I offer a range of tailor-made, affordable one-off services and ongoing consultation packages to build and manage social media marketing for your business. My rates are very reasonable and negotiable dependent on your needs and budget. Services offered include:

- Social Media Strategy Audit / Analysis
- Social Media Profile Setup and Design
- Social Profile Management and Audience Building
- Social Media Strategy and Profile Design Analysis And Recommendations

If you would like more information on pricing or would like to get me on board to help you with social media in any way, please visit the 'Hire Me' page at my website, http://www.andrewmacarthy.com or email me on amacarthy85@gmail.com

I look forward to hearing from you!

About the Author

Andrew Macarthy is a father, blogger and social media consultant from Swansea in Wales, UK. His #1 Web Marketing Kindle Bestseller, *500 Social Media Marketing Tips*, helped thousands of businesses with simple, practical advice to optimize their social media activity and make the most of the sector's marketing opportunities. In his spare time, Andrew enjoys running, Nintendo videogames, acoustic guitar, and Swansea City FC.

Any Feedback or Questions?

Email me at amacarthy85@gmail.com or contact me via my website or the following social networks:

Website / blog: http://www.andrewmacarthy.com
Facebook: http://www.facebook.com/500socialmediatips
Twitter: http://www.twitter.com/andrewmacarthy
Pinterest: http://www.pinterest.com/andrewmacarthy
YouTube: http://www.youtube.com/user/500socialmediatips
Instagram: http://www.instagram.com/500socialmedia

Did You Enjoy 500 Social Media Marketing Tips?

If you found this book helpful and believe it is worth sharing, please would you take a few seconds to let your friends know about it? If it turns out to make a difference in their lives, they'll be forever grateful to you, as will I.

In addition, if you have a few moments now to leave a short review on the Amazon product page, please, please do. Something that only takes you a few moments will help me out today and for years to come.

All the best, and thank you so much for reading *500 Social Media Marketing Tips*.

Andrew.

Made in the USA
San Bernardino, CA
25 September 2018